D0392934

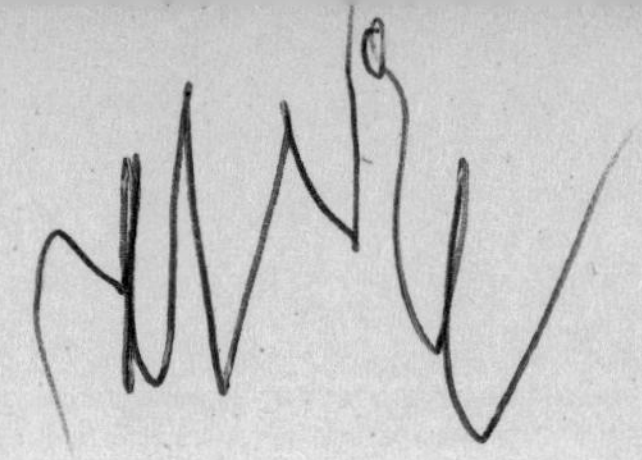

ALSO BY KAY ALLENBAUGH

Chocolate for a Woman's Soul

Chocolate for a Woman's Heart

Chocolate for a Lover's Heart

Chocolate for a Mother's Heart

Chocolate for a Woman's Spirit

Chocolate for a Teen's Soul

Chocolate for a Woman's Blessings

Chocolate for a Teen's Heart

Chocolate for a Woman's Dreams

Chocolate for a Teen's Spirit

Chocolate for a Woman's Courage

77 Stories that Celebrate

the Richness

of Life

A FIRESIDE BOOK
Published by Simon & Schuster
New York London Toronto Sydney Singapore

Chocolate
for a
Woman's Soul
Volume II

KAY ALLENBAUGH

FIRESIDE
Rockefeller Center
1230 Avenue of the Americas
New York, NY 10020

For information about special discounts for bulk purchases,
please contact Simon & Schuster Special Sales at
1-800-456-6798 or business@simonandschuster.com

Manufactured in the United States of America

1 3 5 7 9 10 8 6 4 2

Library of Congress Cataloging-in-Publication Data

Chocolate for a woman's soul II : 77 stories that celebrate the richness of life /
[compiled by] Kay Allenbaugh.
p. cm.
1. Women—Conduct of life—Miscellanea. I. Allenbaugh, Kay.
BJ1610 .C529 2003
305.4—dc21 2003042575
ISBN 0-7432-5019-2

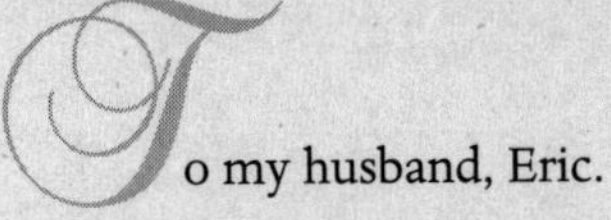

To my husband, Eric.

Thank you for clearing a path

and lighting my way.

You absolutely add richness to my life.

CONTENTS

Introduction xvii

I
LOVE'S TWISTS AND TURNS

Callie's Daisies *Ruth Lee* 3

My Robert Redford Moment *Sande Boritz Berger* 5

A Tale of Two Weddings *Janie M. West* 8

Dear John Letter *Lynne Biango* 11

First Winter *Karen C. Driscoll* 15

To Tell the Truth *Ande Cardwell* 18

Finding the Right Ring *Kathleen Coudle King* 24

Of Hope and Ski Socks *Mary Dixon Lebeau* 28

II
HEAVEN SENT

Angel in the City *Patricia C. Fischer* 35

The Throwaway *Jennifer R. Finley* 39

Chocolate Heaven *Gayle Montanez* 44

Rocky *Anne Culbreath Watkins* 46

A Timely Gift *Dawne J. Harris* 49

Mother Knew Best *Diane Fleming* 52

"All Mighty" Shark Repellent *Jennifer Galvin* 54

The Princess and the Rescue *Laura Stanford* 56

III

A WOMAN'S INFLUENCE

Rattlesnakes Do Not Lay Eggs *Jean Jeffrey Gietzen* 63

Boys Keep Out *Marilyn McFarlane* 66

The Best Day of My Life *Susan DeMersseman* 69

Southern Delicacies *Sheila S. Hudson* 72

Nights in Blue Gingham *Linda C. Wisniewski* 74

Comforting Connection *Marla Hardee Milling* 77

Along for the Ride *Jennifer Gordon Gray* 80

Tips to Feed Your Soul *Kay Allenbaugh* 83

Sexual Sea Bass *Ly Nguyen* 85

IV

FUR AND FEATHER LOVE

Better than Therapy *Susan Parker* 91

Cleo, My Empty-Nest Cat *Felice R. Prager* 94

That Dog *Kathleen Coudle King* 97

Heart Songs *Anne Culbreath Watkins* 101

My Husband's "Other Woman" *Eileen Modracek* 105

The Cat's Meow *Joanne M. Friedman* 109

Conversations with Zoe *Elizabeth P. Glixman* 113

The Last One Picked *Pamela Jenkins* 117

V

MOM'S MAGICAL MOMENTS

Ice Cube Wars *Peggy Vincent* 123

Paid in Full *Tracey Henry* 127

Birth of a Mom *Lisa Sanders* 131

Puddle Talking *Shirley Kawa-Jump* 134

Fat Days *Melissa Gray* 137

Leaving the Glitz Behind *Jennifer Bialow Zeidler* 140

The Outsider *Kathy Briccetti* 143

VI

GIVING AND GETTING

I Wish I Were Here *Julia Rosien* 149

The Reason for the Season *Chris Mikalson* 153

My Sister Sam *Lyssa Friedman* 156

Do It Like a Survivor *Laurel A. Wasserman* 160

Just a Daughter *Beverly Tribuiani-Montez* 164

Teaching the Teacher *Cheree Moore* 167

Choosing Sides *Amy Munnell* 170

VII

THE GUYS IN OUR LIVES

Jennifer's Feet *Peggy Vincent* 177

Cultivating Character *Michelle Guthrie Pearson* 181

The Wedding Hankie *Kathy Hardy Rhodes* 183

Dylan's Derby *Susan B. Townsend* 187

Enough Love to Go Around *Christy Caballero* 190

Magic Words *Kay Bolden* 193

Risk, Dare, and Try *Nancy Maffeo* 196

VIII

LIFE'S BIGGEST CHALLENGES

Shaman's Flight *Sheila Stephens* 201

Two Pink Lines *Annette V.* 203

Unleashed *Teri Brown* 208

A Place We Call Home *Sheri McGregor* 211

Something in Common *Patty Swyden Sullivan* 215

One Out of Four *Patricia R. Reule* 218

A Fruitful Obsession *Edna Miner Larson* 222

The Keyhole *Diane Payne* 228

IX

FINDING PEACE ALONG THE WAY

A Bluebird's Lesson *Kelley Bowles Albaugh* 233

Exactly Like Me *Jennifer Nelson* 237

Taking a Chance *Harriet May Savitz* 240

Mom's Kiddie Pool *Carol Sjostrom Miller* 244

Egypt Calling *Kyla Merwin* 247

Raising Daughters Differently *Barbara Carr Phillips* 252

Christmas Crunch *Linda Aspenson Bergstrom* 255

X

LAUGH LINES

Doughnuts for Heroes *Jennifer Gordon Gray* 261

The No Treat Retreat *Elizabeth Kann* 263

Praying for Deep Water *Lana Robertson Hayes* 266

One Day at a Time *Eileen Thiel* 268

Doris *Tammy Wilson* 273

Of Golf Tees and Evergreen Trees *Dawn Goldsmith* 278

Mechanical Pariah *Alleyne McGill* 282

The King of Hearts *Carole Moore* 286

More Chocolate Stories? 289

Contributors 291

Acknowledgments 311

Chocolate *for a* Woman's Soul Volume II

INTRODUCTION

Chocolate and women just go together! I've been saying this* ever since the publication of my first book, *Chocolate for a Woman's Soul*. But when I gathered that first collection of rich and delicious stories, I never imagined that it would begin an entire series of bestselling books, of which *Chocolate for a Woman's Soul Volume II* is number twelve.

Now that we have reached an even dozen, I want to pause and acknowledge all the Chocolate sisters who have shared so much with us. I myself feel a deep sense of gratitude for being divinely inspired to create the series, and I have marveled at the joy I've gained from listening to the small, still voice that has urged me on. We are all here to learn and grow and discover the things our souls are calling us to do, and for me the Chocolate series has surely been one of those things. I am honored that women from around the country have shared—again and again—their endearing moments and moving true tales that lift the spirit and warm the heart.

In the best Chocolate tradition, the stories in *Chocolate for a Woman's Soul Volume II* are poignant, touching, even downright funny. They celebrate a woman's experiences negotiating the path of love, listening for the divine, discovering meaningful work, cherishing friends and family, believing in oneself, and finding peace while overcoming life's biggest challenges. All women are gifted with the ability to be both strong and soft, smart and intuitive at the same time. No doubt you'll smile as you recognize yourself and your friends in these experiences we all share.

I continue to learn a lot about myself while compiling these inspirational stories. My wish for you is that they will affect your life as positively as they have affected mine. May you recognize and appreciate the messages, magic, miracles, and synchronicities that inform the events of your own life.

So, in keeping with the Chocolate tradition, open a box of chocolates, find your favorite quiet place to get cozy, and then savor each story, one by one, knowing that these pages were meant just for you.

I
LOVE'S TWISTS AND TURNS

When first we fall in love, we feel that we know all there is to know about life, and perhaps we are right.

MIGNON MCLAUGHLIN

CALLIE'S DAISIES

"So."

I smiled and hesitated, wanting to pose my question just right.

"Callie, what can you tell me about romance? Specifically about the romance in your life."

Callie's blue eyes sparkled. "Oh my goodness. I don't know." She looked across the well-worn kitchen table at her husband. "What would you say about romance, John? What can we tell her?"

My assignment was to interview John and Callie, then write the story of their sixty-four years of marriage for our local newspaper. A love story for the Valentine's Day edition.

John's voice was soft and quiet as he answered. "Maybe you should tell her about the flowers," he suggested. Then to me he added, "I always get her flowers on our anniversary."

"That's right, he does." Callie chuckled. "We've been married so long he's just about run out of ideas as to what kind he should get next."

"I surprised her a couple of years ago," John said. "You see, we met and fell in love at church so it seemed like a good idea to have her flowers delivered to church. That's where she got them. Right there in front of everyone before the preacher gave his sermon for the day."

I listened and smiled as I took notes. Their stories were interesting, but not quite what I hoped for. Romance was my assignment, so I tried again.

"Callie, of all the flowers you've received from John, which were your favorites?"

She gave me a gentle smile. "The daisies," she said as she reached for her husband's hand. "John knows I love daisies. One day he came in from the pasture with a fresh-picked bouquet. Not because it was our anniversary or anything, just because he saw them and he knew I'd be pleased."

John's shoulders lifted a bit higher and he sat taller in his chair as Callie continued to praise him.

"And then do you want to know what he did next? He went back out to that field, dug up some of those flowers, and planted them in a garden bed alongside our back sidewalk. I couldn't have been more pleased. We tend those daisies together and they mean so much to me."

I felt like an intruder in a private moment as she patted his hand. Then, almost in unison, they said, "It's the little things that count, you know. It's the little, caring things that make a marriage work."

And I smiled. I knew I had my story.

Ruth Lee

Before we love with our heart,
we already love with our imagination.
LOUISE COLET

MY ROBERT REDFORD MOMENT

On a balmy August afternoon, several years ago, I was stuck in traffic on the way to the airport to pick up Steve. The sun's rays were so brilliant that I had to shift the visor whenever I changed direction. With traffic at a dead halt, I looked in the rearview mirror. Not bad, I thought . . . finally a good haircut, free of frizzies, each hair obediently in place. Steve had said he loved my hair, calling me Sister Golden Hair after the song by America. In a few weeks, the two of us would be married.

Now, looking forward to seeing him, I began to feel a surge of joy. I imagined his coy look as he walked toward my car, smoking his pipe, his deep-set brown eyes intent on finding me. I was grinning like a Cheshire when I arrived at the American terminal about fifteen minutes early and begged the security guard to let me stay at curbside. I always get lost looking for the parking lots. Once I'd exited the airport by mistake.

When I stepped out of the car to stretch my legs, the smell of the cars' exhaust in the stagnant air made me dizzy. I leaned against my old Pontiac and peered at people coming and going through the terminal doors. A young couple wearing matching floral shirts carried straw bags and balanced their suitcases. They looked badly sunburned, but very happy. I guessed they were returning from their honeymoon. Steve and I would grab a weekend away, eventually, if we could manage to find a baby-sitter for the children.

After a few minutes of people gazing, I noticed a tall, serious chauffeur walking quickly, carrying two black bags. A few steps behind him, wearing dark glasses, a powder blue shirt, and a navy blazer, walked a short but strikingly handsome man. Who? Who is that? It finally registered; my hands flew up to my face in total disbelief. I reappeared slowly, like a toddler in a game of peek-a-boo, to see the man chuckling, his head tossed back. He seemed amused at my display of shock. Was this a mirage, a dizzy daydream on a hot summer's day? No, no, I was sure. It was really *him*. It was Robert Redford!

I felt a sudden surge of adrenaline. "Oh my God," I shouted to no one in particular.

"You still here lady?" the security guard asked.

Breathlessly, I babbled on, trying to make him my friend. I pointed in the direction of the white stretch limo, sending the guard to investigate, to see for himself. I realized the limo would have to pass me when making its exit from the one-way lane in which I was double-parked. In my mind I did what any normal divorced woman, about to be remarried in three weeks, would do. I reached into my bag and touched up my lipstick. Then I posed against the Pontiac covering the neon graffiti someone had once sprayed on my car door.

I waited, my heart beating relentlessly in my throat. A leading lady in some untitled B movie. But none of that really mattered. As predicted, the vehicle passed in front of me ever so slowly. The window was rolled halfway down, just enough for our eyes to lock in an intense, burning gaze. This was a scene I'd remember, take with me, whenever things got really rough. I saw him gently smile, not mocking at all and, as he passed me, his head turned in my direction, until all that was visible was the black glass of the rear window.

Dazed, I fantasized him suddenly stopping. Then he opened the door, beckoning me to enter. What would I say to this icon of the silver screen? The heartthrob of millions of women just like me. Would I surrender myself completely, then ask him to please get me home in time for my girls' baths?

"Lady, that was him all right. Tiny little guy, ain't he? Lady, you gonna move that car now? Yo, lady!"

As the limo descended the exit ramp, someone called out my name. It was Steve grinning from ear to ear, lugging his own heavy bag, no chauffeur, no valet. As we embraced tightly, I felt my flushed cheeks sizzle against Steve's cool smooth-shaven face. And just the slightest tinge of guilt.

Sande Boritz Berger

A TALE OF TWO WEDDINGS

History repeats itself when you least expect it—even family history. I am reminded of this twice each year: on my wedding anniversary in June, and on Valentine's Day, the anniversary of our oldest daughter and wonderful son-in-law. The repeated events began before this daughter was even born.

It was a beautiful June, and my fiancé and I were anticipating a relaxing summer vacation before returning to college in the fall. Quite unexpectedly, he was offered, and accepted, a job out of state. Did I want to go with him? Of course I did! Separation was unthinkable and unnecessary from our youthful perspective.

We would simply get married and go.

I was not quite twenty and we had known each other less than a year. He was all of twenty-one. However, with two years of college under his belt, we honestly could think of no reason not to marry immediately.

We informed our families and friends of our plans, unleashing a frenzy of activity. Pastoral counseling, blood tests, marriage license, bridal clothes, flowers, photographer, wedding cake, gold bands, a showering of gifts, and even house hunting led up to a lovely wedding and reception—all in a time span of three weeks.

Hindsight provides an amazing picture of our parents at that time. They accepted our impulsive decision with love and support. If they complained or cried, they did it privately and we were blissfully unaware of it. Blinded by love and incurably optimistic, we assumed that they were as happy and excited as we were.

They may not have shared our enthusiasm at the time of the wedding, but they certainly did a year later—at the birth of the prettiest baby anyone had ever seen.

In a few years we returned to our hometown where we welcomed the birth of three more children. We were all sitting around the dinner table one evening when the prettiest baby you ever saw, who was now not quite twenty, announced her engagement to a young man she had known only a few months. They wanted to be married on Valentine's Day—three weeks away. I reminded them that there would be another February 14 next year, but of course, they could see no reason to wait. We comforted ourselves with the fact they would live only a few miles away.

We began three weeks of wedding preparations for the second time in my life. Pastoral counseling, blood tests, marriage license, bridal clothes, flowers, photographer, wedding cake, gold bands . . . wait a minute.

We had been here before, but I did not remember it being so stressful the first time around. It was fun and romantic and exciting when I was the bride, but the same events can look quite different when seen from a mother's perspective. She was too young, they were moving too fast; this was not what we had planned for her life! We were not ready to let her go, but we did. Perhaps we were following the example of love and support set for us by our own parents when we married.

I phoned my mother and apologized profusely for what we had insensitively subjected her to twenty years earlier. She laughed and said something about sowing and reaping, going around and coming around. I think she enjoyed seeing us receive our just desserts.

It was a warm February that year. The Valentine's Day wedding was beautiful with red roses, red velvet cake, and a glowing bridal couple blinded by love.

And one year later—the birth of the prettiest baby anyone had ever seen!

Janie M. West

DEAR JOHN LETTER

I *am driving home from work. It is Friday night, and I* can't wait to arrive home and relax for the weekend.

My boyfriend, Larry, is coming to New York from New Jersey next weekend to take me out for my birthday. I smile, reflecting on how we have successfully maintained a long-distance relationship for *more than* a year! I had received his usual two telephone calls that day. He told me, "I will catch you later."

The hot bubble bath feels wonderful. I put on my aerobic clothes and have a bite to eat. I am ready to work out for a half hour, then relax and watch television. I will spend the weekend preparing for Larry's visit in a week.

I decide to check my e-mail first.

It surprises me to see an e-mail from Larry since we have communicated mostly by telephone for the last six months, his choice. The subject is "Us."

> *Dear Lynne. It's been a little over a year now that we have been communicating, and I can't imagine how difficult it would have been for me during this year if it were not for you. You have been the brightest spot in my life . . . and truly, a great friend. I do love you very much but, as I have said before, I am not "in love." And that is a problem, Lynne. After a year of having a relationship with you, I am still not "in love" with you.*

I start to shake after reading the first paragraph. In the letter he calls me a "friend" twelve times, which is the most painful word a woman can hear from a man whom she is in love with. Larry is not in love with me! He wants to start looking for another woman to date and informs me this is the most "honest" thing he can do.

I stare at the screen, a deer looking at headlights. Quietly sitting, I catch my breath. I am in trauma. Printing out the e-mail in tears, I call my friend Tony and read the letter to him. There is a rock in my stomach. I cannot function. Having taken my makeup off, I look awful. Tears are streaming down my face.

Tony is very supportive, but he lives in the country forty miles away. I call my other friend, Naomi, and she drops everything and meets me for coffee.

I don't even remember what she says to me this night.

Larry informs me in his devastating e-mail that he will give me the weekend to recover from the "heartbreak" of losing him! Then, after I process the shock, I can e-mail him back. It will take time to get used to the change, but he hopes that I will adjust and get comfortable with him "just as a friend."

He adds that after we e-mail each other for a while, he will call me and we can communicate by phone. He has enjoyed all the wonderful times spent with me this past year, but now he wants to see me only "occasionally—just not as often." Prior to this, we had seen each other once a month.

The next morning feels strange not getting Larry's usual Saturday phone call. My sister takes me shopping. Mechanically I browse the shops, feeling like a zombie.

Sunday I get another e-mail from Larry. He feels terrible, imagining me in tears and at a loss for words. He misses me and hopes to hear from me soon.

I do not respond.

Taking Larry's suggestion, I begin to "process" his words.

Reflecting back on his e-mail, he stated he has never been "in love." He is fifty-one years old, still legally married, although separated and out of the home. I realize I have no business dating a married man.

His whole identity is about "honesty." I realize that he has not been honest with me and I have not been honest with him. I had ignored the yellow flags in our relationship—the fact that he had not said anything meaningful or intimate to me in months, although he had told me he was very much "in love" with me at the *beginning* of our relationship.

Larry has never been betrayed, rejected, or heartbroken by a woman in his entire life. He has no idea how it feels, as *he* is always in control of a relationship and calling the shots.

I receive two other e-mails from him during the week. I don't respond. On Thursday I receive a third e-mail from Larry informing me that he is *still* planning to come up for my birthday. I can't believe it!

Again, I do not respond.

The day before my birthday I receive another e-mail from Larry titled, "I guess I won't be seeing you this weekend." He writes that he realizes I must be angry and hurt and that he hopes some day "when I get over this" we can be friends. He informs me there are a lot of decent men out there and he hopes that I will not be like his wife and give up on the thought of finding someone else. He tells me he hopes I enjoy my birthday the next day, although he knows "it will be tough."

The time has come for me to respond.

On my birthday, I get a "heartwarming" online birthday card from Larry. That evening I send off my response to him, which is a gift I am giving *myself* for my birthday. I let him know that I have come to a realization that after having been with him, I now know what I do *not* want in a man. *I* desire a man who is honest with himself, God, and others. *I* desire exclusiveness and stability in a relationship. I also let him know that I am *not* interested in a friendship with him. I end the letter by stating that my birthday was not a tough day for me. It was a celebration.

Larry is furious. I get two responses from him, and a few days later he e-mails me asking if he can call me on the phone.

I do not respond.

Eight weeks have passed since I received my "Dear John" e-mail from Larry. I have no intention of *ever* interacting with him again.

Hats off to Larry! He may have broken my heart, but his letter allowed me to give *myself* a wonderful birthday gift. I am giving back to myself dignity, honor, and self- respect. I have come to the realization that I will never again settle for crumbs of affection from any man.

LYNNE BIANGO

FIRST WINTER

The well-worn shag carpeting gave me the creeps. The furniture was upholstered in cracked brown plastic. The linoleum was decrepit, not to mention exceptionally ugly. And could I really stand to look at faux-wood trailer paneling for endless days throughout a long New England winter and not go crazy?

For lack of anything better, my husband and I took it.

"Oh, you mean that little shack in the woods?" one of my friends asked when I tried to describe the location of the place we had just rented.

"Yep," I assured her glumly. "That's the one."

It didn't seem much like the newlywed house of my dreams. How was I supposed to turn a place like that into something that felt like a home? I was so depressed about the way it looked inside, I didn't even consider the view.

It was a small cabin located halfway up a steep hillside on a country road. It was sheltered by a stand of sugar maples and partially blanketed by hemlocks and ginger. We moved in with the help of my eighty-something-year-old grandparents in the pitch-dark and the pouring rain and were off to a soggy start.

At first I was so busy despising how ugly it was inside that I was blind to the fact that it overlooked a cow pasture cradled by rows of distant mountains. But by the time we got ourselves settled, replaced the ratty curtains, and hung our few wedding-present pictures on the trailer-paneled walls, I was feeling a little better. And once we had seen a few breathtaking sunrises from the strategically placed picture window in the bedroom, I was hardly even noticing the Naugahyde or the linoleum.

We had no television, no children to look after, no lawn to mow, and no homeowner compulsions to maintain, improve, or renovate. So we had time. More time than I can ever remember having before or since. We read our favorite books out loud to each other. Brilliantly colored leaves fell to Tolkien's *The Hobbit* and *The Lord of the Rings* trilogy. I made batch after batch of Christmas cookies to chapter after chapter of *Anne of Green Gables*. The snow blew into glittering drifts to James Herriot, and melted to Orson Scott Card.

We read, played chess, carved pumpkins, strung popcorn and cranberries, and made snowball lanterns and snow angels. We went sledding and skiing. We were frequently awakened by moonlight. We had picnics on the floor in front of the fireplace—and I don't even recall the awful shag carpet.

And then, too soon, a gorgeous spring came and went, and it was time to move on out of state from the country to the city. I cried with the certain premonition that our lives would never be the same.

We went back to visit a few years ago. So many trees had been cut down. The hemlocks had been hacked away and the ginger uprooted. The pasture, where cows no longer grazed, had been violated by two of the ugliest prefab homes I have ever seen. My grandparents, whom I think I really believed would live forever, were now somehow, impossibly, gone—their own farm looking neglected and tired.

I wished for a long time that we hadn't gone back. I couldn't help the feeling that something had been stolen from me, and that the way things had changed somehow totally eclipsed the way they had been. Then I remembered the utterly dark night in late February that my new husband and I stood, holding hands in the heart of our little sugar bush, transfixed by the sound of a million droplets of sap pulsing from the earth, plinking into hooded metal sugaring buckets. There was no wind, no light but starlight, no distant sound of car or plane—only us. It was as if the stars were singing. I stood there in awed wonder, in the dark stillness, feeling the anchoring warmth of my husband's hand, and in that moment the word "home" was defined for me. It had nothing to do with four walls and nice carpeting, nothing to do with a geographical location, and everything to do with the man whose hand I held and our ability to appreciate as sublime the simple, beautiful moments of life. Together.

It is true that a place I came to love deeply has been totally changed by time. But I look over and smile at my husband roughhousing with our kids. The baby is pulling on his graying hair. Everyone is shrieking with laughter.

Nothing in my life has stayed the same. We have moved six more times since our first winter together. We have had four children. We've said more good-byes to places and people than I would have liked. But I have not lost a thing, because home isn't a place you leave, it's a place you bring with you.

Our first winter in the country gave us the foundation for something that has been a work in progress ever since. Our Home. It's not an address, but a word that has been written with the indelible ink of shared experiences across the pages of my heart.

Karen C. Driscoll

I think everybody should have a shrink.
I don't know how you could get through life without one.
Neve Campbell

TO TELL THE TRUTH

I *followed my husband into the bedroom, forgetting to* breathe. The word "trust" rolled over and over in my mind. John was unaware that I was preparing to tell him something that could transform our lives. For me, one of the most exciting things about life is that one decision, one act, one statement, one single word can change your life's course. But the declaration I was getting ready to make did not excite me. It frightened me. It could end my marriage of seventeen years.

Our new life on five acres, fourteen miles northeast of Colorado Springs, was growing more and more complicated. My hormones raged louder than ever, John's depression deepened as he battled to find work, all four of us were struggling through the children's adolescence, and I'd just brought home a new puppy. Our son, fifteen, was being overtaken by acne. The cure the doctor prescribed made the skin on his lips peel off and bleed and caused an alarming rise in his triglyceride levels. Cheyenne, thirteen months younger, was experimenting with starving one week and bingeing the next. Even our home was at risk; it looked like we were going to lose a battle with the IRS, which would mean we'd be moving—again. Just two years before, we'd left an upscale suburb in Southern California for rural Colorado to "simplify" our lives.

I was a wreck. My cheerful, blind, and busy rush across the surface of life was skidding to a halt. I was being forced to stop—and take a deeper look at my life, at my family, and mostly . . . at myself.

One sunny, superficial morning as I smiled and joked during Cheyenne's regularly protested visit to her internist, a common miracle occurred: One human being saw fear and pain in another and reacted with insightful compassion. Dr. Norris motioned me out of the exam room. She led me down the hall to her office, jotted something down on a scrap of paper, and handed it to me. "Call her," she said. "She's rather unconventional for 'The Springs,' but I think she may be just the person to help you."

Six days later I was sitting with Megan in the basement of a church annex in town. A gold plaque bolted to the bricks outside read "Mercy Center." The walls were unadorned, soft white. Megan relaxed on a loveseat, barefoot and pretty without makeup, her knees tucked up underneath earth-toned gauze. Pillows of all sizes were placed around the room; some were covered in East Indian prints that reminded me of skirts and dresses I wore as a teenager. A windy instrumental breezed through speakers that rested on the floor. I sat in a well-worn armchair across from her and in no time was rambling rapidly, my whole body helping to tell my story. She was stone quiet, listening to every word I said, and somehow (I knew) hearing every word I didn't.

During our next visit Megan urged me to talk with my eyes closed, my back comfortably straight, and my feet flat on the floor. She instructed me to keep my hands and arms still by resting them on the arms of the chair. She was teaching me to breathe, and to slow down, and to go within. She was teaching me to communicate without looking for approval. She was teaching me to see the truth, and to tell the truth. She had suggested I start with those I loved and trusted the most.

That morning I shared with Megan that I was distancing myself from John. I told her I questioned the stability of my marriage because of fantasies I was having about an old friend's husband; our families had recently met for the weekend in Vail. I relayed to Megan that during a Saturday hike Mike and I ended up alone—his wife, Kim, had gone back to their van and when our teenagers sprinted ahead, John took off. I explained how I got winded and Mike surprised me by slowing to a stop. How he turned to face me on the thin dirt path and without asking, slipped my daypack from my back and slid his arms through the straps. I told her how he gave me a sip of water from his bottle even though I had my own. I confessed that when he convinced me to step off the trail to rest on a big rock under the trees, I found myself wishing he would come and sit beside me. Then . . . I imagined him kissing me. My God—I sat there—his wife (my friend!) waiting in the car, my husband possibly within earshot—and imagined Mike kissing me.

"Megan . . . I've been thinking about him a lot." My face burned and my stomach churned. "I don't know why this is happening—I want it to *stop.*"

"What do you think John would say if you told him?" Megan questioned easily.

"I don't know." I was even sicker at the thought.

"What are you afraid of?"

"He'd probably be so hurt he'd want a divorce."

"Are you interested in staying in a relationship where you're afraid to be honest? These feelings are separating you unshared. What do you have to lose by opening up and trusting John with the truth?"

I was leery. But I was listening.

My mind screamed all the way home: *Being this honest is nuts.* But my gut kept insisting: *Not only is it sane, it's essential.* It was Trust that walked me into our bedroom that afternoon.

"Honey . . . I need to tell you something." My voice quavered—I was quaking inside. John leaned back, stiffening, in one of our seafoam-colored swivel chairs. He looked uncomfortable and it wasn't only because he hated that chair. Life had not been easy lately and we were both exhausted. He was chasing an elusive light beyond the darkness of his depression. I spent most of my time fighting to keep our daughter healthy. We had little strength left over to listen to and support each other. I stood silent, facing him, but not fully in the room physically or mentally. John waited for me to speak.

I was more scared than ever. I loved this man and now I was going to hurt him. I didn't know what I was going to say, just that I had to be as honest as possible without spilling unnecessary details. I sat down on top of the crumpled pinstriped sheets at the edge of our king-size bed. My eyes met his, then focused past him through our front window and onto a tall, enduring stand of ponderosas, the green of their needles prominent against the bright blue Colorado sky. After a few deep breaths I looked back into his almost-as-blue eyes.

"B-baby," I stammered . . . "I'm attracted to Mike."

I couldn't believe I said those words aloud. I held my breath, dreading his response.

He stared at me, squinting . . . then asked, "Are you in love with him?"

"No!" I said. But I didn't really know. Could I be in love with two men at the same time?

And then words tumbled out. "I don't understand what it means . . . I'm feeling so guilty, but I can't get him off my mind. I'm afraid of what could happen; I could destroy our lives . . . I could destroy lots of people's lives. I'm so confused. I'm sorry. I don't know what to do. . . ."

"Do you want to split up?"

"No!" shot out again, my word slapping his. Separation did not feel like the answer; our marriage had survived tough times before. I was boosted by my conviction.

Again, silence. A bolt of regret struck. I felt empty and dazed knowing I couldn't take back what I'd said. I was sure that he was going to want to split up. Then, strangely, I was relieved that I had told him; I was no longer alone, keeping a secret that had cut me off from my best friend—my husband. I basked in the frankness of the moment, still fearing what John might say next.

Finally, he took a deep breath. "Well . . ." He exhaled. Then he slowly sucked some more air up through his nose. "Let's see . . . Mike's a tall, handsome guy. He's strong—and he's tan. He's kind."

John paused. I puzzled. He began again. . . .

"He's great with his kids . . . and he loves his wife. He works hard and has a successful business, which makes him a good provider. Hell—I'm attracted to Mike!"

I sprayed out a laugh and melted into tears. In a split second my fear and confusion were eliminated. I leaped forward, threw my arms around John's neck, and buried my face beneath his sandpapery chin. I wept in relief, both of us swiveling in that silly green chair.

I used to think this incident was about honesty; the rewards and freedom it brings. I've told friends about John's reaction, trying to talk them into opening up with their husbands. Thank God none of them took my advice.

When we relocated to Oregon a while later, I wanted to tell John about my latest attraction, Brad. But something always happened to stop me: The phone would ring, the dogs would bark, and I'd chicken out. After several attempts, I finally got it. John doesn't want to hear about my every crush! Blurting out confession after confession would only hurt him. If there's nothing to gain but the release of my guilt, I need to deal with these feelings on my own . . . or with a friend or a counselor.

John and I celebrated our twenty-fifth wedding anniversary this year. We renewed our vows sitting alongside the McKenzie River. Flowing water, moss-covered trees, and tiny yellow flowers bore witness. Tears slipped down my cheeks as I held John's hand and read, "I take you for this day and for all days as my husband. . . . I believe in this marriage more strongly than ever. Baby, you were and are my love for life."

ANDE CARDWELL

FINDING THE RIGHT RING

*Ours was a whirlwind courtship. We met in No-*vember when Alan was visiting New York City for a conference. By May I'd moved to North Dakota, and by October we were engaged. True to the pace we'd kept up thus far, we chose a December wedding in New Jersey since we would be back East for Christmas.

There were some wrinkles on our way to the altar, such as the ice storm on our wedding day, but when the minister pronounced us "husband and wife," I knew we had done the right thing. The day after our wedding we watched the New Year's Eve fireworks over Central Park from our bedroom window high in the St. Moritz. It was a fairy tale.

But all fairy tales have challenges. The lore of love seems to require that true love be tested. Alan and I felt as though our marriage was put through the gauntlet immediately.

It occurred during our honeymoon on Isla Mujeres off of Cancún, Mexico. Instead of shipping home all the wedding gifts and Christmas presents we'd received, we hauled thirteen pieces of baggage through airports, customs, cabs, and water taxis. That was the endurance portion of our test. To increase the challenge, I had left my one pair of comfortable shoes at the hotel at which I'd dressed for my wedding. On my feet was a pair of quickly disintegrating, white lace pumps. We recognized, however, what an absurd sight we made and were able to hold on to our sense of humor, laughing as we loaded all our "stuff" into the water taxi that threatened to capsize in the Gulf of Mexico.

Once at the hotel, we began to relax and spent one idyllic day on the beach where we swam in clear, blue water. We dined by candlelight and walked down sandy lanes from which chickens scattered. It seemed like we'd come through the worst of our honeymoon horrors. The next day, however, a cold I'd been battling before we'd left North Dakota descended with a thud. I ran a high fever and needed to seek medication at the local pharmacy. It took some effort on my part to convey it wasn't Montezuma's revenge I was battling, but the common cold.

"Die-a-ria," insisted the pharmacist, trying to be helpful.

"No, sore throat," I replied, gesturing with a finger to my mouth.

"*Si*, vomit," he said, turning toward the stomach medicines.

It wasn't Vicks VapoRub Alan had imagined smearing on my chest. Yet he never let me feel like I was ruining his honeymoon. Finally, when I was feeling somewhat better we planned a snorkeling expedition at the end of the island. We donned the masks and snorkels and soon the beauty of the sea creatures lured me out beyond my husband. Minutes later I heard him shout to me. From the fear in his voice, I thought he must have seen a shark. It was worse. He'd been holding on to a rock formation when his wedding ring slipped off his finger and disappeared into a crevice below.

"I heard it land," he said. "I'll never forget that 'ding' sound it made." Then he asserted, "I'm not moving until I find it."

He still held firmly to the rock so he wouldn't be swept away by waves, which tugged at him. We searched for a few minutes, feeling that sick lump of dread in our bellies, and then I decided to run up to the snorkel shop. Maybe one of the staff could help us. I came back with a young man who spoke very little English. I pantomimed the loss of the ring, and he seemed to understand. He took a few dives sans snorkel, but came up empty.

It was time for my new husband and I to walk away. Letting go of that rock meant he'd given up on finding his four-day-old wedding ring. He'd wanted a thick band of gold, and we'd looked at many before he found the one that he knew was his. He said he wanted it to be large enough to announce how proud he was to be married to me. Now it was lost in some recess of the rock.

In a last-ditch gesture of hope, Alan offered to pay the young man two hundred dollars if he found the ring after we left the island and mailed it to him, or three hundred if he found it before we left.

We gave the man our information and grudgingly returned our snorkeling equipment. Back at the hotel we went over the incident, rewinding it between us as though we could press the STOP button and it would never have happened. We waited all day for news from the snorkel shop, and at about eight o'clock that night we went out to dinner, attempting to shake off the feeling that losing one's wedding ring was a bad omen for a marriage. In Cancún we would shop for a similar ring, but we both knew that the ring blessed during the wedding ceremony would always hold greater significance.

When we returned to the hotel, we got the surprise we'd given up on. The snorkel shop attendant had left us a message. In poor but understandable English, he stated he had found the ring! He had walked the length of the island, had waited for us, but needed to return home. He would be back the next day. It seemed impossible. First that he'd found it; second that he'd return it. We were offering him a reward, but he could so easily have kept it or sold it, or simply not have bothered to look.

The next day my husband met him in the hotel lobby and placed three crisp hundred-dollar bills into the young man's hand. Both men had tears in their eyes as they made the exchange. For the young man that was more money than he could make in many months at his job. He and his family would live well for a while. As for my husband, the return of the ring felt like a seal on our marriage. All that had occurred on our honeymoon we'd endured as a pair, never resorting to blaming the other.

We recognized we were partners in this thing called life. Loss of the ring hadn't been an omen, but a test of sorts. Losing the ring would be a minor event in the course of a lifetime together. Nevertheless, the return of it holds great symbolic meaning to us. Accidents will surely happen, but sometimes we get lucky, and it seems the universe works together to return that which is lost to its proper place.

I slipped the gold band back on Alan's finger for a second time, and there it has stayed for twelve years and counting.

Kathleen Coudle King

OF HOPE AND SKI SOCKS

"Y*ou know what a second marriage is?" my friend* Mike asked me. "It's the ultimate triumph of hope over experience."

An odd response, especially when the question was: Will you marry me?

Actually, I wasn't asking for Mike's hand—just his assistance. He's more than my oldest friend; he's also an ordained minister, and I had just asked him to perform the ceremony when I would take that leap of faith, once again, down the rabbit hole of marriage.

I tried to form a rebuttal, but stopped myself short of actually speaking. Mike and I fight a lot—we are gold card members of the Devil's Advocate Club—but this time I couldn't disagree.

"You know something? You're absolutely right."

I guess if I rely on experience alone, I would never dare this second trip into that dark, scary tunnel of marriage. I mean, who would? Marriage is hard, even at the best of times—when the bride is fresh and lovely, the groom is young and strong, and the world seems to be blossoming with posies and possibilities. Even when you fervently believe in love song lyrics, you learn pretty quickly that those crooned tunes are little more than pretty background music to the dirty dishes, the tight budgets, and the daily compromises that have to be made to keep a marriage even relatively healthy.

Actually, my first experience in marriage wasn't a bad one. What it was, in a word, was lonely. My ex and I were always very different people—he was an introvert, conservative, and a hard-working realist. I' was—and still am—extroverted, liberal in thought and lifestyle, and someone who loves her work but sees it as simply a part of life, not a life in itself.

In the cotton candy ideals that brides-to-be often swear by, I actually believed that marriage would give each of us the best of both worlds. That by joining our lives together, we would always be learning new and different things, experiencing things we never even contemplated, living lives that were full of adventure and companionship and, of course, love. I thought we would set out side by side on that road, and each would bring what the other lacked so we could safely navigate our way together.

Forget about "abracadabra." I thought "I do" were the magic words, the ones that would make all our differences fade away into the sunset, just like the couples in every fairy tale.

Yes, I really thought that.

What happened instead was that we remained two individuals. The paths never did converge—instead, it turned out that we were on an obstacle course, and we were having a hard time making it through. And then, slowly, the realization dawned—instead of helping each other over each roadblock, we were the ones putting them up in each other's paths. Slowly, the anger at each other, ourselves, at the entire situation emerged.

"I know we can't fix this," I said to my ex-husband at a counseling session. "There's no place in our entire marriage that I'd like to go back to."

It was the saddest statement I ever made.

I hadn't been single very long when I met Scott—if you call what we had a "meeting." It may sound cliché at this point, but we met over the Internet—not in a chat room (perish the thought!) but in a trivia tournament. I had been assigned to a team; he was the team captain. For a long time, that was the extent of the relationship.

And then we developed a working relationship. I had a freelance writing assignment that needed pictures; my trivia team captain had spoken of dabbling in photography. I asked him if he could provide photographs, and he came through. Soon I was writing words and he was taking pictures—and together, full articles were created and sold.

An added bonus: We were becoming friends.

We communicated mostly through e-mail, which of course put me at a distinct advantage. From my e-mails he could learn that I was a fascinating, driven, intense writer. What he couldn't see was the mountain of laundry, the maple syrup in my hair, and the four kids who were in constant need of attention, homework clues, and peanut butter sandwiches.

It's loud here, I wrote him. *There's so much confusion.* It was easy to explain; he could read it in silence.

If you need a friend, I'm there for you, he responded (he was three hundred miles away from my home in New Jersey).

And in a way he was. I complained about my cold, and UPS delivered a Tupperware container full of homemade chicken soup with a postmark from out of state. My son scribbled on his face with Magic Marker, and a package of washable felt tip pens appeared in my mailbox.

Then, one day, a package arrived. Of course, I receive a lot of packages—books to review and samples of laundry detergent, magazine subscriptions, and free address labels.

But in this package, a note read *Wear these when you need to feel close.* I unfolded the tissue paper and found a pair of warm woolen ski socks. I wore them to bed that night, and whenever I was feeling alone. I even carried them in my pocket at times, to touch when I needed a hand to squeeze tight.

It was a dubious beginning. Eventually, he moved closer. He was transferred from Massachusetts to Philadelphia and, eventually, we grew closer. Again, I was on an obstacle course, but this time, someone was helping me around the hurdles. I warned him about me as we became something more than e-mail buddies.

It seemed fair to warn him. After all, his life as a single man was his own. My life involved four children, two jobs, a mortgage, and the pile of bills that came as part of a divorce settlement.

"There's a lot involved here," I told him tentatively. "Sometimes it's hard to handle everything."

He smiled a brave and simple smile. "My hands are free," he told me, so I took one.

So yes, in spite of my experience, I'm going to travel this road again. I'm a creature of hope, not of habit, after all.

I'm not even worried about cold feet. After all, I have more than ski socks. I have my new husband and all the things we have in common to keep me warm.

Mary Dixon Lebeau

II
HEAVEN SENT

As we let our own light shine,
we unconsciously give other people permission
to do the same.

Marianne Williamson

ANGEL IN THE CITY

I *was born and raised in a small town in the South.* We never locked the doors and left the windows open in the summer to help escape the heat. We slept confident that no harm would come to us during those humid nights filled with singing frogs, chirping crickets, and blinking fireflies outside our bedroom windows. As a young girl, I did not know fear.

Years later, I left that small-town existence and headed for the bright lights of a prominent city in the Midwest—and an unfamiliar, exciting lifestyle. I was a flight attendant based in Chicago.

One night, after an exhausting four-day trip, my plane touched down precisely at 11:30 P.M. in Chicago and taxied slowly to the gate. It was the middle of January and my arrival announcement included the frigid 20-degree temperature. After saying my good-byes to the deplaning passengers, I gathered my belongings, said good night to my flying partners, and hurried to the front of the terminal, hoping I had not missed the last limo to the city. As luck would have it, I made it just in time. The limo left O'Hare Airport and joined the Kennedy Expressway to the loop and the well-known Palmer House Hotel in the heart of the city. As the limo snaked through the bright lights of traffic, I closed my eyes and relaxed. The long trip had taken its toll and I was glad to be on my way home.

Upon arrival at the Palmer House, I walked the short distance to Monroe Avenue and waited only briefly for the Lake Shore Drive bus. The next stop would be directly across the street from my apartment building near the Lincoln Park area.

Unexpectedly, a young man I had not noticed before appeared from the shadows of a building and boarded the bus with me. He was wearing sunglasses, a black stocking cap, and a leather jacket. He sat down directly across the aisle from me. Although he remained masked behind his sunglasses, I intuitively felt him watching me. The bus was all but empty due to the late hour and I felt a little uneasy. I concentrated on other things to reassure myself. I hoped my roommate, Sally, had returned from her trip. Returning home to an empty apartment late at night was not something I enjoyed.

Sally and I had days off to look forward to. We always made sure we scheduled the same days off so we could shop, sample different restaurants, or attend a play together. Chicago had a host of things to do and see, and we never grew tired of exploring the city's vast labyrinth.

I was looking forward to a good night's sleep in my own bed. Hotels were often noisy with people coming and going at all hours. I preferred the feel of my down comforter and soft pillows. It was a small apartment, but for Sally and I it was cozy and it was home.

Suddenly I realized I had missed my stop and was at least a block past my apartment building. I walked to the front of the bus and explained my dilemma to the driver. He immediately stopped and let me off. The young man wearing sunglasses got off, too. Had he missed his stop as well? That was highly unlikely. An adrenaline chill surged through my body. My uneasy feeling turned to icy fear.

As I walked down the sidewalk in the direction of my apartment building, he cautiously waited for the bus to pull away, surveyed the dark neighborhood, and began walking at a brisk pace behind me. A blast of icy wind whipped at my coat and I wrapped it closer around my body as I hastened my steps. I glanced over my shoulder several times and noticed, as I walked faster, his steps also quickened. I felt panicky and my heart was pounding so hard I thought it would explodc in my chest. I started to run, and so did my stalker. I could hear the falling of his threatening footsteps closing the distance between us. I felt caught in the web of one of those terrible nightmares, struggling to run to escape something sinister, but never managing to gain any ground.

The street was completely deserted, and I knew I would not make it to the safety of my apartment without being apprehended by the menacing stranger. I slipped on a patch of ice and almost fell, but managed to regain my balance and continue running. My breath caught the cold air in small evaporating clouds as I ran. With every step I prayed, "God please help me!"

Suddenly out of nowhere, a yellow taxicab went by. Before I could scream for help, the cab came to a jolting halt and backed up quickly. "Get in!" the driver yelled. I ran toward the taxi crying and gasping for breath at the same time. My lungs ached and my legs felt like limp noodles. "Get in, get in!" he continued to urge. I threw my luggage in the backseat and leaped in behind it. Immediately we sped away. I looked back just in time to see the silhouette of my aggressor dart between two buildings and disappear in the dark shadows.

The cab driver wasted no time reprimanding me, "What were you thinking . . . out walking a deserted street alone at this hour?" he bellowed. Choking back tears, I told him what had happened and the reprimand in his voice turned to the gentleness of a fatherly lecture.

When we reached my apartment building he refused my efforts to pay him, shaking his head adamantly and waving my money away. He helped me out of the taxi and escorted me to the door of the lobby. "Be careful from now on," he said firmly, waving his finger in my face. I nodded and, stumbling over my words, managed a weak, "Thank you. I'll never forget you." He smiled slightly, gently patted my cheek, and waited until I was safely inside the lobby before he returned to his cab. I waved good-bye as he pulled away from the curb. I didn't get his name, yet I probably owe him my life.

I spent a restless night thinking about my terrifying experience.

"Thank you, thank you," I prayed. A stranger I would never see again had delivered me from harm's way. For a long time now, I've asked God to bless this guardian angel and keep him safe, and I no longer worry that I didn't get his name. After all, God knows whom I mean.

Patricia C. Fischer

THE THROWAWAY

I *wouldn't shed one more tear. Four years of back and* forth in the torrential relationship had been plenty long enough to break my spirit and drain me of any hope. His cruel words had been too harsh this time and, although they were familiar, the sting was deeper than usual. He wasn't sure what he wanted again. So be it. There could be no going back. I wouldn't judge him. I wouldn't try to convince him again. I wouldn't make excuses for him or try to help him heal. I would do the only thing left to do—leave him in his uncertainty, locked alone in his world of solitude. Did he really love me? Probably. Could he ever allow himself to be loved? Probably not. My head ached from the continual bang on the wall.

Throughout the night, I packed my clothes as I waited for dawn to bring the light needed to travel the solemn back roads of the low country. He had been my reason for living for so long. Now, I was lost. I had been certain that it was God's will for us to build a life of service to Him together. Apparently, the plan had changed, against my will. I had no idea where I would go now or how I would serve my purpose. The silence of the morning, gray and still, offered time for a gentle good-bye. With one last kiss on his mouth, I squeezed his hand firmly, and emotions from the years flooded me, making me yearn for an alternative, but one was not coming. How I wished he would take me in his arms and ask me to stay. How I longed for one more false promise from him so I could close my eyes to the truth for just a little while longer. But his eyes were dead. He no longer looked at me, only through me. He was gone.

The world drizzled on me, and I felt each individual splash of coldness as I closed the trunk and got into my car. I watched the door to his house close slowly behind me as I pulled out of the dirt driveway. My emotional exhaustion left me numb. I did not cry. Surrounded only by country, my thoughts turned to the sky as I focused my mind on prayer. "How will I serve you now, God?" I said out loud.

I knew that if I couldn't believe in a higher reason for my pain at that moment that I would not make it in one piece over the bridge and off the island that I had called home for so long. My sadness was complete. My feelings of defeat lulled me into a grief that I had only known with the passing of my mother. I chose silence over song. The two-lane road through the marsh was slowly but surely winding behind me, pushing the pain away one mile at a time. I was truly leaving him this time.

The roads seemed desolate that morning. It was the day after Thanksgiving. Most people were still tucked in bed with their lovers, slumbering off the remains of the big holiday meal. The deserted stretch of pavement through the backwaters seemed to be out of place, as if the asphalt had been dropped by accident. It did not make sense, but then again not much did anymore. I accelerated despite my fear of the falling rain loosening the oil on the roadway. The miles passed too slowly.

In the distance, something caught my eye, something in the right lane, coming right at me. The rain and the reflection of the car lights blurred my vision. What was it? A rat? A squirrel? I swerved to the left to avoid crushing it. I slowed as I passed and realized it was a tiny puppy, howling and running as fast as its little legs could carry it.

I braked and slowed and was overcome with feelings of self-pity. "Oh God, why me, why today?" I bellowed. I knew that there was no way I could just leave it out there, alone to die. With some skillful maneuvering, I carefully turned the car around and headed back to look for the baby. There were now cars coming toward me, and I feared that the puppy would be struck before I could get to it. Finally, I saw it in the distance, still running.

I pulled up parallel to the animal and pulled off to the right shoulder. He was crying at the top of his lungs for his mama. I opened the car door, and he looked up at me with the desperate love in his eyes that only another lost soul needing a home would recognize. He raced across the road into my open arms, and I lifted him to my chest, cuddling him closely to my neck. His body filthy and bones protruding with starvation, he began to whimper. He nestled up to my throat, cooing with gratefulness. I melted.

He was so sickly, so puny. I sat for a moment, confused by the change of the winds, waiting for clarity. I picked at the large fleas that were racing over his scalp and circling his tiny blue eyes. He wasn't old enough to be away from his mama or the rest of the pack. I wondered how in the world he ended up way out here, alone, in the middle of nowhere. There were no people, no homes or businesses for miles. Without a doubt, he must have been a throwaway. Surely, I thought, there was a special place in Hell for those who do this to the helpless. He shook from the cold. What a little trooper, I thought. What a fighting spirit he had. He could have simply crawled off into the woods. I took off my sweatshirt and placed him in the middle, his pink belly now faced upward. I swaddled him tightly on my lap and cried harder when I realized that he must have really trusted me to lie on his back. I longed to feel worthy of that. He seemed so vulnerable.

It wasn't long before I began to sob because I realized that God had answered my prayers, and done so immediately. I had asked Him how I might serve again if I was to leave and had been given an immediate assignment. I felt shivers all over my body. Suddenly, I knew that I had made the right decision that morning and that I was headed in the right direction. I had ended up exactly where I was supposed to be at that very moment. Overwhelmed and humbled, I cried out with thanks.

His name would be Petie. I promised him that he would be just fine now. My mind raced as I tried to decide what I should do next. Medical help. I should get him to a veterinarian. I swung the car back around and raced for the closest town. It was early, but the vet was in. The workers cooed over the new baby, but also explained that they could not keep him or offer him free service. I explained that I didn't expect that. I just wanted to get him started off on the right foot. The exam brought good results. Petie was just three and a half pounds of healthy Jack Russell terrier, probably only six weeks old. Before he knew it, he was sitting at the end of his very own rainbow. He was given his first meal; he had his first shots; he had his first worming; he had his first bath. The colors of his life were changing; warm water had turned his coat from a dingy gray to a soft white. It wasn't long before he was yapping and playing with his new friends.

New love was in the air. I knew I couldn't just leave him there, only to be taken to the humane society, so it was also true that Petie now had a new mama. The animal hospital workers wished us luck as they sent us off to start a new life together. We climbed back into the car and again I wrapped him in my shirt and laid him across my lap. He fell into a deep sleep. Once again, I wasn't sure whether to turn right or left out of the parking lot, but then again, I knew it didn't really matter. God was driving.

I looked down at this tiny miracle that had been given to me. "Petie, we serve an amazing God," I whispered.

I asked myself why I had continued to question God's answer for my situation. Why had I stayed for so long? I tried to recall what I had feared would happen if I freed myself. I could no longer remember. I was more determined than ever to learn how to let go of the steering wheel and simply follow. Petie knew how and so would I. Petie and I drove deliberately into our new life that day. I threw away my pain and feelings of failure and replaced them with renewed hope and great life expectations. The ticking of my life clock once again began to beat my very own rhythm, and I was on the road to healing.

JENNIFER R. FINLEY

Any dessert that doesn't have chocolate
is a pointless dessert.
KATE BECKINSALE

CHOCOLATE HEAVEN

One afternoon, I was standing in my kitchen trying to decide what to fix for lunch when I noticed a commercial for an Almond Joy candy bar. I realized that it had been at least thirty years since I had eaten an Almond Joy. Everyone in my family knows that my favorite candy bars are Mr. Goodbar, Hershey's with almonds, and PayDay. I stopped what I was doing and looked longingly at that commercial and said out loud, "I wish I had an Almond Joy to eat right now." Then I forgot about it and went back to making my lunch.

Approximately three hours later there was a knock at the door. I knew it was time for my son to get home from school, but I did not think it would be him because he never knocked. I opened the door and there stood my son, Abraham, holding something out for me. I remember how shocked I was when I realized that he held an Almond Joy in his hand.

Every day Abraham took fifty cents to school to buy some ice cream, or whatever snack he decided to have after lunch. His snack was something he looked forward to and he never brought a snack home, especially not for me! When I asked him what made him bring it to me, he said he really did not know. I asked him what time he bought it, and it happened to be the exact time that I had been wishing for one.

He said he was standing there, trying to decide what he wanted to eat, when something "just came over him" to buy an Almond Joy for me. When I told him that I had wished for one earlier, he didn't know what to think. We split the candy bar and enjoyed every morsel—knowing that those up above have a sense of humor and we were experiencing a little bit of Heaven.

Gayle Montanez

ROCKY

R*ocky was a large, powerfully built Alaskan malamute.* Tall enough to put his front paws on my shoulders when he stood on his hind feet, his muscular body was broad and strong. He had coarse, thick hair that begged you to run your fingers through it and short pointed ears that were silky soft to the touch. Silver and black with touches of cream, he was a beautiful animal who enjoyed howling at the moon on dark, starlit nights. His voice created eerie, mournful music that made the hair on my arms stand up whenever I heard him.

An avowed outside dog, the big husky hated to come in the house and I could usually get him inside only after bribing him with chunks of his favorite food. As soon as he finished his treat, he was ready to go right back out. No matter what I tried, I just couldn't convince him that it would be fun to be an indoor dog.

One Friday evening, my husband left for an out-of-town weekend business trip. With only Laura—my two-year-old daughter—and Rocky for company, I looked forward to spending a couple of quiet days catching up on my reading. To my surprise, just before dark that night Rocky began whining and pawing at the front door. There was no mistaking his meaning. He wanted in! Puzzled, I held the door open and he sauntered inside like he owned the place.

With one swish of his bushy tail, he swept everything off the coffee table. Laura giggled in delight as I pretended to scold him. Rocky grinned at me and strolled away to investigate the rest of the house. Laura tagged along behind him. Before long, the two settled in her room, where Rocky decided to lie in the doorway. Halfway in the room and halfway in the hall, his shaggy body filled up the narrow space. He gave no indication that he wanted to go back outside.

Before long it was Laura's bedtime. As she drifted off to sleep, the dog curled in a tight ball and dozed off, too. A little surprised by his insistence to stay in her room and miss cuddling with me on the sofa, I shrugged and left them alone. I got myself a snack and a magazine, and settled in to read. The house was so quiet, I forgot all about Rocky.

Sometime later a loud vehicle drove up in front of the house. Somebody turning around, I thought. Then the engine shut off and a door slammed. I hurried to the window and peeked out between the mini-blind slats. A scruffy-looking young man was stepping on the porch.

He looked vaguely familiar, like someone I might have met before. Cautiously, I opened the heavy wooden door a crack. The man pulled open the outer storm door and propped against it.

"Hi," he said. His tone was friendly, but the icy look in his eyes sent a warning chill rippling up my spine. "Your husband told me he was going out of town for the weekend and I promised to check on you."

Alarm bells clanged in my brain. In the space of a second, the horrible thought that I had to get rid of this man or both my daughter and I would be in serious danger raged through my mind.

"I'm fine," I replied as firmly as I could. My mouth felt like it was full of sawdust. "There's really no need for you to be concerned. Thanks for stopping."

I reached for the storm door but he jerked it open wider and parked one foot on the threshold. My heart pounded wildly.

"I think I'll visit for a little while," he said, and started to step into the living room.

Terrified, I tried to shove the heavy wooden door shut, but he blocked it and forced it open, pushing me back into the room.

Suddenly, the man froze, his eyes riveted on something behind me. I glanced around and there stood Rocky, his lovely plumed tail waving gently back and forth. The dog's lips were curled back in a huge nasty smile that exposed every sharp, wicked-looking tooth in his head. My knees went weak.

"D-does that dog bite?" the man stammered.

"Yes," I said. "He sure does."

"Sorry to have bothered you." The man abruptly let go of the door and stumbled backward, his eyes fixed on Rocky.

I slammed the door shut and turned the locks. A few seconds later, the truck engine roared to life and sped away.

Trembling, I dropped to the floor and threw my arms around Rocky's neck, burying my face in his beautiful fur. He panted cheerfully as I hugged and kissed him and told him what a wonderful boy he was. There was no doubt in my mind that he had saved Laura and me from something too horrible to think about.

As if he sensed that the danger had passed, Rocky asked to go outside. Overwhelmed with emotion, I watched him romp around the moonlit yard. How had he known that we would need his protection? Why did he pick this particular night to ask to come in the house? After a few moments of wonder, I decided not to question his knowledge. Instead, I thanked the heavens for my beloved dog, Rocky, who knew how to protect my little girl and me at just the right time.

Anne Culbreath Watkins

A TIMELY GIFT

Things were rough for me that year. I'd lost my job and, despite more than ten years of experience in my particular field, had been unable to find a new one. As financial problems descended, I was filled with self-doubt. I was past thirty years of age, unmarried, and, now, unemployed. Was I doing everything right? Was I doing *anything* right? What kind of example was I as an unemployed and unmarried female minister?

Feelings of being a failure had been my breakfast, lunch, and dinner when a friend and I went to hear a senior colleague preach one Sunday. His message took an unexpected turn, as he began to lambaste women in ministry. He spoke passionately, saying we were out of place. He said that women could barely help one another, and most certainly couldn't minister effectively to men. I was surprised to hear this preacher talk that way, since our prior conversations led me to believe he felt differently. Usually this type of sexist talk would have rolled off my back, but this time it cut me to the quick.

As my friend drove me home, I forgot about the testimonials in the form of letters and phone calls I'd received over the past few years, quite a few from men telling me how my ministry had helped them. Maybe the guy was right. Maybe I'd been out of place, and that was why I'd been having such a rough time. Retreating to my own thoughts, I rode along quietly. Sadness and depression overwhelmed me.

When I got out of her car, I thought of my own SUV and how

an accident a week earlier had left me without transportation. *Good Christians don't lose their jobs and have car accidents. Good Christians don't experience one disaster after another.* Perhaps I *should* focus on becoming someone's dutiful wife and stop giving so much attention to ministry.

Weeping, I sat on the side of my bed and considered canceling a revival I was scheduled to conduct that night. Without a car, I didn't even know how I was going to *get* to the revival. Oh, how I hated asking for this kind of help! I decided it would be unprofessional to cancel, so I'd go through with it. I prayed for strength but felt hypocritical, ministering to others when my life was going so badly. When my sister and I arrived, we could see the church was filled with exuberant people. I worried for a moment that my mood wouldn't match their enthusiasm, but we had a great service. Men and women stopped me afterward, telling me how blessed they had been by the night's message. As I was leaving the building a few minutes later, one of the ministers from the church came to me and placed a man's watch in my hands. He said that a man had put it in the offering basket, and further explained that "around here, we give the best thing we have as an offering if we have no money." I thought it odd, but put the watch in my purse and went home.

I sat on the same edge of the bed I'd sat upon a few hours earlier. I'd done my job, but wasn't feeling much better. Just then, a Voice said to me, "Go get that watch." When I had the watch in my hands, a comforting loving feeling wrapped around me like an encasement. It filled my heart with peace and my eyes with tears. My doubts were locked out and His love was locked in. I pictured some man overwhelmed with gratitude after hearing the message tonight, taking off his precious watch and placing it into the offering basket as an offering to the Lord. The Voice spoke again to me, saying, "It is not you who touches the hearts of men and women, truly. It is *Me* who touches them *through* you. Be encouraged." I reveled in His presence as the sadness and depression lifted. These days, I wear the watch on those occasions when I need a little extra courage to minister. It reminds me of what I am there to do and Who has sent me to do it. I look forward to the day when I will pass on this "timely gift" to another young woman in ministry who needs a special kind of courage of her own.

DAWNE J. HARRIS

MOTHER KNEW BEST

"Here is a gift I made for you to put on your* kitchen table," exclaimed my mother. My mother had learned to crochet in her senior years and had made some lovely things. As she advanced in age, she developed many serious health problems, including dementia, producing a decline in her mental faculties. Because of this, I had thought she stopped crocheting long before.

I opened the box and pulled out what seemed to be a beautiful tablecloth, and then I noticed the jagged edges making the piece look bizarre. There were clumps of material bunched together, ruining the otherwise well-handcrafted gift.

I thanked her, took the tablecloth home, and put it in the linen closet. I couldn't bring myself to throw it away.

Whenever my parents came to visit, my mother would ask, "Where is the tablecloth I made for you?" I made up excuses saying it was at the cleaners, or I was using another one for a change. I couldn't break her heart by allowing her to see how awful it looked on my table.

Mom died several years later. Her death was a blessing because she was very ill. We had a wonderful funeral with family and friends and life moved on, taking us with it.

In 2001, I decided to renovate and paint my kitchen. My husband and I saw a very unusual kitchen set at a garage sale, which we thought would look great in our newly redecorated kitchen. I have always liked things that are a little different from the "run-of-the-mill" furniture. This table was square with extremely large rounded corners. I remarked to everyone that I would never be able to find a tablecloth for it because it wasn't round or square but a combination of both shapes.

A few nights after we bought the set, I dreamed of my mother. In the dream she gave me a box saying it was a gift for my new kitchen. In the box was the strange, uneven tablecloth.

The next day, I had the urge to take another look at the last item my mother made before her death—the tablecloth with the ghastly bunched up uneven edges. I don't know why I put it on my new kitchen table. I smoothed the folds over the edges of the table and gasped in amazement. The material gently cascaded down from the rounded corners. The straight sides complimented the rest of the table. How could my mother have created such an exquisite custom-made tablecloth for a table that was bought five years after her death? And what about the dream? Did my mother really come to remind me about her gift?

My husband and I agreed it was one of life's wonderful mysteries that may never be solved. We still enjoy our new kitchen and most of all we love the main feature—our "made-to-order" tablecloth.

Diane Fleming

Prayer is a long rope with a strong hold.
HARRIET BEECHER STOWE

"ALL MIGHTY" SHARK REPELLENT

My *husband, Mark, used to be a submariner in* the navy. Sailors and their families have little contact during a deployment, but my children and I prayed every night for my husband's safety. The first night Mark was gone, Matthew and Alex realized Daddy was in the ocean with the sharks. Every night thereafter, they prayed sweetly, "Dear God, please don't let Daddy fall into the ocean and please don't let the sharks get him."

Thinking they needed some clarification, I told them that although it was good to pray for Daddy to be safe while he was gone, it wasn't likely that he would fall off the submarine or be eaten by sharks. But they would not be dissuaded from this prayer. Since we have a "say anything you want to God in your nighttime prayer" policy at our house, I just let them go on praying rather than argue with them. And if their prayers made them feel their daddy was safe, so much the better.

For most of the time the crew is under way, the submarine is underwater, so the likelihood of falling off is very low. In an emergency, however, someone on board may need to leave the submarine while it is far from land. If a submariner needs emergency medical attention, a medical transfer, called a "medivac," occurs. If someone in the submariner's family is very ill or dies, then another emergency transfer called a humanitarian transfer, or a "humavac," takes place.

In either case, a helicopter flies out to the boat and sends down a harness to the sailor. The submariner gets into the harness and the helicopter pulls him up and flies away. These transfers can be very dangerous because high seas may come up without warning.

While Mark was deployed on this patrol, he was on the bridge of a Trident submarine during a humavac. The humavac went off without a hitch and the sailor was removed from the boat safely. However, after the humavac, the sea started to get rough. The bow of the sub plunged into the sea and the submarine was actually eight feet underwater with Mark on the bridge. Hanging on as tightly as he could, Mark watched ocean waves rush over his head as he was thrown to the floor of the bridge.

Mark said that they had never battened down the hatches as quickly as they did at that moment. Both he and the lookout got back down safely into the submarine. About half an hour later, he was in the Corpsman's office and still in shock. If he had fallen into those frozen seas off the coast of Alaska, he could have easily gotten hypothermia and died before the crew could rescue him.

When my husband returned home from patrol and told me the story of how he almost fell off the boat, I was astounded. I never thought he would be anywhere *near* the surface or have any danger of being in the water. Thankfully, my children had been praying for the right thing all along.

JENNIFER GALVIN

THE PRINCESS AND THE RESCUE

I've been off and on diets my whole life, concerned with my appearance always. I bought into the romantic fairy tale of the princess being carried off by her true love to live happily ever after and, beginning at a young age, I yearned for him to come find me. In the meantime, looking great was part of the formula. One had to be ready for the prince's arrival. As early as elementary school, I learned how to hold in my stomach all day to look thinner. It's still a habit, even now.

I usually looked fine through the years, but was seldom satisfied. I got quite thin once during a particularly captivating romance but when that ended, my weight gain gradually began.

At forty-seven I was thirty pounds overweight and became aware of a strong force within that seemed determined to sabotage my every dietary effort, casting me adrift in a wild, uncontrollable sea of steady weight gain. I wanted to understand what this childish inner tantrum was all about and finally told my best friend and spiritual teacher of my concerns.

She had heard plenty of this from me over the years, and I could tell it strained her patience to be discussing it yet again. She said I needed to get past this obsessive attention I paid to my appearance—it was blocking my spiritual growth. "Don't you think you can be heavy and still serve God?" she asked.

"Yes," I grumbled. "But I don't feel good this way, and my clothes don't fit me anymore!"

"Then buy clothes that are looser," she answered. "Stop being the princess that has to look just so. All she thinks about is how her waistband feels against her belly button."

Something inside rose up angrily against this. *What, I have to be fat to serve God?* I seethed inwardly.

"You're putting too much emphasis on the material," she added, "which is starving the soul. It's like spiritual anorexia. Let it go so we can move on."

I imagined how huge I could become if I did indeed let it go. It was a frightening thought.

"But I want to understand what this inner battle is all about," I persisted. "I try to make reasonable choices—God wants that—and something inside demands ice cream, which isn't good for me!"

"Ice cream *is* good for you," she responded. "You need the calcium."

"Hey, I can't eat all the ice cream I feel like eating!" I cried, frustrated.

"I know what's happening with you," she said finally. "Your spirit has indicated many times that you never give it enough room, that you don't listen to it. You're so concerned with what other people think of you that you don't hear what God has placed inside you. The still voice of truth. Well, now it is determined to challenge the beliefs that are stifling it."

It struck me then. "Oh, my God," I breathed.

I got it.

And it was the opposite of what I'd been assuming.

It was the spirit of truth that was demanding my attention, seeking to get bigger, and it would use a physical avenue if necessary. The fairy tale princess, on the other hand, required that I maintain an attractive façade in order to be valuable. She was holding on to a destructive lie. How much would it take to crush this lie that stood between God and me? Twenty pounds? Fifty? Whatever; a soul was at stake, bound by falsehood, and it had to be shaken awake.

So it wasn't the princess being rescued from the castle.

It was the castle (or inner temple) being rescued from the princess.

She was demanding the youthful skin, shapely waist, stunning hair. She had to have stylishly coordinated outfits that turned heads.

The castle reverberated with her needs and so was being dominated by a petulant brat in a tiara and cute shoes.

I was speechless at the discovery.

"So if I want to feel better about myself and try to accomplish that just by losing a couple of dress sizes . . ." I thought aloud.

"Then what are you really feeling?" my friend prompted.

"The belief that something physical makes me valuable. That my worth lies in how others see me."

"And if that's what you believe, that's the message you pass along to others. It's what you teach."

"Still . . ." I hesitated. "I can't teach that God wants everyone fat, either."

"Fat?" she echoed. "That's just the particular physical attribute *you're* focusing on. The underlying problem is attaching spiritual value to *any* physical appearance—whether you see it as desirable or undesirable."

"I know He doesn't see us as bodies," I conceded. "That's how we rate one another."

"So what is it He really wants for everyone?" she challenged.

A lot more than I seem to want for myself, I thought. I recalled religious diet books I'd followed where weight loss for God was encouraged, and failure implied lack of faith. The reasons for wanting to get thin could be based in false values, however, so that failure is just as well. I knew that God cares most about the beliefs fueling my behavior, and whether they're based in the truth or not. But I was deeply moved to realize that when I over-focus on my body—on creating a fantasy image that will draw people's admiration—I'm helping neither them nor myself toward what really matters. *I'm encouraging the lie.*

"I have to let go of the fairy tale," I announced. "It's become a tyrant. It demands I meet a worldly standard that's totally worthless."

"Well, good plan. That princess should never have been allowed to rule the castle."

How interesting to realize that often what I see as an enemy attacking is really a savior rescuing. It had never occurred to me to think of a weight gain itself as a rescue mission—I was so desperate to battle it that I couldn't hear the message.

I won't be following a particular diet anymore. On a deeper level, I'm rededicating myself to daily meditation. Reading more on topics that have to do with healing. Affirming consciously that my worth lies in my divine creation. Casting myself, fat or thin, into God's arms . . . and accepting His love for me.

LAURA STANFORD

III
A WOMAN'S INFLUENCE

One is not born, but rather becomes, a woman.

SIMONE DE BEAUVOIR

RATTLESNAKES DO NOT LAY EGGS

Because *their parents prized education, my grand-*mother and her sister were packed off to college in 1902. Scrapbook notes from that time give us a look at what the young ladies ate for a "spread" (biscuits, cheese, and tea), the names of their most ardent swains, and the cost of a yard of grosgrain ribbon—ten cents. There are no scrapbook notes describing the classes the two young ladies attended, but my guess is that my grandmother majored in Trivia and in place of a final exam, she must have been instructed to pass these "facts of life" down to succeeding generations.

My mother recalls that from the time she was an infant, she heard such motherly pearls of wisdom as "Butterflies taste with their feet instead of their mouths," and "Rattlesnakes do not lay eggs. They give birth to their living young."

As my mother sat down to practice her piano lessons, her mother never failed to say, "The first piano was built in Florence, Italy, in 1720." Working in her garden prompted my grandmother to spout, "A bean stalk will climb the bean pole from right to left, but hops will climb the pole from left to right."

It was only natural, then, that along with my mother's milk, I drank in "The first pure food law was enacted in the United States on June 26, 1848." And while most mothers and grandmothers were reciting, "This little piggy went to market," my caretakers were advising me that a person who has six toes on one foot is said to be afflicted with hexadactylism. At age two, expecting applause after singing "Twinkle, Twinkle Little Star," I was reminded instead that the twinkling of stars is entirely an atmospheric illusion. The lesson of the beans and hops outdid itself when I began to write my name. "Always write from the left to the right," I was told. "Think of yourself as a hop and not a bean."

As a grade school student, I had many outstanding teachers, but I was convinced that none of them knew as much as my grandmother and mother. Mrs. Hanson made us memorize the list of U.S. presidents, but it was my mother who knew that Abraham Lincoln was the child of cousins who had married; Andrew Jackson once carved his name on Lookout Mountain; and President James A. Garfield was a member of the House of Representatives, a senator-elect, and the president-elect all at the same time for a period of four days. And who but my grandmother knew which three presidents of the United States—Chester Arthur, Grover Cleveland, and Woodrow Wilson—were the sons of clergymen?

Dinner table conversations often brought out the fact that there is at least some sugar in practically every food, including meat, and eighteen newborn opossums can be placed in a teaspoon. Because I had a sweet tooth, I was pleased with the information about the sugar in my meat, but somewhat unnerved by the thought of opossums on my teaspoon.

When I fell behind in math, my mother took it upon herself to teach me the times table and set a six-week goal for this monumental task. Six weeks was decided upon as the limit because of Patrick Henry, who began his study of the law only six weeks before he was admitted to the bar. His "Give me liberty or give me death" phrase is, in my mind, all jumbled together with "nine times seven equals sixty-three."

Facts fell as gently as raindrops all throughout my young years, culminating with the purchase of my first piece of intimate apparel when my mother informed the clerk, "Queen Isabeau of France was the first woman in recorded history to wear lingerie."

I was so embarrassed by my purchase and the pearl of wisdom that I could hardly speak to my mother for days after the event. I vowed I would never spout trivia to my children as my maternal ancestors had done.

I was quite surprised, then, to hear myself tell my daughter on the occasion of her first heartbreak that King Louis of France played tennis with such abandon that he caught a chill and died. My daughter was so caught off guard by my seeming lack of sympathy that she started to laugh through her tears. Swept into her laughter, I began to state all the other trivia facts passed down from generation to generation.

We nearly split our sides over "Rattlesnakes do not lay eggs," became hysterical about the eighteen newborn opossums cradled in a spoon, and held a contest to see which of us could most quickly write their name from right to left.

"How come you never taught me any of this stuff?" my daughter asked as the night and her grief passed. "And where did you learn all of this?" she probed, repeating some of the lines.

"I got it from my Alma Maters," I said. "By the way, did you know that that is a Latin term meaning 'bounteous mothers'?"

And so they were. And so, my daughter now thinks, am I.

JEAN JEFFREY GIETZEN

BOYS KEEP OUT

My little sister Marian (in her fifties now, but still short, cute, and younger than I) has a bazillion women friends who support one another through thick and thin. Chocolate chip cookies, a ride to the hospital, balloons, a walk in the park, a shoulder to cry on . . . you name it, they're there with whatever is needed. Once it was planting a garden.

The garden was mine, too. At the time, Marian and I were in the throes of painful divorces; our long-term marriages had crumbled and we were on that crazy roller coaster ride of exhilaration one moment and intense depression the next. We mistrusted all men we didn't despise, an attitude that didn't change when we began dating again. Our mistrust was usually justified. After yet another date with a guy who turned out to be a drunken oaf, and married to boot, we'd commiserate over the phone. "Not again!" I'd say. "What is it with these guys? I will never go near one again, and certainly never get married."

"Me, too," she'd say. "Me, neither."

We were not alone. Several of those many friends who clustered around my sister were in relationships that were breaking up. We were all furious with the world and the rotten creeps in it.

Somebody came up with the garden idea. Next to Marian's little house was a plot of ground, maybe twenty feet by twenty feet. It did not look promising; even weeds struggled to grow in its rough dirt clods. But spring had arrived and we were determined. "Think of the money we'll save on groceries," we told ourselves. "We'll have beautiful salads. No men involved."

On a cool Saturday morning in May, six of us showed up with hoes, rakes, shovels, and trowels, eager for the attack. We chopped weeds and dug until the sweat poured. Each bit of chickweed, each dandelion was another chance to strike at the unfairness of it all. "That's for you, you jerk," I heard more than one woman mutter as she stabbed at a tough root. By the end of the day, the plot was cleared and the clods raked smooth, and we had shoveled in seven bags of manure and mushroom compost. We wiped our brows with muddy hands, sipped lemonade, and grinned at one another. This was just the beginning. We were back the next Saturday, this time with packets of seeds: peas, beans, radishes, carrots, beets, parsley, lettuce, cabbage.

"I want eggplant," one woman announced. "My ex-husband hates eggplant. I'm going to eat it every day." We agreed; she should have eggplant.

Another said, "No man is going to touch a single bean from my patch! These are mine!" We laughed and applauded.

We planted our seeds and marked the wobbly rows by jabbing sticks into the ground and putting the empty seed packets on them. The bits of paper blew away before the next Saturday, but we didn't care. We knew what was pushing deep into the earth and reaching for the sky. Within days green shoots appeared, and we tended them as anxiously as if they were preemie babies, watering, weeding, and removing slugs by hand. "Organic only," we said, massaging aching shoulders and backs. "No poisons in this garden. Boys keep out!" The only male allowed to set foot in the garden was my sister's three-year-old son.

Long summer days passed, and our garden grew and flourished. We pulled radishes and lettuce and shared a salad. We carted peas and carrots home to our children. Our aches faded and our arms tanned; we sprouted muscles and talked knowledgeably of the virtues of steer versus chicken manure.

One day in September, as I was gathering a basketful of richly scented basil, I realized that I hadn't heard any grousing about men for weeks. Well, it turned out that a few of us had found boyfriends who were nice, good men, and it didn't feel right to gripe anymore. The divorces were over or under way; life was moving on. "You can stay mad forever," someone said, gently tugging a carrot out of the ground. "But I'm tired of that. Plus, there aren't as many jerks out there as I thought."

Someone else nodded. "Yeah, true, but you know what? I think the garden helped. I needed to be mad and have a place to work it out."

There was a chorus of agreement.

"Oh, me too, definitely."

"I'm stronger and healthier now."

"I could take on the world. And I don't need to."

We had dug our pain into that garden, and it had transformed into nourishment.

We picked up our bags of produce. There was less of it now, with cooler days approaching. As we headed toward our cars, the woman with the bean patch grinned and said, "By the way, I'm cooking dinner for my boyfriend tonight. And I'm serving him beans from the garden."

Marilyn McFarlane

THE BEST DAY OF MY LIFE

It started the night before, with a phone call from my friend Kathy. She lives on one coast and I live on the other, but our bond is solid and even if we don't talk for months, we can always start right where we left off.

In graduate school she was a few years behind me and helped with my doctoral research. Then, when housing became tight in Berkeley, she lived in an extra room in my house for a semester.

Kathy is the oldest of eight children and I'm the youngest, with four older brothers. It was nice for me to have a sort of little sister friendship and for Kathy to have a big sister friendship.

When she called, I thought it was to share more news of her firstborn, new baby Matthew, but the call had a very different purpose. That morning she had been diagnosed with colon cancer and treatment would start immediately. It was wrenching news. This new mom, my precious friend, was facing a horrible disease and the sad truth that even if she survived she would never have another child.

We talked and cried, and when we got off the phone I kept crying. There would be nothing I could do if I were by her side, but I felt helpless being across the country.

Kathy and I were both raised as good little Catholics. We were taught by the sisters to offer up our suffering for some purpose or for the "poor suffering souls in purgatory." I'm sure that in my youth I helped release more than a few of those suffering souls. Every cold walk to school, every toothache, every disappointment, I offered up. It might have bordered on the superstitious, but it always made the suffering a little easier to think it had a good purpose.

In fifth grade I had a nun for a teacher who went a step further. She taught us that prayer did not need to begin with "Dear God," but could be any act offered up for His "Honor and Glory" or a special intention. She told us a story of a little nun who typed all day and she reminded herself that every stroke of a key was a prayer to God. She taught us that we didn't need to be on our knees to pray. We just needed to do our very best at whatever we were doing and offer that as a prayer to God.

I fell asleep praying and making bargains with God. "Dear God, if you just let Kathy make it, I promise . . ." I couldn't think of anything that would feel like enough. I could do nothing, but I had to do something. What I finally promised was to live the next day as the "best" day of my life.

I woke early the next morning and got right out of bed. I made the bed. I flossed. Throughout the day I mixed in lots of "Dear God's," but mostly I just tried to do everything as well as I possibly could.

In traffic, I looked for ways to be more careful and courteous. I didn't even complain under my breath about the terrible drivers. At work I did nothing in a mindless or automatic fashion. I wrote my reports in the best way possible. I counseled children and parents with as much mindfulness as I could muster. Instead of munching on the chips and donuts in the faculty room, I ran to the corner store for some yogurt. I tried not to waste a single minute.

At home that evening I was patient and thoughtful with my family. I was still sad and worried that night, but I felt right, as if I had accomplished something remarkable. I felt that if God were accepting such bargains, he surely would have thought this counted for a lot.

Twelve years later, Kathy is healthy and daughter Joanna has joined her family. She still lives too far away, and we can still take up where we left off. I will never know if the best day of my life counted, but it counted in my heart and gave me a way to express my feelings for my friend.

Since then, I have tried to balance off negative events of all kinds with "best days," if not to bargain with God, then to create something positive to counteract the negative, and to regain some sense of control. It's well documented in mental health literature that in times of crisis, those who have something productive to do come out in better shape emotionally. Efforts at best days have been my strategy for dealing with little personal crises of all kinds. Whether from faith, love, or desperation, striving for "best days" has brought peace and comfort, available from no other source.

No day has ever equaled that "best day," but many days have been much better than they might have been because of that day.

SUSAN DEMERSSEMAN

Her artistic sense was exquisitely refined,
like someone who can tell butter from I Can't Believe It's Not Butter.
BARBARA COLLIER

SOUTHERN DELICACIES

Everyone in my family is a good cook. Everyone, that is, but me. Not being a good cook is a serious offense, especially in the South.

It's not that I don't try. I took three years of home economics classes. Three long years. Armed with all the tried-and-true recipes from the family matriarchs, I faithfully clip recipes from *Woman's Day.* My husband, Tim, trying to advance the cause, ordered recipe books from the Julia and Jacques cooking show, taped all Natalie Dupree's specials, and subscribed me to web links from Emeril's World. In spite of everything, I still scorch boiling water. NASA is analyzing my gravy, which when cubed makes a perfect paste for astronaut use. My daughter Melissa used my first cheese omelet as a doorstop.

It isn't heredity. My mother is an excellent cook. She can whip up a spaghetti and meatball dinner that would make Caruso croon. Every birthday of my life, she makes her legendary lemon icebox pie instead of a birthday cake, tossing off complaints that the candles fall over in the meringue.

My grandparents were also excellent country cooks. Mama Sewell's sweet potato pie won blue ribbons at the county fair. If piecrust were an Olympic sport, my paternal grandmother would have taken the gold.

Alas, to make matters worse, I married into a family of food connoisseurs. My mother-in-law crowns our traditional Thanksgiving feast with a freshly grated coconut cake and homemade pecan pie. My sisters-in-law know better than to comment when I arrive with a Mrs. Edwards pie straight from the frozen food aisle of Kroger. They pretend not to notice as I slip it out of the cardboard box onto a china pie plate.

Tim, in Hudson family tradition, began a legacy of cooking as soon as he could reach the stove dials. He is a BBQ Gold Crown Master's Platinum Level and Bread Baker Extraordinaire. I can't even toast a bagel without setting off the smoke alarm. Once I tried Beef Wellington and let's just say that I'm still cleaning the oven racks. The children don't even speak of it publicly.

I don't know how I've eluded becoming a *chef de cuisine.* Excellent culinary skills are part of every Southerner's DNA right along with hospitality and *Gone With the Wind.* Every woman of Southern extraction can bake, puree, stir, or frappe a three-tiered gastronomic extravaganza for the ice-cream social, carry-in dinner, or holiday drop-in that we Southerners are so famous for. If we could have gotten Sherman to a family reunion or Southern wedding reception, he would have forgotten all about the war. Tecumseh would have been too full of fried chicken, buttermilk biscuits, mashed potatoes, and gravy to travel.

I've pondered how the cooking gene could have somehow been omitted from my genetic makeup. Perhaps an alien experimenting with gene splicing spirited away my cooking chromosome. Or, maybe I'm adopted.

Sheila S. Hudson

NIGHTS IN BLUE GINGHAM

"O*h-h-h-h-h-h the-e-e-r-e's nothin' half-way about* the Iowa way to treat ya."

That's the first line from the curtain-opening song in *The Music Man.* In the summer of 1963 when I was a high school senior, the director chose me to be one of the five River City women who opened the show. We stood at stage left and belted out the words to an audience of family and friends. I wore a blue-and-white checked gingham dress with a full white apron and bonnet.

Our little town's Parks Department presented a show every summer, and that year I made the cast. I was prouder than I'd ever been to be on stage, singing "almost solo."

As a child, no one wanted to hear me sing. Mom said my voice was flat, and Mr. Milewski, our girls' choir director, sometimes told me to silently mouth the words while the other girls sang out loud. In third grade, Sister Felicia made each of us stand alone at the front of the classroom and sing a few bars of a favorite song as a kind of test. I chose "Playing Lady," a song I'd learned on the piano. When my turn came, I began in a loud voice.

"Playing lady is the finest game I know . . ."

"Sit down, Linda. That'll do." Sister Felicia lowered her head and wrote in her notebook.

I sank into my seat like a deflated balloon while Annie Haber sang four whole stanzas of "How Much Is that Doggie in the Window?" Imagine my glee, nine years later, when Mr. DeRose, director of the summer theater program, chose me to be one of the opening singers in *The Music Man*.

The magic night came and I was ready. The audience chattered as they took their seats. I peeked around the curtain and saw Mr. Dylong, our next-door neighbor, and his wife fanning their faces with their programs. I searched the crowd for my parents, although I didn't expect to see them. They never saw me sing, except in church, and they never knew I was lip synching in the choir. Mom hardly ever left the house anymore, and Dad criticized me so often, I almost didn't want him there anyway. "Don't show off," he'd say when I pranced around at home. Still, I felt disappointed when I couldn't find them.

"Break a leg," Mr. DeRose softly told each of us as we quickly took our places. He'd taught us that real actors never say "Good luck" before a performance.

"Break a leg," we whispered, grinning at one another. The lights dimmed and the crowd fell silent. A few coughs echoed in the hall. My big moment had arrived. The curtain rose slowly and I began to belt out the song with the others, projecting to the back of the hall.

"Oh-h-h-h-h the-e-e-r-e's nothin' half-way . . ."

A thrill of pride raced through my body. *I'm up here, on stage, in a beautiful gingham dress, singing! Listen up, Sister Felicia! Hear this, Annie Haber! I'm singing, and hundreds of people are watching and smiling up at me.* The lights were so bright I couldn't see past the first row, but Mr. DeRose told us the house was packed.

Almost forty years later, I can still feel the thrill of that wonderful night. I can well understand why people go into show business. The applause, the adulation, the attention!

My parents raised me not to be a show-off, and they weren't in the crowd that night. I was hungry for their attention and rarely fed, but for a few glorious nights in the summer of 1963, I was satisfied. I wasn't a star, but heck, I opened the show! Although I had no speaking lines, I was happy to do the fake conversations and head wagging of a "townsfolk" woman. I was an actress.

Thanks to *The Music Man* and Mr. DeRose, my confidence grew. I've faltered many times since those nights in blue gingham, but I've kept on going. I've learned to speak with clarity and self-assurance before large groups of people. Last summer, I joined the "Can't Sing Singers" at my church. After ten laughter-filled lessons from our choir director, we delivered a spirited rendition of "This Little Light of Mine" to the entire congregation.

"You looked like you were having a good time up there," my friend Judy said. Nobody called me a show-off.

I make it a practice to be in the audience for all of my son Matt's public appearances—the school plays, the soccer and basketball games, the band concerts. Yesterday, I proudly watched him take fifth place in his school spelling bee. Matt is quiet and shy like his mom, but he stood bravely at the microphone before hundreds of his schoolmates. I was amazed when he turned to the moderator and calmly said, "Use that word in a sentence, please."

On the ride home, I asked him what he liked best about the spelling bee.

"Being up on the stage," he answered.

I bought him a pizza for dinner with everything on it.

Linda C. Wisniewski

COMFORTING CONNECTION

"*What's the baby's name?*"

The question hung in the air as I wondered how to answer. The hospital records clerk sat with pen poised at her clipboard waiting for my reply.

I stroked the head of my newborn daughter on her first day of life. She fit perfectly in the crook of my arm, her chubby neck pressed against my flesh and her toes extending into my cupped fingers.

"I don't know her name," I whispered. "We haven't settled on one."

The clerk smiled and said she would come back the next morning. I eased back, letting my head drift into the pillow. My lungs filled with a deep breath as I enjoyed the brief reprieve from the struggle of deciding what to call my baby.

When we entered the hospital the night before, my husband, Tim, and I felt fairly confident about our name choices. We didn't know the baby's sex, but if our second child was a boy, we decided his name would be Samuel James Milling. A girl would be Kathleen Jamie Milling, and we would call her Kate.

Moments after birth, as Tim held his daughter for the first time, he studied her face and said, "She just doesn't look like a Kate." I had to agree. She didn't. But what would we call her?

During my pregnancy, we both checked our preferences in a baby name book. There were few names, however, that made both our lists. Where I would opt for McKenna or Erin or Sierra, Tim's top picks included Maggie and Rebecca. Kate had been one name we both agreed on. Now we were choosing to start over.

I yearned for the opportunity to discuss my dilemma with my mother. A massive heart attack had taken her from us suddenly in 1992. I wished for a way to bring her back, even for a short period of time, so she could meet and hug her two grandchildren. I wanted to talk with her about how she selected my name, and what advice she would give about her granddaughter's name. Beyond that, I wished for a renewed connection with my mother, despite the reality of death.

My mind carried me back to a day when my mother showed me her high school yearbook and explained her own name. My grandparents did not give my mother a middle name. They simply named her Geraldine and called her Gerry for short. When my mother was a senior in high school, she recalled that she added a name to her yearbook listing so she would be like all the other kids who had a first and a middle name. Beside her picture it read: Grace Geraldine Shuford. "Why Grace?" I asked her. She explained it was simply a name she really liked.

Alone with my baby in our hospital room, I spent that day praying for guidance in choosing an appropriate name. The responsibility of helping create a portion of someone's identity seemed huge. We wanted to pick a name that would fit our child's personality. We also wanted it to be one that she liked, and that others wouldn't twist into some horrible nickname.

Tim and I tossed around a few names when he arrived at the hospital later in the evening with our son Ben. All of our suggestions seemed too bland or just didn't feel right.

That night, before I drifted off to sleep, I envisioned God putting our baby's name inside an envelope and revealing the contents to me before the clerk came back to fill out the paperwork.

The next morning, Tim and I continued our name search. I was leaning toward the name Megan, but the sound of Megan Milling bugged me—too much of a tongue twister. "Right now, right at this moment, what is your first choice?" I asked Tim. He paused, and a small, still voice inside of me said, "The next name you hear will be the name of your child."

"Hannah," said Tim.

It seemed to fit. Hannah.

Tim picked up my packed bags and headed out the door, greeting the doctor as she walked in. She reached in the bassinet, picked up our baby, and then cuddled her tiny body close to her chest.

"Does she have a name yet?" she asked.

"Yes, it's Hannah Jamie."

We had previously decided to give her a middle name of Jamie after Tim's dad, James. Tim arrived back in the room just in time to hear the doctor say, "Well, it's a beautiful name." He looked at me, startled, and waited until she left to ask, "What *is* her name?"

"Hannah Jamie," I said, and his face lit up.

Later on, I started second-guessing the name. Did we make the right choice? Will she like it? Should we change it? Again, I heard a small, still voice inside of me. It said, "You will find a connection to your mother with this name."

When I arrived back at our house, I looked up Hannah in the name book and found my comforting connection.

The name means Grace.

MARLA HARDEE MILLING

Inner beauty is highly overrated.
Just kidding.
PAMELA ANDERSON

ALONG FOR THE RIDE

I *have a friend who is about as down-to-earth and* sensible as any who ever lived. She takes care of a family, a dog, and a house—like many of us.

But sometimes, she is someone else, someone exotic. Someone I've never been. Sometimes she is a rock and roll blues singer.

I've known Rebecca since we were girls feeling our way into adulthood. Even then, she always had different guts than I. But now we are in our late forties, and after years of sitting in smoky bars watching her strut her stuff, I took a page from her play list.

Vamp dresses. Yep, I took the leap.

Now, Rebecca has an excuse for the clothes she wears to a gig. It's business, right? As a member of the Crunchy Frogs, she has to wear high-heeled boots and purple streaks in her hair. I am a northwoods woman, happiest in fleece and sport pants.

But secretly, I yearned for the panache that would allow me freedom from such apparel. Not that jeans and turtleneck shirts and wool plaid blazers aren't a good look for me, but they certainly don't help me break out of the usual. Sometimes, I don't want to be me.

It started a few weeks ago when Becky made me try on a leather skirt, then a skin-tight dress of giant-sized sequins. I blushed and made excuses, but stuff like that gets you thinking.

So keeping an upcoming club date in mind, I took a spin over to the local Goodwill Store to comb the racks. I wasn't going to spend a lot of money on this new venture, after all. What if I chickened out?

Part of me prayed that there would be no naughty dresses on hand. The lack of the seriously slinky would give me a way out.

No such luck.

I found my dress, neighing to me from a round rack in the middle of the size eights. A black-and-white zebra stripe, halter top, no-back spandex affair. A true vamp dress if I ever saw one, and for only $4.25. It was certainly an affordable mistake.

I slid it on in the dressing room, telling myself all the while that I was buying it for Becky. But as I turned around in front of the mirror, my perception changed. I looked hot! Even my breasts looked happy to be there. This was my dress, my first tawdry dress, and I was going to gird my loins and fly my flag.

Saturday night came. I teased my hair, painted my nails, and emerged from Becky's bathroom. The effect was clear. Becky's boyfriend grabbed the camera. She hugged me and put on a leopard-skin skirt in support.

I buttoned on a black velvet shirt as a last-ditch cover-up, and we drove to the bar. The band was already there setting up, and there were greetings all around.

I got myself a drink, sat down on a red plastic stool, and slid off the shirt. After all, it was hot in there. I glanced around, hoping not to attract too much attention.

And then, depression set in. Nobody seemed to notice. Not the band, not the bar, not the bikers playing pool. I adjusted my hair and sat up straighter, hoping my aging bosoms would take the hint.

Still nothing. People wouldn't meet my eyes. I wasn't sure what I'd expected, but I had expected something. Eventually I found myself slumping.

Becky sidled over. "Nothing's happening," I wailed. "My first vamp dress, and nobody's even noticed!"

She gave me a look—one of the sensible, down-to-earth ones—and shook her purple-streaked head.

"They noticed," she said. "You can bet they noticed."

I sighed, she went off to sing, and I sipped my drink. And after a while I realized she was right. A few polite yet astonished glances shot my way from the stage.

They were confused. I'd been the pal, the girl who helped coil cords when all was done, someone to have pancakes with after the gig. They didn't know the new me. They'd have to adjust.

And they soon did. I grabbed Becky's boyfriend and began to dance. I stomped my feet and whirled in circles. I noticed the bass player coyly focusing in on my cleavage while we chatted during a break.

I made the grade.

Emboldened, I eventually strutted to the ladies room in the back of the bar. On my way back, a man at the bar stopped me.

"Uh," he said astutely, "do you have a boyfriend, or live with someone, or anything?"

"Yes." I smiled, thinking of my cat, and sauntered on.

I pranced up to Becky, who flashed me a smile of acceptance, like I was the member of a club only a few select girls knew about. "How's it going?" she asked.

I grinned back. "I own this bar."

She laughed. "Now you know what vamp dresses can do."

I've bought a few more since then. I try them on at home and will soon try them out in public. Vamp dresses haven't exactly changed my life, but they have reminded me to never box myself in. Maybe I'm still the northwoods girl, but I have learned I can be all that and a bit of a hussy, too.

Jennifer Gordon Gray

TIPS TO FEED YOUR SOUL

1. Start each day with a desire to make a difference.
2. Live each day bringing more love wherever you go.
3. End each day with a moment of thanksgiving.
4. Acknowledge the unique gifts and talents of your loved ones; it reinforces their best.
5. Pray for yourself and others and you will bring more light into the world.
6. Play as hard as you work. Joy and laughter are therapeutic.
7. Embrace the journey of discovering and living your soul purpose. We are all here for a reason.
8. Share your heart's desire with those who believe in and support you. The power of your dream will be magnified.
9. Look for the learning when difficult moments occur. We grow the most during challenging times and end up stronger, wiser—and often more fulfilled.
10. Nurture the relationships you have with your girlfriends. The older you get the more precious they become.
11. Provide a "hand up" to someone less fortunate. It will be helping yourself as well.
12. Go to a special place that feels sacred to you when you need to relax and renew.
13. Record the important events of your life. Your children will cherish reading them when you're gone.
14. Spend time with a pet when you are feeling blue. The unconditional love you receive will lift your spirits.

15. Remove the clutter in your home. Keep only those things you and your family treasure.
16. Remember that the answers are within. Approach each major life decision using child-like imagination and the wisdom of a wise woman.
17. Create a new tradition or celebration for you and your family to experience each year.
18. Save consciously, spend wisely, and enjoy your deliberate prosperity.
19. Add richness to your life—eat a morsel of chocolate now and then.
20. Stay on speaking terms with God. Inner peace comes when you include Him in your daily life.

Kay Allenbaugh

SEXUAL SEA BASS

One of the greatest things a mother can pass on to her daughter is the ability to create in the kitchen.

I remember one time in my life when I had a secret crush on an acquaintance. For a short while, I was unsure whether this would remain an unrequited love. I began to strategize ways I could try to win his heart. I decided my best chance was to create an extravagant dinner. If the crush wasn't returned after a home-cooked meal, I would lose all hope.

A week before inviting him to dine at my place, I began to plant some gourmet thoughts in his mind. During the next few conversations, I raved about the out-of-the-ordinary cuisine my girlfriends and I would simmer up during the week. I referred to "Sexual Sea Bass" and described it as "juicy" and "tender." Shortly after, I extended an invitation and he accepted. I don't think that he knew what was in store for that evening.

On the day of the trial dinner, I made a trip out to my favorite market. I weaved through the aisles looking for the magic ingredients for my love-potion dinner and searched the produce section for the ripest avocados, golden pears, and freshest red leaf lettuce. I reached the seafood counter and gestured to the man behind it.

"One sea bass filet, the piece in the middle," I hollered. I watched carefully as he threw it in the plastic bag and placed it on the scale. It read, "1.5 lbs., $8.40." I smiled at the bargain I was being blessed with; the sea bass was on special today! I continued on to pick up the last few items, crab paste and magi seasoning.

When I arrived home, I checked the clock and realized that I had just enough time to prepare the meal with delicate pinches of seasoning. As I listened to the Brazilian beats from Bebel Gilberto, I began to prepare the spring salad. I topped it with sliced boiled egg, pear, avocado, and tarot strips, then sprinkled it with fresh cracked pepper. Shortly after, I squeezed fresh lemon juice on the sea bass and sprinkled it with salt, pepper, TJ's 21 seasoning salute, and fresh garlic. I wrapped it up in foil before my kitty, Choco, could get to it.

I glanced at the clock, 6:45 P.M. He would be arriving soon. I placed the sea bass in the oven and turned my attention to the rice. I pulled out all the secret ingredients of my mother's special side dish. I knew that this would be the perfect compliment to the richness of the sea bass. My music continued to play and the butterflies in my stomach began to flutter rapidly as the clock ticked closer to seven o'clock. After I added the crab paste to the aromatic rice, I checked on the fish filet broiling in my oven. Choco stood near and meowed for just a taste. Even he knew how good it would be.

A quarter past seven, everything was set. I had just enough time to put on my favorite blue jeans and red shirt. I thought I would put my hair up and paint my lips with vanilla lip gloss. With only a few minutes to spare, I lit my favorite incense. Thirty-five minutes past the hour: My phone rang and it was my crush outside the gate. I took a deep breath and pressed "9" to let him in.

We were both nervous, but Choco broke the ice and purred up against his leg. I asked him to take a seat at my polished dining table and offered him pear juice. I brought our salads to the table in ceramic Japanese bowls. I gave him the choice of bleu cheese or ranch and he responded, "Bleu cheese." I let out a sigh of relief; we would definitely get along. I could tell at this point that the extra color and texture I added to the salad impressed him.

After small chitchat over our tossed fruits and vegetables, I announced that we would be dining on the Sexual Sea Bass. He laughed and remembered that I had made many references to this special dish. The sea bass sizzled as I placed it on each stoneware plate. I placed the orange-hued crab rice on the palette next to the fish. Perfection. I took another deep breath and headed to the table. His eyes lit up when he saw what was in front of him; he was a virgin to the sea bass.

We both were silent as we savored the creamy fish and flavored rice. He looked over and gave me the thumbs up. *Mission accomplished,* I thought to myself, assured that I had just nurtured my crush in a way he didn't think was possible.

After the meal was complete, we moved over to my velvet couch as Choco lay between us. We sipped on Indian tea and munched on Belgian chocolates. We talked about our lives and some of our pet peeves.

I asked him, "Do you have a crush on me now?"

Speechless and intoxicated with food, he simply nodded "Yes."

LY NGUYEN

IV

FUR AND FEATHER LOVE

We don't get over them,

we just get used to living without them.

SONYA FITZPATRICK

BETTER THAN THERAPY

A*unt Rita was the butt of many family jokes. Married* to Uncle Bill, my grandfather's brother, Aunt Rita never had children. Instead, she had a dog.

Even as a child I knew that Aunt Rita was not well liked. "Aunt Rita was a cocktail waitress," my mother whispered to me. "She met Uncle Bill at a bar. He was a drunk and she was a barmaid."

"She was much older than Uncle Bill," Aunt Jennie added. "Plus, Edith, calling Rita a cocktail waitress is too generous." My mother and Aunt Jennie nodded at each other knowingly.

My father didn't have much to say about Aunt Rita except that he hated her dog. "Who cares that they met in a bar?" he asked. "Uncle Bill always liked to have a good time. But that dog of theirs . . . I can't understand how a grown man, a full-blooded American, a fireman for Heaven's sake, could put up with a dog like that."

The dog my father was referring to was Fifi, a diminutive poodle, adorned with pink ribbons in her fluffy white fur and faux rhinestones around her scrawny neck. She was Aunt Rita's constant companion.

In our family we called dogs like Fifi punting dogs—dogs that were only good for kicking around. We didn't mess with wimpy little mutts. We owned shepherds, boxers, Dobermans, and Great Danes—real dogs. Dogs with big barks and enormous slobbering tongues. Dogs that bit the milkman and the mailman. Canines with names like King, Ace, Mickey, and Mack.

Our dogs were never allowed to sleep in the house, not even on the coldest winter nights. They roughed it outside in a huge doghouse with an extensive chain-link fence surrounding an exercise "pad" that gave them plenty of room to move. Our dogs didn't squirm. They paced.

After such an upbringing, imagine my dismay when one day a miniature schnauzer was placed gently on my lap, a present from a friend. "Try this," said the gift-giver. "She's better than therapy. You won't need Zoloft anymore."

"Thank you," I said graciously, but to myself I thought, *Oh no, a punting dog.*

Accompanying the perfume-smelling furball was seven months of puppy chow, a pink plastic toy, canine combs and brushes, a sheepskin dog bed, and a book entitled *How to Train Small Dogs.* The pooch's name was Misty. "That has to go," I said when no one was listening.

I changed my new companion's name to Whiskers. I stopped combing her curly hair and soaking her in perfume. I took her for long walks in my neighborhood.

Slowly I've begun to appreciate her small charms. Her poops are minuscule. She fits into my crowded house quite well. She doesn't eat much. She barks like she means it, and even though it is more a high-pitched squeal than a low menacing woof, she sounds vicious and ready to tear apart, limb by limb, anyone who dares to threaten me. When we walk by schools, children flock up against the playground fence, begging me to stop and let them pet her. Elderly men and women pause from their gardening to tell me about their own pets. Homeless people with shopping carts give us a wide berth, and delivery men ask if she bites.

I got rid of the sheepskin dog bed. Whiskers really didn't enjoy sleeping in it. She prefers to curl up with me in bed, wrapping her furry body around my neck, emulating those coats old ladies used to wear to church, foxes clenching tails, head to hind end.

One day as I was cuddling Whiskers in my arms I looked into the mirror and saw our reflection. "Oh no," I gasped. "Aunt Rita!"

It was true. I'd turned into Aunt Rita. It had happened overnight. One day I was a depressed, Zoloft-taking, big-dog lover, and the next I was staring into the soft brown eyes of a little panting creature. The gift-giver was right. Whiskers is better than therapy.

SUSAN PARKER

CLEO, MY EMPTY-NEST CAT

She is sitting on top of the TV right now, her head resting on the remote control. She doesn't belong there and I know she knows it. She also knows that it doesn't matter, just as it doesn't matter that she sits on the table and the counter, other places she doesn't belong. Just as it doesn't matter that she's breaking a lot of rules these days, and we're half-heartedly trying to point her in the right direction but not putting a lot of effort or emotion behind our words.

Cleopatra has taken over. And no one really minds.

I'm watching as she sits up straight and stretches her body to its full height. Her petite mouth opens to a hearty, healthy, lion-sized yawn. One paw, the white one with the stripe, goes forward. Then the other foot follows, as she arches her back and dismisses the sleep from her body. She's up and ready to go.

I watch as she cocks her head. She hears something the rest of us don't hear. She uses her chest to balance and jumps down from the TV, her back legs often attempting to pass her front legs as she races down the hall. Out of the picture, noiseless, out of mind, Cleo is learning about her world.

Today she saw birds for the first time. She sat on a pillow looking out the window as birds flew from branch to branch in the acacia tree behind our house. Cleo, destined to live indoors because of the harsh realities of desert life, instinctively knew birds were important to her. I can't wait for Cleo to see the rabbits that visit our back lawn during the summer. I hope the owl we saw last summer, sitting on the wall that separates us from the desert arroyo, returns. Safe behind her picture window, maybe she'll see a coyote or a snake or a bobcat.

I'm not sure whose cat Cleo is, although my sons each claim she's theirs. Each of them continues to call her different names. She's still Britney to my younger son and Kenshin to my older son.

My older son speaks to his cat, Kenshin, in self-taught Japanese. We look at him sort of cross-eyed, the way most people look at teenagers, hoping this stage will be short-lived, trying hard to dig back to our own pasts to remember being sixteen years old. I think Jeff genuinely believes that Kenshin will understand his attempts at Japanese more than our English, and perhaps he's right. But I'm not convinced she's even listening.

My younger son has pulled out the stuffed animals he put away a few years ago because he was too old for them. "They're for Britney," Steven said. "She told me she needs a lot of toys to play with when I'm at school because she misses me so much." This son is still walking the young adult/little boy tightrope, and I'm not forcing him to get to the other side any faster. I don't want to disappoint him and tell him the cat is very busy during the day and needs little extra to keep herself entertained.

Cleo has brought back the kitten in both of our older cats. It's not uncommon to hear all three cats running up and down the hall. Cleo has reminded Bumper and Smokey just how much fun it is to play. I watch as they take turns winning and losing.

But the time comes during the day that even the older cats grow tired of Cleo, and they find a favorite spot to curl up and sleep. That's when the reality of Cleo surfaces. When all is said and done, Cleo is mine.

My husband knows this and there's been no argument. I've explained to him that Cleo is my empty-nest kitty. She's there when each of my boys leaves for his too-busy-for-the-cat/too-busy-for-the-mom social lives. She's there when my husband heads out to his someone-has-to-have-a-real-job job. She'll be there when the boys, one after the other, move away to begin their own lives.

Cleo is mine.

She comes to me when she's hungry or frightened or lonely, and she cuddles into my body when I sleep.

Right now I'm watching Cleo as she chases her tail atop the wall unit. I keep partially getting up to catch her as she almost falls to the floor. But she's so clever. She chases her pretty pencil tail and never once misses her footing. And when I start to rise, thinking she's about to fall, she looks at me with that "Don't worry, Mom, I can do this" face.

I watch as Cleo deliberately leaps down from the wall unit and gallops over to where I'm sitting. She does two or three circles and falls, perfectly placed, on the arm of this old chair, her head resting on my chest, her back against my upper arm, as I sit here and write.

Cleopatra has taken over. And no one really minds. Especially me.

FELICE R. PRAGER

Dogs are a habit, I think.
ELIZABETH BOWEN

THAT DOG

"That dog," *was the phrase my husband, Alan,* and I often used when referring to our basset hound, Maybelline. We had her and her pup, Norma Jean, years before we had kids. I've always believed she made me a better parent. She definitely taught me about unconditional love.

I think the feeling was mutual, but she sure didn't listen to me. Mayb often ran away, fast on the trail of fresh garbage. When she managed to break out of the yard, I usually found her in the alleyways behind my neighbors' homes, standing on her hind legs, long snout deep in their trash. However, there were times when this quick hound could not be found. That's when her name tag on her collar brought her back to us. One night, after calling her and cruising the neighborhood for more than an hour, a couple of men pulled up with Maybelline. She'd been greeting fans arriving at the nearby hockey game. Another time she decided that there were very good smells indeed coming from the carnival, so off she trotted. It didn't matter that she had to cross four lanes of traffic to get there. Phone calls from strangers informing me she was in their garage, children sighting her at the park, and the mailman bringing her home in his mail truck. "Is this your dog?"

But Maybelline wasn't all fun and games. She had a neurotic

side, too. For all her hyper ways—she could vault over the back of our sofa with her stubby legs—she would withdraw when put in a moving vehicle. One time on our way to a campground, Mayb got carsick. She was in the backseat with Norma Jean, Alan was driving, and I was in the front passenger seat. Mayb kept insisting on putting her front paws on the back of Alan's headrest, sort of like an anxious backseat driver. "Watch that curve! Not so fast! Do you have to hit every pothole?" she seemed to say. I kept telling her to sit down, but each time she did, she'd get back up moments later.

Alan said, "Oh, don't worry about it. She's fine."

Except she wasn't. And the dead bird she'd scarfed down at the last rest stop was making a repeat appearance—right down Alan's neck.

"Oh, geez!" my husband cried, swerving off the road. "That dog . . . !" he shouted.

Once at the campground, Norma Jean ran off, but Maybelline was not particularly fond of camping. No matter how many dead birds she found, they could never make up for her worst nightmare: flies. When she was a pup, she'd been bitten on the rear by a black fly during her first camping trip. Since then she had equated camping with black flies, even when there were none. Mayb would whip her head around, like she was hearing voices, her long ears smacking herself in the face. She'd snap at the empty air and when she could stand it no longer, she'd go into the tent and curl up in a tight ball, with eyes scanning her surroundings.

After having two children within a couple of years, I found it difficult to care for the dogs. I had never been able to housebreak Maybelline, so we kept them in the yard where they shared a doghouse. This became problematic in the winter when our North Dakota temps drop below freezing. We tried everything to keep them warm and at one point the dogs were in the laundry room, but I had to continually hose it down. With the children, I no longer had the time for this—or the inclination.

Finally, I made the decision to give them away to a good home. A kindergarten teacher answered my ad in the paper. She and her children readily granted my request that they keep Maybelline and Norma Jean together. The woman said her husband would have them housebroken in no time. I couldn't stand to be home when she came back to get them a few hours later. I sobbed over the loss of them in my life. But when I called the woman the next day to see how they were doing, she regaled me with stories of the dogs playing in the snow with her little boy and how even the housebreaking was going well. I hung up, heart still heavy, but pleased they were getting the kind of attention I couldn't give them. The basset hound chapter of my life seemed to be over.

Then the phone calls began. Every so often I would get a call from someone where Mayb and Norma Jean lived. "Are you missing a dog?" Well, yes, I always missed them, but no, they didn't belong to me anymore. Mayb was found wandering the streets and had jumped into a pizza delivery car. The tag on her collar had our number on it. I told the caller I'd phone the new owners. The kindergarten teacher sounded less than pleased to hear from me. The lilt in her voice when she'd first gotten the dogs was gone. Well, I knew how stressful it was when Maybelline got loose, so I tried to shrug it off.

A couple of months later I received a call from the sheriff in Mayb's new town. Again, she'd been picked up roaming the streets. The sheriff revealed that Mayb looked neglected. She was dirty, her ears needed cleaning, and she was on the thin side. This seemed odd. What had happened to the perfect family I had found? I called her owner, only to discover that the kindergarten teacher had divorced her husband, taken the cats and kids, and moved away. The husband was left holding the pooches.

I begged my husband to go with me on a recon mission. We'd visit where the dogs lived, and if they looked like they were okay, we'd leave matters alone. Alan grudgingly conceded, and we strapped the kids in the car and drove the two hours to spy on

Mayb and Norma Jean. We found the house and them in the backyard on a metal chain. Disney never drew two more forlorn-looking dogs: eyes all droopy, rib bones protruding, ears hanging low. They just sat there gazing off, not even stirring when our car moved past slowly. I looked at Alan, who began to shake his head.

"No, no, no!" he stated firmly as he drove. "Absolutely not!"

"I'll place another ad. Please?"

When the guy opened the front door and I explained who I was, he looked at me like we'd just driven up in the Publisher's Clearing House van. He was moving, trying to find a new home for the dogs. I didn't hesitate to offer to take them off his hands. Alan didn't say a word on our ride back home. The dogs slept the whole way, content to be back with their family.

In one of those, "Why didn't we do this before?" moments, we put in a doggy door and Mayb and Jeanie actually used it! We had to keep them gated in the kitchen, no small feat for a dog that was part Houdini, but eventually it all worked out. It had to. After all, how can you give away animals that keep coming back to you?

Mayb passed away in 1999 and Jeanie is nearing twelve years old. I believe that there's some sort of karma being worked out through my relationship with my dogs, but Alan doesn't believe in my canine karma. I fear my basset hound days are now coming to an end, but I'll never forget the friendship of *that dog.*

Kathleen Coudle King

HEART SONGS

My *heart ached for the troubled young woman* who came rushing breathlessly into the bird store. Her face was pale and drawn and there was a sadness about her that was almost physical. "Does anybody want a canary?" she blurted out. "He's free to anybody who will take him."

For some reason, she seemed to zero in on me. I shook my head and replied, "No, thanks." Waiting at home for me were three parakeets, my Blue-crowned conure Rio, and a room full of zebra finches and cockatiels. There was no way I could squeeze another bird into the house. Everyone else in the store refused the canary, too, and turned away to finish their shopping.

The woman's shoulders sagged. "Well, if nobody wants him, I don't know what I'll do. I can't take care of him anymore."

"Why are you getting rid of him?" asked the store owner.

The woman sighed and explained that she had purchased the bird nearly a year earlier, hoping that he would bring a few bright moments to her unhappy marriage. Shortly after buying the bird, the woman had a baby. Born with a tragic birth defect, the infant died within a few weeks. That put a nearly unbearable strain on the already tense marriage, and the young woman was emotionally wrung out. To top it off, the canary had been silent the entire time. "He hasn't sung a single note in all the months I've had him," she told me, dashing away a tear. "I think he's depressed."

Her air of desperation frightened me, and I suddenly feared for the little bird. Before I could change my mind, I spoke. "I'll take him."

"Oh, thank you!" exclaimed the young woman. She hurried out of the store and returned a few moments later clutching a shiny brass-colored cage containing a bedraggled canary.

Splotchy black markings and soft lemony yellow patches accented his white feathers. "His name is Sugar," said the woman, setting the cage on the counter. I bent down to peer at him through the bars. He regarded me steadily with tiny jet-black eyes.

"He doesn't sing?" I asked. The woman told me that she had heard him sing at the breeding facility, but as soon as she took him into her home, he fell silent. And silent he had stayed.

"Well," I said after a moment of study. "He looks healthy. Maybe I can at least make him comfortable."

Thanking me again, the young woman left the store. I purchased a box of canary diet to go with the twenty-five-pound sack of cockatiel seed I needed and loaded everything into my car. The canary cage was fastened into the front seat next to me and we set off for home.

Winding my way through the heavy traffic, I wondered if I had lost my mind. What was I going to do with another bird? True, he was small and wouldn't take up much space. I was sure he didn't eat a lot and couldn't be that much trouble to take care of. But I already had nearly thirty birds!

Then a soft sound reached my ear. Startled, I checked the rearview mirror. Nothing looked out of the ordinary, and anyway, I could have sworn the sound came from inside the car. Then I heard it again. It was Sugar!

I stared at him in amazement. Fluffing his feathers in the sun, he took a deep breath and released a few more tentative notes. It was as if he wasn't sure he remembered how to sing. But each note was a bit stronger and by the time we got home, he was singing clearly. I was thrilled beyond words.

As the days went by, my other birds grew accustomed to the strange sounds coming from the newcomer. Soon they stopped squawking and flapping in alarm every time he opened his beak and it wasn't long before it seemed like Sugar had always been with us. Eventually I even heard some of the young male cockatiels trying to imitate him.

Sugar sang all day, every day, and long after his cage was covered each night. Sometimes he even woke us up, cheerfully singing away in the dark. He sang throughout the winter months, during thunderstorms and gray days, heavy molts, and frequent shuffling from room to room while we finished building our house. He enjoyed singing along when my husband played guitar or mandolin, and he would sometimes match pitch with the notes. Even the antics of our orange-winged Amazon parrot, Pancho, didn't bother him. Sugar sang on, oblivious to the big green monster perched on top of his house, chewing holes in his cage cover.

Late in his tenth year with us, he began to slow. Molts took longer to recover from and, more often than not, he would softly twitter instead of singing the full-throated songs we loved. He still relished the fruits and vegetables I offered, and he took daily baths in his water cup. Although he didn't sing as frequently, he liked for me to sit next to him and whistle. He never failed to respond with a few rolls or trills.

One morning as I stumbled into the kitchen to put the coffee on, I heard rustling from Sugar's cage. I carefully lifted the cover and found him in the throes of a seizure. Frightened, I gathered him up in a soft cloth and held him. His bright black eyes gazed directly into mine as he cuddled against the cloth. He twittered at me and seemed not to think it strange that I was holding him cupped in my trembling hands.

After one terribly long seizure, I kissed the top of his beak and told him it was okay to go. His jet-black eyes looked earnestly into mine and he whispered a few muted notes. Then he rested his head against the cloth, relaxed his body, and his lovely voice fell silent.

We buried Sugar in a place of honor in the backyard, under a young, strong oak tree. Though I never knew why he had chosen to present me with the precious gift of his voice all those years ago, I thanked God that he had.

Anne Culbreath Watkins

MY HUSBAND'S "OTHER WOMAN"

I *passed right by the cute face in the cage. I was on a* mission. Four months ago, my beloved dog, Smokey, had passed away. Two months later our cat of twenty years had been bird prey on our five acres. Coming home after work and having no "greeter" was lonelier than I could bear. Not that I thought I could replace any of my special creatures. I just wasn't ready for the total lack of furry companionship.

My husband, Bob, was pretty easy to convince. Even though he was the logical one, I could still wrap him around my little finger when I put my energy into it. So off we went to the pound "just to look," I told him. I thought that maybe a black lab would be a good choice. Then I heard Bob's voice, "What about this one?" There sat the most beautiful face looking at Bob with big, brown eyes and a snappy scarf draped around her neck. She truly did not need anything to make her more cute! Well, German shepherd, husky, and Border collie was an interesting combination. Later I realized this made up the Molotov cocktail of dog breeding.

What can I say? Bob was always a sucker for a pretty face. Her name was Katie and we decided to keep the name. We were told that someone had dumped her off without divulging her history. Apparently, Katie had had puppies and then was tossed aside, abused and lonely. We had to wait for a few days so Katie could be permanently "pup-less." We read some pamphlets on how to introduce a dog into a new home. After having several dogs, we thought we would do it correctly this time. New life in the home started to excite us. We believed we had everything on hand; however, nothing could have prepared us for the experience we were starting on.

Our first challenge was getting Katie into the car to take her to her new home. She was terrified to get in and threw up before we arrived home.

She quickly took the toys we had for her and brought them to the head of our bed. There she sat, leaving her spot only with great coaxing. This was strange behavior to us, but the real problem occurred when we tried to go to bed at night. For about a week, a forty-five-pound dog shared our pillows with us, and we woke up with hair balls in our mouths. One night I awoke to find Bob sitting with Katie on her dog bed, which we brought in our room for her. He was trying to convince her that this spot would be better for all of us. She wasn't buying his line of reasoning, and so he sat there for hours petting her and soothing the fears she was harboring.

When Katie finally left the bed, she decided to see who belonged in her pack. That's when we began to notice her wild and crazy traits.

The main person in her life was Bob. Bob was a great lover of animals, but he fell *in love* with Katie. Nothing was too good for the Kate. Bob never checked the price when buying toys for Katie. We needed to build a fence when we discovered that the husky part of her would head straight to the North Pole when loose, and Bob decided that she should have an interesting yard with plenty of space to run. The fenced area turned into a plot of land with more square footage than our house. Yet, Katie usually sat at the gate waiting to come into the house.

While watching television at night, Bob would throw a ball to her for hours. At first she was the biggest klutz I had ever seen. After a while, she became the picture of grace, leaping into the air to retrieve the ball for Bob.

It was not hard to figure out that she had also fallen in love with him. When we would come home from any activity, she would tackle Bob and almost sweep him off his feet. She would wait for him to go to bed and then get on his chest, groom his beard, and meticulously clean each of his fingers. This process could take quite some time, but Bob patiently sat through all the care she was giving him.

Bob and I were so happy to be able to make a move to another location where we would have a view of the water we loved so much. Bob had plans to take Katie out on his small boat. We could walk on a rocky beach not far away and Bob bought a long leash so Katie could go out into the water as far as she wanted. He even had a fence planned to keep his girl safe.

Shortly after we moved Bob became very ill. We were both stunned and devastated to get the diagnosis of cancer. An immediate treatment plan of chemotherapy and radiation was scheduled. Bob became very thin and slept a great deal of the time. Last winter Katie faithfully sat at his bedroom door, only leaving to eat or for a short trip outside. The sadness in her eyes was a reflection of my own sorrow. Still, when Bob came back from a treatment, Katie would leap up and now almost knock him over. He sat in his recliner for short intervals and Katie would jump up on him and fall asleep on his chest and lap. Not an easy load for Bob to bear, but he never could ignore those huge brown eyes.

Almost five months ago, Bob was coming to the end of his journey on this earth, and he was sleeping most of the time. In the last week of his life he would sometimes wake up at about eleven at night and want a small snack. So, Katie and I curled up with him with cookies and milk and gave Bob whatever comfort we could.

On the last day of Bob's life, Katie had to stay outside because of his fragile condition. When he went into a coma, I let Katie onto the bed. Her ears cocked from side to side as she heard the different sounds of his breathing. She did the last act of love she knew—she groomed his beard and licked his hands. Then with one final kiss, she jumped off the bed.

It hasn't been an easy road for Katie or me. In the beginning of our grief, we curled up together and I sobbed on Katie and clutched her for dear life. Gradually we started going for walks again. Already I am known on my street as "Katie's mom." Eventually, I took Katie to the beach where the three of us had walked and visualized all our dreams. She trotted on the sand, oblivious to my tears, pulling me along as if to say that life had to go on and that she was willing to drag me through some of the hard times.

Every time I look into her eyes I remember the love affair between Bob and her, and I am so grateful to still have a piece of his heart that he left behind.

Eileen Modracek

THE CAT'S MEOW

It's been quiet around the farm lately. So when my daughter, Jess, stalked into the garage, cat carrier in hand, and called, *"Mom?"* with an obvious question mark, it signaled trouble on the horizon.

As anyone who owns any amount of land will attest, farms attract living, breathing "gifts" from neighbors and friends. While other homeowners are given cheese-and-crackers snack plates and "Welcome to Our Home . . . Now Go Away!" doormats, farmers—no matter how "gentlemanly"—are more likely to receive live offerings. Chickens that won't lay eggs ("Figured you'd like to have them to make the place more homey."), horses that can't walk, sheep, goats, and other assorted visitors with hearts and stomachs requiring tending appear on the doorstep without warning. The question has long since stopped being "Why?" and weathered into "How many?"

So, I asked the obvious question. "What's in the carrier?"

I received the obvious answer. "Well . . . it's a cat, sort of."

Only my daughter could come up with a "sort of" cat. He must be part of the set that began with the "sort of" garter snake that was "broken" in the middle (her grip on biology at that time was tentative and didn't include snake pregnancy). The "sort of" baby bunny (in a fear-induced coma following a confrontation with the lawn mower) followed when she was "sort of" eight. She's twenty-three now and determined to complete the collection of "sort of" animals.

With a cautious glance in my direction (she's big on eye contact when there's an element of fear involved in the transaction) she babbled a long, involved story about disease, death, and disaster. At last the carrier door opened to reveal perhaps the ugliest cat in the world. The kindest thing she could have said about him was that he was orange. Sort of. His fur was matted and filthy so his color was left to the imagination. A tick clung tenaciously to his crusty chin, practically invisible amid the clumps of dirt.

Perhaps most distinctive about his appearance, however, was that his head sported a baseball-shaped lump. The cat also smelled awful.

We stood in silence for a long minute, my daughter and I, watching the orange cat doze in the carrier. Then began the frenzied discussion. Yes, the cat was male; "intact" we determined as we inspected his nether region. Not a good thing with three neutered male cats already in residence. Fleas? Certainly a possibility. He was lounging in my arms, firmly attached to my jacket by his incredibly sharp claws when he sneezed mightily. Sick? No doubt about that. I gingerly replaced him in the carrier. Jess entered into manic mode, and in moments there were bowls of food, water, and milk on the floor, which the cat ignored in deference to his nap.

He'd made his presence known, she said, just as she'd been finishing up in the horse barn. It was nearly dark; the cat was walking up the long driveway, yowling as he came. What else could she have done? He had climbed into the carrier willingly, and now seemed determined to live there forever.

After spending an hour driving door to door as Jess searched for the rightful owner of this disaster with paws, we came to a meeting of the minds. The cat would stay in the garage until morning. At that point, if he was still alive (and that was definitely by no means a certainty), we would reassess the situation, and reassess we did.

Come morning, he was sicker than ever and looking for all the world like a plague come to visit. In hushed tones (so the cat wouldn't hear), we decided it would be best to find a vet who would send him to his final reward in the most painless possible way. I left for work a little saddened, but moving cheerily into denial about the verdict we'd just handed down. Jess headed for her room, phone book in hand.

Had I thought the problem through, I would have realized that never in her life has my child been forced to issue the death sentence for an animal. It's always been me holding the sad creature's shivering body for the vet and crying in the dark when guilty nightmares came home to roost. She'd been adept at absenting herself from the premises at those terrible moments. This was not going to be the time when she would ford that stream and leap into the adult world of hard decisions and morning-after remorse. I remembered that she'd cried, inconsolably, for hours after her favorite cat had met the vet's kind needle two years before. We all spent a restless night, anticipating the coming sadness.

Home from work the next day, I found her note on the kitchen counter: *Mom—lesson at 3:30. Meet me at the vet's if I'm not home by 3.* Glancing at the clock, I saw there was no time to spare and hustled back into my truck. I hadn't gone far when I passed Jess coming from the opposite direction. Through her windshield I could see the unhappy look on her face. I swung a hurried U-turn and raced home to offer a shoulder of support.

I could have taken my time. When I got home, there was the orange cat, still alive and still looking like a child's distorted crayon drawing. Jess was spitting the story rapid-fire and proffering a bottle of antibiotic drops as she talked. The cat, it seemed, was even sicker than he'd appeared. He suffered from FIV (the cat version of AIDS) and the lump on his head was a brain tumor. Could it get any worse for this poor animal? The cat was between five and ten years old. His tenure on this planet was bound to be short, but the vet had decided that this creature needed to go back to our garage where we could dose him with Amoxicillin and listen to him sniffle and sneeze at our leisure.

My daughter insisted that she'd been forceful with the vet regarding this sudden change of plans, but he'd ignored her. She is definitely capable of great determination, yet I silently wondered if this was an occasion that simply squashed her burgeoning adulthood where it stood.

So the orange cat slept on, waking only at our insistence at medication time.

Days have passed. The cat—called, alternately, "Orange Cat" by my partner, "Tumor Cat" by my daughter, and "Velcro Kitty" by yours truly—has made both a startling recovery and a nest for himself on the cushy backrest that used to decorate the bed in Jess's dorm room. We've put out feelers for a good home where he can live out his days (or weeks, or years) in the best health possible, but, almost imperceptibly, the family is reorganizing around this newest heart. Don't tell Jess, but I've already planned the vet appointment that will render Velcro Kitty—minus reproductive organs—a viable member of the household.

As time goes by we'll add his story to the others and he'll add immeasurably to ours.

Joanne M. Friedman

Dogs act exactly the way we would act
if we had no shame.
CYNTHIA HEIMEL

CONVERSATIONS WITH ZOE

Yesterday I had a conversation with Zoe. It went like this. "Let's go this way. Zoe, listen. Listen Zoe, Zo . . . e! Lis-ten. LISTEN ZOEEEEE. This way girl. THIS WAY GIRL. I'm counting to ten. ZOE, I AM IN CHARGE!"

I jumped up and down on the sidewalk to get Zoe to listen to me. I wanted her to be a model citizen, to walk down the street with me so it looked like we were together. I wanted Zoe to hold her head high, to show she had manners.

It was Zoe's quality time, her time to relax, to see the sky, and look at the grass, to enjoy the great outdoors. I also hoped Zoe would stop and smell the roses. Instead, my forty-five-pound pooch was pooping on the best-groomed lawn on the street. The landscape truck drove away as the irate owner watched Zoe from an upstairs window. Why couldn't this intelligent animal poop on the grassy area between the sidewalk and the street like all the other well-behaved dogs?

As a parent I had to set limits. Zoe's creative impulses needed to be curbed. Since I am not a confrontational type, I decided to use reason.

Trying to trick her, I said, "Zoe, is that a gun in that man's hand?" pointing to the man in the window. "What if he's good with a gun, Zoe?"

Zoe looked at me as if to say, "You worry too much."

What is really going on is a test of who is leader of the pack. When I took a personality assessment test not long ago to see what job might suit my temperament, my leadership skills were low. Zoe acted as if she had corrected the test. She challenged my weak ability to lead.

When all else failed, I said firmly as I yanked her leash, "I am the alpha dog." I had studied books on dog's social dynamics since Zoe was born. Zoe was not impressed with my knowledge and refused to budge.

I sat down on the sidewalk and cried. I could no longer listen to the comments and laughter of people passing by. "Who's taking who for a walk! Get a choke collar, lady, and wear it."

The next day, Zoe listened. I said, "Zoe stay." She stayed.

"Good job, lady," said a man who was watching. "The world needs more well-trained dogs like yours."

I felt proud. I was a good parent. Zoe was a remarkable dog. After all, what could have made me doubt this?

Peace of mind can be fleeting and sitting dogs don't sit forever. In a matter of seconds I realized that Zoe had fooled me. She was not listening but hunting. Before us was Rocky the squirrel. Zoe was intent on getting the disheveled rodent, who was out looking for nuts. The calm always does come before the storm. The squirrel dashed away from Zoe. Zoe was frenzied, tugging at her leash. A bell had gone off, a gun fired, the rabbit released. The chase had begun. The squirrel was in first place. Zoe was in second. I was in third.

"That's it, Zoe," I said, sitting on the curb again. "I'm giving you away."

Zoe stopped suddenly, long enough to lick my face, to make me feel guilty for thinking about abandoning her. It worked.

"I was only trying to teach you to be a good puppy, Zoe."

Now that Zoe had kissed up to me and felt secure, she took the lead. Rocky or a Rocky look-alike appeared. I followed Zoe home. She was faster than Amtrak. I know my feet were off the ground for at least a split second as Zoe showed me the sights: empty soda cans, a discarded pizza, and raw eggs.

The sun was setting. Zoe had done her stuff. I had enough aerobic exercise for a couple of years. The squirrel was dancing on the treetops. Our quality time together was about over. She hung her head low and glanced at me soulfully with those chocolate eyes as she tugged the leash and leaned her body toward the park.

"No, we are going home," I said firmly for the first time that afternoon. Possibly for the first time in my life.

At home I told Zoe what a bad dog she was. She wagged her tail. I gave her a dog biscuit. She wagged her tail. I told her I didn't like her. She wagged her tail. Zoe didn't know what I was saying, or did she? I could have sworn that Zoe winked at me. She had an ally next door to give her confidence. He was a psychologist who supported her theory that people are easily manipulated.

I could end by saying dogs are difficult, but they aren't. Zoe taught me that dogs aren't the problem, people are. They don't know how to communicate with dogs (many don't know how to communicate with one another). To make matters worse, people have no clue that yelling at a dog is like yelling at a deaf person.

"What do dogs want?" I asked Zoe that night. I looked into her sleepy eyes. The answer was as clear as day. "Dogs want to eat."

"Oh come on, Zoe, be serious."

"Dogs just want to have fun."

"What else?" I asked, waiting for a profound truth.

Was that snoring I heard? Zoe's eyes were almost closed. I looked into them as she drifted off to sleep. The answer came. "Dogs want you to put them in their place in the pack."

"So dogs want to be bossed around?"

"Kind of," said Zoe's eyes. "I'll tell you more in the morning. Go to sleep."

I left Zoe's side feeling better about our relationship. We were communicating. I knew that one day Zoe would poop in that grassy strip of land next to the curb and that we would walk together down the street. With Zoe's help I will learn to be the leader of the pack, and what a great leader I will be.

Elizabeth P. Glixman

THE LAST ONE PICKED

I *held the warm, fuzzy body in my arms during the* two-hour drive home, breathing in the sweet puppy scent. As my husband drove, the puppy watched the moving scenery through the window. Occasionally he would stretch up and touch his moist nose to my cheek, as if wondering who I was and where I was taking him. As the miles passed, I felt the aching in my heart ease a bit.

It had been seven months since we lost our elderly schnauzer to cancer. Being married to a veterinarian and working in an animal hospital should have prepared me for the loss and grief that would follow. I help people deal with these difficult situations every day. In the end, though, I cried just as hard as anyone else did. I missed my little buddy. I didn't think I'd find another dog I would ever love as much.

Time goes by, however, and the kids were asking for another pet. My son, especially, wanted a dog he could teach tricks. To an eight-year-old boy, there could be nothing as cool as a dog that would fetch and roll over on command.

I researched all the breeds I could think of that would fit our family lifestyle, and finally decided on a wire fox terrier. They are popular in circus acts, so surely one could be taught a few simple tricks. We were able to locate a breeder in our state, and I called to ask about her puppies.

"Yes, I have three males left," she said. We talked for several minutes about pedigrees and temperaments. I began to feel a small rush of excitement at the prospect of a new puppy—and guilty at the same time. I would never be able to replace my old dog. I told the breeder that I would discuss it with my husband and let her know.

The next day, I called again to set up a time to look at the litter. I began to feel a little anxious when she told me that she now had two puppies left.

When we arrived, only one puppy was left. My husband and I were both apprehensive. The litter had been a large one. Out of eight puppies, this was the only one that hadn't been sold.

We were pleased to find that the puppy was healthy, bright, and alert. We could find no faults in his physical conformation. Even his spots were in all the right places. It took less than a minute to make our decision. We would take him home.

As my husband drove, he turned to glance at the puppy I held close to me. He said, "I know he got passed over seven times, but I can't help but think that we may have gotten the best pup in the litter. I honestly can't see a thing wrong with him."

Our children were overjoyed when they saw the new arrival. They named him William Tell, and he quickly adapted to his new home. My children enjoyed hearing the story about getting the last puppy from the litter.

This morning, my son was throwing a stick in the yard. Tell was dutifully bouncing after it and bringing it back gripped tightly in his puppy teeth.

"Look, Mom! His first trick!"

Then he dropped down on his knees and hugged Tell. The terrier wiggled with excitement at the attention, but my son looked up at me with watery eyes. I asked, "Honey, what's wrong?"

"He was the last one picked," he said sadly. "I hate to be the last one picked!"

Suddenly, my mind went back in time. I was once again a gangly young girl with bad eyesight, clumsy at sports, holding back tears because I was one of the last to be chosen for gym teams.

"Oh, sweetie, I know Tell was the last one left, but look at how wonderful his life has turned out! He lives on a farm in the country. He has a fenced yard to play in so he doesn't get lost. He has lots of barns to explore when he walks with us. Your daddy is a veterinarian, so he'll always have the best of care." I gave both son and puppy a hug as I added, "And the best thing of all is that he has his own boy to play with every day. I think being the last one picked turned out pretty good this time, didn't it?"

"Yeah, Mom, it did!" he answered. I watched him throw another stick across the yard. In a flash, the spotted puppy raced after it.

"Thanks, Mom," my son said. "I'm glad he was last, because you know what? Now we've got the greatest dog *ever*!"

I watched as William Tell pranced back to us, proudly holding the stick in his mouth. I wondered if what my son had said would turn out to be true. This puppy had some mighty big paw prints to fill. Then I noticed the look of joy on my little boy's face. I don't think I have anything to worry about now. Tell may have been the last puppy, but he's off to a fine start in our hearts.

PAMELA JENKINS

V
MOM'S MAGICAL MOMENTS

We learn the inner secret of happiness
when we learn to direct our inner drives, our interest
and our attention to something outside ourselves.

Ethel Percy Andrus

ICE CUBE WARS

I heard ice cubes rattling and turned to see my adult son pouring a Coke. Talking a blue streak, he grabbed the last ice from the bin and emptied out four new trays. Tall, broad-shouldered, and handsome, he looked every inch a man. But I needed one last bit of proof that he was well launched into adulthood, so I watched.

He filled the trays with water and replaced them in the freezer. I gave him ten points, rejoicing at how far we'd both come. During his adolescence, ice cubes had triggered our biggest fights.

Just old enough to have his own set of car keys jingling in his pocket, he had developed an ice cube passion. My husband and I went to sleep at night to crunching sounds coming from his bedroom and were frequently jarred awake an hour later as he mindlessly rattled more cubes in a plastic mug. Ice cubes were his crutch, his pacifier.

While I worried about possible damage to his teeth, the fact that he didn't refill the empty trays rankled me even more. Our neighbors grew accustomed to my appearance at 5:30 P.M., clutching an empty ice bucket like a saffron-clad monk in Tibet with a begging bowl.

In increasingly heated exchanges, I stressed that it wasn't about ice as much as it was about responsibility within the family. Ice cubes became the metaphor for all of my issues with his teenaged self-centeredness. As the empty trays remained unfilled, my complaints veered off into messy bedrooms, dirty dishes on the kitchen counter, smeared toothpaste in the bathroom, or the car parked across the driveway. The list went on and on, but it always began and ended with ice cubes.

One evening at dinnertime, after a difficult day at work, I opened the freezer for ice. Nothing. Furious, I turned and saw the empty trays at the far end of the counter. Gripping one tray like a war club, I rounded on my son and, if words could do bodily harm, he might still be in a cast. As it was, I yelled, he swore, I hit him on the arm with the empty tray, he pushed me against the counter, and I screamed, "Out!" In tears of rage, he slammed out the door, and I threw the tray against the wall.

I stood still, ashamed of the things I had said, but certain that all fault lay with my son. My husband shook his head sorrowfully and made another trip next door with the ice bucket. My son circled the house, came in the front door, and went upstairs to his room. We ate dinner, his unoccupied chair speaking volumes.

At bedtime, I listened outside his door. Silence. I knocked, and when he didn't throw something at the door, I interpreted it as permission to enter. He lay with one arm across his eyes. His adolescent body filled the narrow bed, and my memory flew back in time to when he was nine months old.

I heard once again his palms slapping against the wooden floors as he crawled at top speed toward me when I came home from work. Chubby hands then, with grubby bits of graham cracker stuck between the fingers.

Now those same hands were broad and tanned with tendons where lovely dimples once lurked. Scrapes from dirt bike injuries marred his knuckles. His broken nails needed trimming, but I no longer had the job of imprisoning his fat little hands to clip the fingernails after his nightly bath. His overlapping bare feet looked like Christ's on the cross, pale and long and narrow. A surfing sock line separated his chalky feet from the deep tan above. Peeking from beneath his frayed cutoffs were knobby knees scarred by surfboard collisions with coral reefs. Those same knees had been his most ticklish spot in infancy, and I ached to squeeze again the once-squishy flesh above them. I wanted others to love him as much as I did. I wanted a guarantee that his selfish, thoughtless behavior would disappear and that he would turn into the mature, compassionate son that I had always expected to raise.

What had I done wrong?

I knew I couldn't touch him yet, not yet, but in my heart I yearned to kiss his fingertips or bury my nose in the sweaty male scent of his tousled hair.

I wanted to whisper my love, to hold him in my arms once more and sing Kumbaya. Instead, I knelt and said, "Colin, I'm so sorry I lost my temper, but I don't know what to do. You not refilling the ice trays is driving me crazy."

Only a strangled sniff came from the bed.

I watched my hand move toward his fingertips—and I touched him. He didn't flinch, so I held his hand. He squeezed my fingers, and my heart soared like a bird released from a cage.

"Mom . . ." he began, but paused. I held his fingers and kissed them. He tried again. "Mom, there's something I don't understand. I just don't understand why you get so upset about this."

I took a deep breath, choking back a resurgence of irritation. *Speak calmly,* I told myself. "Because when you leave us without any ice cubes, it makes me . . ."

He lowered his arm with a jerk and stared up at the ceiling. "Mom, listen to me. Just listen, will you? Look. I've never been arrested, I don't use drugs, and I don't smoke. I've never gotten a DUI, I always let you know where I am, and I've never gotten anybody pregnant." He paused, turned his head, and stared at me. His chin trembled as he continued. "I just don't understand why you get so upset about ice cubes!"

Ice cubes.

I swallowed around an enormous lump in my throat. Then I kissed his damp forehead. Looking into those blue, blue eyes, I relaxed for the first time in hours.

"I'll make a deal with you," I said. "You keep taking care of all that stuff, and from now on I'll do the ice cubes."

Every afternoon till he left for college, I emptied ice cubes into the bin and refilled the trays. First thing each morning I did it again. I made so much ice every day that he never had to deal with the trays at all. I kept my part of the bargain, and he kept his. I figured that, by far, I got the better part of the deal.

PEGGY VINCENT

One can never pay in gratitude;
one can only pay "in kind" somewhere else in life.
ANNE MORROW LINDBERGH

PAID IN FULL

For as long as I can remember, my parents have always gone to great lengths to insure that things were fair between my sister and me. I would always get a little present on her birthday so I wouldn't feel left out, and she would likewise get something to open on mine. If I had a friend spend the night, she would have one, too. Choices regarding television shows, movies, and books were all accounted for precisely so no one's turn would be inadvertently missed.

I don't remember when that accommodation stopped; when we were deemed old enough or mature enough to handle a sibling rivalry that never really was allowed to fester. But I do remember when I noticed the greatest inequity of all, when the scales would be tipped in my favor forever.

Our mother died two years ago, and we both knew how fortunate we were to have had a wonderful relationship with her, and to tell her that often before she died. And so my only regret was not even my own, it was for my sister. Her words that were left unspoken, that float out there reminding me of the heartbreaking disparity that exists between us.

She never got to say, "Mom! I'm going to have a baby!" She

never got to hear the pure joy from the other end that radiates when your daughter is going to become a mother. She never got to tell Mom all of her plans for the nursery or what names she and her husband are considering. She never got a shower, or a Christening dress, or that moment at the hospital when grandparent and grandchild meet for the first time.

I feel guilty that I did get all those things. I feel like someone gave me a far bigger and obviously better toy on Christmas morning. I feel like I snuck the last piece of cake and just left crumbs on the plate for my sister. I feel like Cinderella's evil stepsister. Just call me Drisella.

Wendy is getting cheated, plain and simple. Yes, I know it's no one's fault, but it is still wrong. You might even argue that maybe she won't realize just how precious a moment she's losing, since this is her first, but I know what Wendy is missing, and I ache for her.

We both mourn my mother differently, but fiercely. I play this masochistic game on the days that I need to cry, called, "If I Could Bring Her Back for One Day . . ." It used to be for the day my son graduated from kindergarten or when my second took his first steps. That has all changed since Wendy called with the news just a couple of months ago. I now have a new Day. It would be for that not-so-distant moment in October when Mom would see her third grandchild.

I wish for Wendy that special time during the first week. When she brings him home and has not slept except on her feet and Mom reaches over and takes the sweetness from her weary arms and says, "You go take a nap," and Wendy feels as though she has just won the lottery.

And so, Wendy, my favorite little sister, I've racked my brain trying to figure out how to give you your fair turn. I want to share just like Mom taught us how. You deserve much more than I can ever give you, so I've decided to give you a promise. I promise that I will try to be a flawed and humble substitute. I promise to tell you that you will lose all of that weight right away, and that you are "glowing." I will carry that first blurry sonogram image in my wallet as if it were the Mona Lisa. I will be in that waiting room drinking stale coffee when he finally graces our family with his entrance. I will bury my nose in his neck sniffing his delicious scent when I hold him for the first time.

When you arrive home from the hospital, I will have arranged all of your flowers around the house and piled your cards of welcome and wishes on the table. That huge stuffed, impractical polar bear will be from me. And when you wake from that precious nap that you don't even realize how desperately you need, the smell of a roast will waft up to you from the oven, and your baby will be bathed and powdered, ready for you to take over again. I promise to tell him stories of his grandmother that you won't remember right, and I will tease him that his toes look just like hers. I promise to blanket my mantel with pictures of his cutest moments and my refrigerator with Crayola artwork. I promise to spoil him when you tell me not to.

On those occasions when I'm baby-sitting because you need a haircut, I promise to give him ice cream right before dinner and keep him up too late. We will sing inappropriate songs and play with toys that are off-limits at his house. On those nights when I am pleading with Mom to haunt me, I will instead ask her to dance across your son's dreams. I wish I could give you a picture of her holding your baby proudly in front of a camera, but I promise to paint you one with my words and stories of how much she loves you, instead.

I can't tell you that Mother's Day now won't become the most bittersweet day of the year, although I can tell you that as your baby grows, it does become sweeter. But the one gift you will treasure the most, the biggest prize of them all, I cannot give. Mom has already given it to you; you just have not opened it yet.

It will sneak up on you when you least expect it. Probably on a quiet evening in a rocking chair listening to lullabies or singing one, there will come that perfect moment. You are marveling at this little life that you have created, cradled in your arms, tracing tiny circles on his translucent forehead to soothe him to sleep, and wondering if anything was ever so beautiful and so loved. And then you will realize with a wave of ancient understanding and déjà vu. Yes, this has happened before. You were once this and your mother felt this for you. Tears will flood your eyes and threaten to spill down your cheeks despite the smile you wear on your lips. You will know now and be at peace. We will be even. And it will be enough, at last.

Tracey Henry

BIRTH OF A MOM

After ten months of waiting and three hours of pushing, the tiny baby was placed in my arms. She was so small. So beautiful. So perfect. As I looked into Torri's bright blue eyes, I could hardly believe that she was real.

Then my husband said something startling: "I love you, Mom!"

Mom? *Oh my God,* I thought, *I'm a mom. I'm a mom?*

It was almost surreal. Sure, I knew having a baby made you a mother, and my husband and parents had bought me Mother's Day cards while I was pregnant, but this was so different. I was actually somebody's mom!

I guess the reason I was so surprised by this realization was because I didn't feel like a mom. I was still young and I had a great career that I didn't intend to leave. I had big plans, and a bigger wish list of things I wanted and wanted to do.

On top of that, I didn't have any intuition whatsoever. My instincts were always wrong, and pushing out a baby didn't change that. I remembered how my mom knew everything, but I felt as though I knew nothing. "How do I know if the baby is getting enough to eat?" "How often should she poop?" "What is baby powder used for?" Yes, even the nurses knew I was clueless. How could I possibly be a mom?

Things got worse after we left the hospital. Everyone told me that babies have different cries for different needs—four years and two babies later I still haven't figured that one out. Whenever Torri cried, I went through the same routine: check diaper, distract with a toy, hold and sing, offer food, sit on the floor and cry along because I had no idea what she needed. Eventually I decided to call it colic. Whether it actually was is still a mystery.

During the first few months, I assumed the role of mother without accepting the title. I felt more like a long-term baby-sitter. When I saw myself in the mirror, I still looked like a high school kid. Worse, I still felt like one! It was impossible for me to believe that I was a frumpy, old married woman with a kid of my own.

After three months, it was time for me to go back to work. I was excited to be guaranteed a shower, nice clothes, and time as an individual rather than a mom. The week before my return, I talked with my boss and coworkers, and they were eager to have me back. I assured them that I was just as eager to come back. However, after the conversation, I looked at my angel asleep in her swing. Her tiny head bobbed with the motion, and she had the sweetest look of contentment on her face.

The next three days were the hardest and longest of my life. I was faced with the decision that I had ignored until now: Will I be Mom? Or will I be Me?

Prior to this, I had convinced myself that I could be both. Thousands of women had done it before me. It would be no problem.

Now I was looking beyond the others and into myself. "Could *I* do it?" "Am I strong enough to share my child so I could save myself?" As I looked at the tiny mass of human who was still unable to play or talk, I knew I was not ready to decide.

I called my office just two days before I was scheduled to return and asked for an extension. I bought myself another month. But instead of using the time wisely, weighing the pros and cons, I refused to think about it.

"I have no choice," I justified. "We did the math, and we can't live without my income. I need to go back to work. That's all there is to it."

A month later, I showered and dressed, and then packed my daughter and her things into the car. I sobbed as I drove to the day care center and bawled uncontrollably when I dropped her off. "Whatever you do, don't love her!" I demanded of her caregivers. She was mine, and I wanted her to learn love from me—not paid strangers.

I tried to gather myself as I drove to work, but it wasn't working. When I arrived, I was a mess of makeup and tears. I was welcomed back and told how much I was missed, but I couldn't help thinking of the one I missed. When I finally had a moment alone, something I dreamed of for the past four months, I was lonely and sad.

Before leaving that evening, a supportive coworker told me that it would get easier. I hoped beyond hope that she was right.

However, after two months I was still unable to make it out the door of the day care without being reduced to tears. My misery was affecting my work, my mothering, and my whole life. I became increasingly depressed, with feelings of complete worthlessness. I prayed and prayed for some sort of resolution, but my pleading seemed to go unheard and unanswered.

A few weeks later I had a dream. Torri and I were playing on the floor. The sun was shining, the birds were singing, and the smell of fresh-cut grass filled the air. My husband came into the room with a huge smile and an arm full of flowers. "Happy Mother's Day!" he said. "You are the greatest mom I know. I'm glad you put yourself on hold to care for our child. I respect and love you more than I can ever say. You are my hero." I woke crying. For the first time since my baby was born, I knew I was a mom.

I gave my two-weeks notice, but requested an earlier resignation. My boss could see that I was serious, so she allowed me to clean out my desk that day. I picked up my daughter from what was to be her last day at day care, and we drove home. I have been here ever since.

My birth as a mother was nearly as long and as painful as the birth of my child. But, in the same way a child cannot return to the womb, I will never go back to being anything but Mom.

LISA SANDERS

PUDDLE TALKING

There's a battle brewing in my house, with a line drawn firmly in the mashed potatoes. "No!" roars my son in a surprisingly loud voice for such a tiny child. "All done!"

It's the fiftieth battle of the day, or maybe it's the fifty-first. I lost count after breakfast. I remember the days when my house was quiet, mostly peaceful, when I only had one easy-tempered daughter to parent, a child who bonded with me from day one.

In the supermarket, while other mothers struggled to keep their toddlers in the cart, preventing them from playing Canned Goods Soccer, Mandy sat patiently, holding the coupons and playing "I Spy" with me, dispensing kisses and hugs with abandon. No tantrums, no discipline required beyond the occasional stern look. She was a child who could be reasoned with, talked to, and, in my naïveté, I thought this was due to my supreme parenting skills.

Then along came my son.

At two and a half, Derek is a charismatic child with a smile that captures the sun and radiates joy back ten-fold. He is as much a part of my heart as my daughter. But ever since he was born, he's managed to turn every notion I had about parenting inside out and upside down.

By his first birthday, he was a walking, havoc-wreaking machine. He undid most of the locks in the house, dismantled the window hardware, and, like a master thief, managed to circumvent every baby-proofing device we installed.

He's grown more inventive as he's gotten taller. He's been known to grab his sister's hair and try to swing from her head like Tarzan. He's stubborn enough to refuse to eat for hours, just because we put something green on his plate. My boy is now the one kicking his way out of the grocery cart, while old ladies shake their heads in disapproval. He has tested my patience to its outer limits, pushing buttons I didn't know I had. Because of that, he's made me question whether I really know how to parent at all.

My worst day as a mom came in Blizzard Beach Water Park. My husband went off to ride the water slide, leaving Derek with me. "Daddy, I want Daddy," he screamed, reaching for empty air, shoving me away.

"Daddy will be back in a minute. Why don't we—"

"Daddy! Daddy! No! No!" More determined shoving and wriggling. "Let go! Daddy!"

My dear, sweet son, babe of my breast, put up such a fuss that three people approached me, asking if I wanted help finding his real parents. I was the kidnapper of my own child. And that hurt. Bad.

After that day, I started devouring the books and articles I'd shunned before. No matter what I tried, I couldn't seem to find a common ground with him. Every day, nearly every minute, was a battle.

Tonight, he's decided giving his toys a bath is far more fun than eating his potatoes. He's shrieking, "All done! Sink! Now!" I explain he hasn't eaten his dinner.

"Sink!" he cries, hands outstretched, like a dehydrated nomad who spies an oasis just out of reach.

"If you want to play in the sink, you have to finish your dinner first." I pick up the fork and make for the carrots. "Do you want Mommy to feed you or do you want to feed yourself?"

He grabs the fork, telling me he'll do it himself, thank you very much, and shovels the food in before I can blink. Finished, he scrambles out of his chair and runs by me, a blur of energy. I scoop him up and give him a hug before he says, "Mommy, I'm stuck," and squirms away. I try not to be upset that he's ignored the hugs my daughter has always readily accepted.

I sit down for a breather and tell myself having Derek has given me more dimensions as a mom. Someday, I know, all these frustrating days will become funny stories we tell over holiday dinners. Someday.

For now, though, I watch my son, his toddler-round face serious and cherubic, his lips pressed together as he concentrates on scrubbing Scooby-Doo. I think about the joy each of my children, with their different personalities, has brought into my life and how much I would miss if I'd only had one child and not the other.

Just as I'm about to get teary, I realize that warm feeling isn't love—it's water. My son has pulled out the sprayer and is flooding the kitchen.

"What are you doing?" I ask, already grabbing for a towel and readying a lecture.

He points with pride to the growing puddle and says, "Derek make big sink!" He jumps up and down in the water, splashing in his homemade puddle. And then, amazingly, he puts out his hand and waves me over. "Mommy, play!"

I let the towel, and the lecture, go. Instead, I stomp around and laugh in the middle of the ocean that used to be my kitchen, with my little boy merrily holding my hand, showing me the best spots for splashing.

Sometimes, I realize the easiest way to communicate is not to talk at all.

SHIRLEY KAWA-JUMP

I don't mind the lines because when I was younger,
I just looked so blank!
SUSAN SARANDON

FAT DAYS

Yesterday was a fat day. You know the kind, shortly after winter hibernation, when you try on a pair of shorts only to find that they either don't fit or they show your cheese knees. With dread I threw the too-tight-to-zip shorts to the side and pulled the scale out. Three minutes later I had the nerve to stand on it. I didn't believe what I saw, nope, I knew the scale was lying. I called my constant-weight spouse in and didn't disclose anything except the fact the scale was broken. He stepped his always thirty-four-inch waist onto it and proceeded to tell me it was working fine, his weight was the same.

Of course his weight was the same, brownies don't do to him what they do to me. However, if the scale was right, that meant one thing: Kiss the chocolate good-bye. I resigned myself to turn my fat day into a diet day. I hid the brownie mixes, poured out the soda, and started counting fat grams.

Shortly after noon it was time to pick my daughter up for her orthodontist appointment, and I swear that when I walked into her school the ground shook beneath my massive frame. I didn't feel that fat the day before yesterday, but after standing on the scale and not being able to zip the shorts I knew exactly how much I weighed and the ground had every right to shake.

As is tradition, dear daughter expected a milkshake after her appointment. I said okay, but warned her that if she ordered chocolate anything I would kill her myself. She gave me that wonderful "I-am-almost-thirteen-and-you-are-so-dumb" look and proceeded to order a strawberry shake. The woman at the drive-thru asked me not once, not twice, but three times if I was *sure* that was all we wanted. After shouting back that I was sure, and muttering some not-so-kind things under my breath, we drove around to the pick-up window. There, another bubbly person, who I know zipped her shorts that morning, stuck her head out the window and gleefully told me I simply had to try their new peach smoothies, they were "divine." Well, I knew without a doubt those suckers weren't fat free, because if they were they wouldn't be divine. I had to tell her twice that I simply wasn't interested, but she looked at me and *knew* I was lying.

The entire drive home, dear daughter graphically described how delicious her strawberry milkshake was and kept asking me if I wanted to try. Oh I was trying, yes trying, not to choke her to death.

Dinner came and, rather than sit down and eat with the family, I excused myself for a walk. To walk around the block at my house is a half-mile and I knew I had three to five miles in me. Well, toward the bottom of my street, yes I walked downhill not up, my breathing became a bit labored and I realized that I was getting a little sweaty. Onward and upward I said; I had at least five if not six more times around.

On the next corner my neighbor came from the opposite direction, only she wasn't walking or jogging. She was running. Following her amazingly sweat-free self were her young son and husband riding bicycles. They looked a bit tired, but she was looking like she could run all night. I figured, maybe they had just started out, but by the time I reached the next corner there they were again.

Suffice it to say that I didn't quite have the three to five miles in me that I planned. I made it one mile. Dear neighbor, though, she passed me a total of six times and was still running when I gave up. I bet, though, when she went to bed last night, she didn't have sweet chocolate dreams like I did. My neighbor would be too exhausted to dream at all, and if she did, they would be full of—I don't know—celery?

MELISSA GRAY

LEAVING THE GLITZ BEHIND

So, there I was gazing into Mel Gibson's ice blue eyes, getting lost in his words, when I realized it was time for my baby class. This wasn't your typical first day back to work after maternity leave, but for me it was just that. As a "celebrity journalist" and television producer, my life has been anything but ordinary. Throw a newborn into the mix and things get really crazy. I've gone from Spago to Spaghetti-Os, from emptying celebrities' trash cans to diaper pails.

I spent my twenties living in Los Angeles pursuing a career in the entertainment industry, mainly gossip reporting. My nights consisted of standing on the red carpet at numerous movie premieres and award shows, asking that age-old question, "Who made your dress?" I met everyone from Tom Cruise to O. J. Simpson. I had a job where going to work meant hanging out with Jack Nicholson on the ski slopes in Aspen or chatting with Charlie Sheen at bars in Malibu. I had to keep a bag packed in my trunk in case a story broke and I had to fly off at a minute's notice. I flew halfway across the country and drove through cornfields to get to Julia Roberts's wedding to Lyle Lovett in Marion, Indiana.

Wife and mother were definitely not on my résumé. But, after spending five years reporting about other people's marriages and babies, I decided it was time to have my own. I traded in my Tinseltown shoes for snow boots and moved to the Midwest where I met my husband.

We knew that instantly after our marriage we wanted to become parents, and I still wanted my career. While pregnant, I pored over such books as *Surrendering to Motherhood* and *What to Expect When You're Expecting.* But, as any new parent knows, you never really know what to expect.

At the time, I was waking up each day at 4 A.M. to prepare for a two-hour live broadcast on a local Chicago station. My son, bless his heart, was sleeping from 7 P.M. to 7 A.M. at the age of ten weeks. So, while most mothers spend their maternity leave deprived of sleep, I was actually catching up on mine. I had promised myself that I would return to work—no matter what. Everyone said, "You will take one look at your son and realize that you don't want to leave him." But after four months of staying at home, I was ready to return to work.

Enter the guilt. On one hand, I was content producing my own home video documentaries—the very exciting ones starring my newborn soundly sleeping in the bassinet. On the other hand, I had worked many years to build my career. The thought of leaving my son to return to work, as any new mother can attest, was heart wrenching. I was definitely torn. But when my executive producer called and said that my first day back to work would be spent interviewing Mr. Gibson, well . . . duty called.

I kissed my baby good-bye, grabbed my cell phone, and headed downtown for the big day. I wasn't used to juggling my thoughts about producing a live broadcast and checking in at home to see how many ounces of the bottle were gone. But our interview with Mel was a huge success. As soon as we wrapped, I raced home to the suburbs to grab my then four-month-old son and get him to a Mommy-and-Me class.

When I entered the room flustered, sweaty, and late, the mothers were gathered around singing the usual "Itsy-Bitsy Spider." One of the mothers looked over at me and said, "You look terribly tired. Are you okay?" My response: "I came from interviewing Mel Gibson and just couldn't get here on time." Silence. Then screams. "Mel Gibson?! What was he like? Is he as cute in person as he is in the movies?"

I really just wanted to sing "Itsy-Bitsy Spider," but I was inundated with questions about Mel. For the first time, I just didn't care. My identity was no longer Producer Extraordinaire Who Didn't Screw Up Today. It was Mom. That's when I realized that it was time to join the ranks of the stay-at-home mothers. Then, I could just enjoy watching the smile on my little guy's face when I got to "Out came the sun . . ."

I gave my official notice the following day. I actually cried in the news director's office. Maybe it was hormones. Or maybe it was that I felt somehow I had failed by not having the energy to "Have It All." I was tired. Tired of the hours and tired of trying to wear such different hats. It is never easy for working mothers. I was fortunate to have a choice, but it wasn't an easy one. I still miss the rush. But after weighing the pros and cons of quitting my job, I decided that the behind-the-scenes story of my son's life was worth more than the Emmy on my living room shelf.

Friends say that when I am eighty, it won't be the work that I remember. It will be the long, tiring days spent chasing my little guy around. They are probably right.

Now, a year later, I have a new career. I am freelancing, which allows me to make my own hours and switch off with my husband, rather than incur day care costs. I make more money. I have freedom. But more importantly, I am with my son every day—who, by the way, has ice blue eyes. And I get lost in his words, too.

JENNIFER BIALOW ZEIDLER

THE OUTSIDER

Every Saturday morning in my mother's study I clicked my violin case open and breathed in the smell of wood and varnish. I pulled my cube of rosin out of its velvet-lined compartment and rubbed it across my bow. Looking at myself in the mirror with the half-size violin under my chin, I compared my stance to my mother's. I was eight years old and for a year my mother, a professional violinist, taught me her instrument. But I couldn't get the hang of vibrato, the bottom of the chin rest rubbed hard on my collarbone, and my shoulder ached from holding the violin up. I didn't play "Go Tell Aunt Rhody" with the right fingering and more and more my mother would look at me and quietly sigh.

After months of lessons the sounds that came out of my violin were still squeaky and shrill, and I cringed when my mother told me I was playing out of tune again. My fingers felt thick and disloyal, as if they belonged to someone else. I was often in tears by the end of the lessons. After a year I begged my mother to let me quit.

While I was still struggling with scales, my younger brother played in piano recitals. At six he was given a walk-on part in a Puccini opera that our father, a symphony orchestra conductor, led. Dressed in a white choir robe that matched his white-blond crew cut, my brother played an angel, the dead child of the soprano. Following our father's cues with the baton, he descended a staircase at center stage while the weeping soprano threw herself on the ground and sang to him. My mother, the concertmaster, sat in the orchestra pit just beneath my father's left arm. In the audience, between my grandparents, I squirmed through the performance wishing that my brother would miss one of his cues or, better, fall off the top step and break his leg.

What finally convinced me I was an outsider in my musical family was the day I performed a cheer for them, which I'd learned at my high school's basketball games. It had a long series of arm bends, thigh slaps, and kicks; and I'd practiced it for three weeks in the driveway, whispering the words to myself so no one would hear them until I was ready to perform.

Finally, in the kitchen one night before dinner, I gathered my family around me. "Okay everybody, watch this. I finally know this cheer all the way through."

"C-H—ARGE!" I shouted. My arms flew and I did the kicks precisely. I finished the cheer with a hop in place. I smiled wide. I hadn't missed a step.

But instead of applauding, my mother, father, and brother exploded in laughter, first with a little sputter and then, after exchanging glances, a crescendo of howls. "She didn't even get the rhythm right," my brother said. My parents snorted. I had no idea what they were talking about, and I began to believe the music genes had skipped me. I never performed in front of them again. To people who wondered why I didn't play an instrument when I came from a family of musicians, I explained with a forced smile, "I'm the audience in my family."

I didn't sing again for twenty years, until my children were born. Then, in a rocking chair that squeaked out the beats with each push backward, in a room lit only by a soft night-light, and with my arms wrapped around a baby in fuzzy pajamas, I tested my voice. I made up melodies and words as I rocked. *You are my sweet, sweet love . . .* and sang songs I remembered from summer camp. *Kumbaya, my Lord, Kumbaya.* I could remember the tunes but not all of the words, so I hummed to fill in the blanks. My first baby clapped his hands and smiled at me. My second nestled his head into my neck and went to sleep. No one laughed.

One day I couldn't get a tune out of my head; it kept repeating like an endless loop. It was a classical piece I had probably heard in a movie, maybe in a scene with soldiers on horseback riding in full armor. I wanted to buy the CD but I needed to know its composer. I called my mother and described it to her.

"The chorus really belts it out. The bass drum booms in a few places and the music is so moving it gives me goose bumps."

"I'm sorry," she said. "I don't know what that could be."

I remembered my family sitting around the dinner table, my brother and parents humming music to one another. My brother would hum to my father, who would immediately recognize the piece. I'd sit in awe at their secret language.

On the phone with my mother, now, I said, "If you promise not to laugh I'll try to hum a little of it for you. I'll probably totally botch it, but here goes."

After a couple of false starts my voice sounded to me like the notes that were playing in my head, but I wondered what it sounded like to my mother on the other end of the line. I hummed it once more and then waited.

"Oh yeah, that's Carl Orff. *Carmina Burana.* You carried that tune nicely."

From that moment something changed. I began to sing "Puff the Magic Dragon" in my living room with my sons. I twirled them around as we crooned, drowning one another out, our voices rough and ragged or soft and sweet. I got pajamas on my four-year-old by making up a song about pajamas with feet, and I no longer stopped singing when my mother visited. In the car my children and I sang preschool chants and songs. Now, several years later, we cuddle together in my bed to watch *The Sound of Music* on our video player, joining in with gusto on every song. We laugh with the pleasure of making music. To them I am an opera star. And, for me, I have become an insider.

Kathy Briccetti

VI
GIVING AND GETTING

The fragrance always remains in the hand that gives the rose.

HEDA BEJAR

After a storm the birds sing. Why shouldn't we?

ROSE KENNEDY

I WISH I WERE HERE

The stones didn't cooperate, and I grew frustrated. I chose the shiny, jagged chunk of granite because it seemed to transport a secret. However, it resisted my attempts to bully it into the neck of the empty bottle. Pushed one way, it seemed too large for its space; from another, too small. Finally, it slid in, but then stopped before the bottle grew wide enough to accommodate its girth. With a grunt, I tossed it back into the bevy of rocks at my feet, and it landed inches from where a passing glacier left it thousands of years ago.

Don't ask me why we sat there on a rocky shore trying to shove tiny rocks into an empty water bottle. The kids stopped helping moments after we began, and my husband and I sat like two overgrown four-year-olds, with our brown legs stretched toward each other, the tips of our toes touching. The kids needed to tend to more important matters, like firing stones into the whitecaps and tormenting each other with earwigs and frogs.

I guess we were there because my nine-year-old thought it would be a good way to spend the morning. The yearning to gather stones wasn't there when we doused our campfire and stumbled into our tent; it must have floated through his dreams during the night. We indulged whims all week, which sometimes meant doing nothing at all, and I watched those whims closely for clues. I figured that if I followed enough of them, they'd lead us back to the family we used to be. Before we lost touch with ourselves.

I hadn't meant to let it happen. I just got too busy with e-mails, teachers who needed to meet, supervisors who needed five more minutes before the end of the day, and that bottomless box full of papers sitting beside my desk. All those monumental and minuscule grown-up jobs collided and completely shortchanged the rest of my life. Everything became more important than books, music, snuggling with my husband, gardening, vacations, my kids, and all the other things I'd always loved doing. The part of me that considered happiness as worthy a day's goal as accomplishment disappeared, like an old friend with whom I'd lost touch.

We didn't get away with that, however. The same old arguments cropped up over and over, and made me wonder why we couldn't resolve any issue and move on. Our arguments funneled down to insignificant things that shouldn't have mattered but had the power to ruin a whole day. Finally we detached emotionally and functioned separately, no longer members of a team. Our marriage began to resemble two disinterested patrons watching a rerun of a once-loved play. It wasn't interesting anymore, and I felt disaffected, as if I were taking part in my life but not really connecting to it or anybody in it. Accounted for but not present.

This disconnection might have continued indefinitely. A minivan in cruise control will reach its final destination, even if the trip isn't very exciting for anyone inside. But something happened that forced us to skid to a stop: Both my brothers faced divorce in the same year that a neighbor's fifteen-year-old granddaughter died from an overdose. We, my husband and I, suddenly realized that all the tiny details we scrambled to remember were worthless without the people that mattered most. If we lost those people, nothing would make sense again, and in the middle of juggling, shuffling, and trying desperately to make it all fit we couldn't remember the point to any of it. We both wanted to make sense of it again.

So we ran away from the real world—not forever, but for a little while. Our tent became our ark as we detached ourselves from e-mail, faxes, cell phones, and anything that needed electricity to function. Instead of the kids watching a video after supper, they re-taught my husband and me the fine art of feeding chipmunks from our fingertips. Instead of rolling over to catch ten more minutes of sleep, I played my flute for the rocky barren shores of a misty lake as a lone loon sailed past.

But to tell you the truth, we made it up as we went along. At first we just tried to be together without arguing. We implemented my mother's rule and pledged to keep our mouths closed if we couldn't say something nice. We used our words to communicate, instead of holding resentment in until it bubbled over like a kettle left on the burner. When we disagreed, we softened it with a touch or smile to let the other know it was said in love. We engaged the time-out routine we'd used when the kids were toddlers, only this time we imposed it on ourselves. And we agreed that space during a conflict can be positive.

We agreed that we needed to be happy alone to be happy together. We gave each other time to relax and reconnect with our higher power. Stacy stayed back at camp and fed the kids breakfast while I walked, played my flute, or just sat quietly on a deserted beach. The kids took me to the nature center to learn about snakes while Stacy swung in his hammock. When we came back together as a family, we felt refreshed and ready to face the challenges waiting for us.

We employed our children in this quest as well. They'd heard the arguing and knew something was amiss, so they weren't surprised when we asked for help. In fact, they were thrilled to be a part of the solution. Our younger children thought silly songs would make us happy, and we rediscovered tunes we'd learned at camp. We ate chips and drank warm orange soda while our swimsuits stiffened in the sun. We built sand castles and moats and filled them with bewildered frogs and snapping crayfish. The shoulda's, coulda's, and woulda's that cluttered my consciousness melted away like ice cream dripping from my chocolate–peanut butter cone—a rare treat from the camp store.

Back from holidays and settled into the daily grind of school and work, we're still trying to belong in our children's worlds rather than just pass through. It takes such immense concentration that we're beginning to understand why we couldn't manage it before. We're aware of the fragility of this edifice, our life together, and a new calm has taken hold.

We've made our life simpler, less tangled. We're clearing a path back home for that nice family that was once chock-full with laughter. They're on their way; I can hear them.

Julia Rosien

THE REASON FOR THE SEASON

As the television tantalizes with still another "per- fect" child's toy, my five-year-old granddaughter points at the screen and shouts, "I want that, Grandma. I want that." It becomes a frequent request, changing as often as the ads do. I smile as I think of what Christmas meant to me at her age and what it means to me now.

I was raised with two sisters and three brothers. And although we never wanted for love and encouragement, money for new clothes or toys was scarce. As the Christmas season approached, our mother and father would emphasize the true meaning of Christmas. We knew they wanted to instill in us a proper spirit of love and giving. We also realized that they were preparing us for another Christmas when our presents would be few in comparison to our friends.

I pour myself a glass of grape Kool-Aid and settle into my hubby's comfortable recliner. Watching our granddaughter dress and undress a Barbie doll, I recall a Christmas long ago when I was only a few years older than she is now. . . .

My oldest sister and I anxiously waited for Christmas. It was difficult not to. The store windows displayed everything we children dreamed of. The crisp winter air vibrated with seasonal songs, as our boots crunched on snow-packed sidewalks. Rushing from window to window, we pressed our little noses to the frosty glass. Mother smiled and shook her head. "Not today," she said, and begrudgingly we followed her to the car, Father placed the bags of groceries in the trunk, and we drove home.

As Christmas neared, we set up our tree and pulled the decorations from the closet. There were many homemade ones. Christmas cards from previous years had been cut into circles and ovals. Two pieces were glued together, pictures facing out. Wooden toothpicks—their ends glued between the pieces—prickled out around the edges, like porcupine quills. A garland of multicolored, linked paper rings was somewhat crushed, but would do for another year. We popped popcorn and strung it by needle onto sewing thread, then draped it around the tree. Although to some our tree might appear shabby, to us it was beautiful. Christmas was around the corner and we could hardly wait.

Christmas morning arrived with banging on our kitchen door. In his long underwear, my father rushed to peek out the window. Mom and all of us kids were behind him. "There's no one there," he said with a shrug. He pulled the curtain back farther and looked again. "Someone's left a big box on the step."

It took some doing, but the box was soon sitting in the middle of our kitchen floor. "Open it," we children chorused. "Open it." And Father did.

Our eyes bugged out as we viewed a turkey, a bag of oranges, bags of candies, and gifts wrapped and named—one for each of us. Mom's eyes filled with tears as she looked at Dad and he slipped his arm about her shoulder, giving her a squeeze.

"And that one too, Grandma," my granddaughter says, drawing me back to the present. She drops the Barbie and points again at the television. "I *really* like that one."

I smile. "How about you come and sit beside me," I say, "and I'll tell you a story."

Loving to hear stories, she climbs into the recliner, as I move over. "What kind of story?" she asks.

"It's a story of Christmas when I was about your age." I put my arm around her and she snuggles against me as I begin the story. . . .

When I'm through, she is very quiet. "Grandma," she says finally, "were you sad when you didn't get presents?"

"Well," I say, giving her a hug, "most years we children received small presents. But that Christmas was made wonderful because someone's heart was full of love for others. Now, I've been thinking that you and I should buy a toy and help brighten a child's Christmas. What do you think?"

She looks at the television as it sputters about another "wonder toy," then she looks up at me, her eyes bright. "Can I pick it out?" she asks.

I nod and pat her hand. It's a small step in the right direction. And after all, every journey begins with a single step.

CHRIS MIKALSON

MY SISTER SAM

J*ust before I turned nine, my parents announced a* baby was on the way. The perfect birthday present: a little sister. Although in 1967 a woman didn't learn her newborn's gender until the doctor shouted, "It's a girl!"

But it had to be a sister. Mom had disappointed me with her second child six years earlier: a stinky boy who cried every time I hid his GI Joe. The word "brother" rolled around my mouth like bad medicine. I'd spent the intervening years dressing Barbies and pulling pranks on Bryon. I wanted a baby I could wrap in Pampers and tie with a pink bow.

"What are we going to name her?" I asked.

"I don't kn—" Mom began.

"Sam," my father interrupted, looking over his newspaper.

Mom looked up from the mint green sweater she was knitting. "Oh, Dave."

"Sam." He turned back to the headlines.

"C'mon, Daddy," I said. "What if it's a girl?"

"Sam." He shrugged.

"Daddy."

"Sam."

After that, instead of saying, "When the baby comes," he said, "When Sam is born."

"If Sam's a girl, you two will share a bedroom," he told me.

I tried reasoning, but I got no backup. Mom turned away when she saw me bristle. And as far as I was concerned, if we told Bryon that Mom was bringing a guppy home from the hospital, he'd believe it.

Finally Mom delivered my sister. Naming turned out to be Mom's job, like ironing. Fern, the birth certificate said. I thought that was something you called ladies who smelled like mothballs and had skin like paper, but at least Sam was prenatal history.

Until they brought her home. "Welcome, Sam," Daddy said. I defended Mom's choice of what I refused to admit was the dumbest name on earth.

"Please call her by her name," I said.

"I did."

The first time the baby flipped over, Daddy bragged, "Guess what Sam did."

When Mom propped her like a sack of potatoes in a half-lean, half-sit position on the floor, Daddy squatted beside her. "Good for you, Sam," he said, giving her a teeny pat on the back.

Fern started crawling. When Daddy came home from work, instead of sitting beside Bryon and me in the living room, she was hurtling down the hall.

"Where's Sam?" he asked, kissing us and peering toward the bedrooms.

"Sam," he called. She turned and broke into a hands-and-knees run.

I fretted about my parents. How could a man who used a slide rule forget his daughter's name? Mom called her Fern, but instead of correcting Daddy she smiled and went back to folding laundry. And this must have confused Sam. I mean Fern.

Around the time Fern took her first steps, we moved to a new town. Daddy took Bryon and me to register at school.

"Names and grades?" the clerk asked.

"Lyssa, fifth. Bryon, second."

"Names of other children?" My breakfast lurched into my throat. I imagined an embarrassment worse than the dream I had where I went to school in my underwear. My father didn't have the right answer, but that was a family secret, like the fact that he watched TV in his boxer shorts.

"Fern," he said, signing the forms. *Fern?* I don't know what made me madder: his trick or my gullibility.

School hadn't started yet, but I learned something that day. That my father had an outside-the-house persona separate from the one I knew. That he loved a good joke and a better foil. That he was constant.

And that I was his carbon copy. Just like he couldn't let go of a gag, I couldn't give up the pranks I pulled on my brother. He persisted in ribbing me, and I kept fighting back. No wonder my mother ignored us: Daddy invented stubborn, but I helped stubborn along. I thought back to what Daddy said before Fern was born. "If Sam's a girl, you'll share a bedroom." I wished I'd teased back, "I'll share if Sam's a boy," honing my developing sense of humor that mirrored his.

Daddy kept calling my sister Sam, but I stopped reacting. He found new ways to tease me and I quipped right back. As I approached puberty, his constancy became an annoyance. *He's as obstinate as life is long,* I thought. Little did I know his life would be cut unexpectedly short.

Daddy died when Fern was not yet four. Since I was a grown-up twelve, Mom let me ride in the limousine. "Father of three has heart attack," the obituary read. End of story.

But the end of one story is just the beginning of another, like a book you open at random. I convinced myself, with the passion of a convert, that life would have grown unbearably difficult for my father. That he was meant to die. That relief from his imaginary suffering mattered more than my earthbound pain. I made sense of the senseless by chopping my grief into recognizable cookie-cutter shapes. *At least I'm free of his nerdy jokes,* I thought, though I knew better than to say that out loud.

But in adulthood I, a nerdy jokester myself, understood that when Dad said "Sam" and Fern answered, they shared a private story. A comedian, he bestowed on his kids the comic's highest honor: He let us each in on our very own punchlines.

Now I'm knitting a genderless mint green cardigan for my father's first grandchild: a girl. Jews name babies after the dead as an honor, but also as a wish: that the namesake's qualities carry on in the newborn's life. I don't know what my daughter's birth certificate will say, but she'll need a nickname. I asked Fern for advice.

"What about Dave?" she said.

LYSSA FRIEDMAN

When I dare to be powerful, to use my strength in the service of my vision, then it becomes less and less important whether I am afraid.

CAROL LLOYD

DO IT LIKE A SURVIVOR

Pushing our bodies to their limits overwhelmed us. Yet, the cancer survivors training with us were serene. What was their secret?

This morning I am one of three thousand women shivering at dawn at Chase Palm Park in Santa Barbara, California. The sky is the same color as the sidewalk, gray and silvery with points of early light piercing the fog. A fine mist settles on my cheeks. The exhilaration is contagious, and my stomach feels the excitement. We are about to begin the Avon 3-Day Breast Cancer Walk.

As I trained for this event, my mantra was, "fifty-five at fifty-five": fifty-five miles at age fifty-five. I had raised two thousand dollars for the cause. My training goal was to walk twenty miles in one day.

But for weeks I couldn't reach that goal; in fact, I couldn't budge past nine miles. My back throbbed and my knees swelled. Walk after walk I tried to get beyond that limit, but I was crashing against a locked door. Invariably I gave up, staggering home, defeated.

For moral support, I joined a group of twelve women who had also signed up for the Avon Walk. Our ages ranged from sixteen to sixty; our occupations were diverse. Two were breast cancer survivors determined to regain physical strength. The rest of us were family and friends of survivors.

"I feel more balanced now that I'm flat-chested," one of my companions, Melody, announced the first morning. Surgeons had removed her second breast fifteen days earlier. That day she walked five miles with a drainage tube still in the incision. Although she wasn't as fit as the rest of us, she never complained. When I asked her about tolerating pain, she spread her fingers, palms up. "Pain is a part of life."

Melody behaved as bravely as my lifelong friend, Donna, who had also overcome obstacles: Years ago she lost a baby in her ninth month of pregnancy; at the same time her husband left for military duty during the Vietnam War.

"I have a lump in my neck," she told me one afternoon. The next day it was two lumps. She was diagnosed with Hodgkin's disease, an often-fatal cancer of the lymph system.

Thirty-one and the mother of two children, Donna saw the disease as another of life's setbacks, another obstacle. She had no intention of leaving her children motherless.

"I separate my mind from my body," Donna told me during her radiation treatments. "As my body gets weaker, my mind grows stronger." Tenaciously, she focused on strength and health. She described her mind as "a well of positive energy." The energy level in her "well" got low at times, but it never dried up.

Courage like Melody's and Donna's was typical of the cancer survivors I trained with. Several of them couldn't walk the prescribed number of hours or days suggested by our guides. Yet, the survivors expected to complete fifty-five miles at the event because their experience with cancer told them they could succeed.

My whining embarrassed me. If women could survive cancer, I could walk for three days. After all, the event was supposed to be difficult. If the walk were easy, it wouldn't mean anything.

As members of the group got acquainted, our common goal connected us. Eventually we increased to nine miles, developing a familiar route along the San Diego coast, treading our way along walkways that overlooked the ocean. We helped one another along.

I missed the next two outings. Little did I know that when I rejoined the group, I would experience an epiphany and break through the door that had been closed to me for so long.

That morning the sunrise was a watercolor. Above an azure sea hung clouds the color of peaches. It was no ordinary day. Again we were twelve. Someone had shaved her head to show support for her sister in chemotherapy. All of us were intent on increasing our mileage.

With our elbows swinging in the power-walking style, we stormed down the sidewalk. After two hours, we reached a rest stop where we stretched and drank water. I was worried about being left behind. Continuing along the beach, we trudged up a steep hill into Torrey Pines Reserve, the most beautiful coastline in the county. At seven miles, my feet felt like concrete blocks, as I struggled in the rear of the pack. At eight miles, I felt fragile, connected to the rest by a thread. Then a veteran walker announced that the halfway point was nine miles. I shuddered. I was already in pain. If I stopped, someone would have to retrieve me in her car at the end of the day. Tears welled up.

I searched the sky for inspiration. Beyond the palms, clouds piled up in layers and tumbled along the far line of the sea. Pelicans skimmed above the surf.

At lunchtime, I wasn't the only one slapping Band-Aids on my feet and taking aspirin. Smiles we shared that morning had thinned into determined lines. Veterans were giving first aid advice to newcomers and describing the route we would take during the Avon event the following month.

On the return, two women dropped out, calling on a cell phone for transportation. Resolved, I lengthened my stride. We stretched every hour, but the hours passed slowly. Nearby, a companion was wincing.

"Feet heal," I was talking to myself as well as to her. "Pain is temporary." I visualized my group advancing to the parking lot at the end of the day's journey. And then it hit me. I was in pain but still walking—well beyond the nine-mile mark! Like Melody, I accepted the inevitability of pain; like Donna, I was focusing on success.

By the time we reached the city of Del Mar, about three miles from the end, we had stopped talking. We shuffled along. Wisps of coastal fog swept in, signaling the end of the day. We had one mile to go. Approaching us were two of our members who had already made it to the parking lot and were returning to escort us to the end.

When I reached the parking lot, I dropped into the privacy of my car and wept.

That evening, as I iced my knees, my husband approached me expectantly. "Well?" he asked.

"Eighteen miles," I grinned. "Double what I could do last week."

By the end of training that month, a few in our group were able to walk the two consecutive twenty-mile days recommended by the Avon advisors. I was still able to walk eighteen. Pain receded as I focused on what was more important: our sisterhood and our progress.

Now it is five o'clock in the afternoon. I'm completing the third twenty-mile day of the event. For three days we have marched along city streets and beaches from Santa Barbara through Ventura, and now to Malibu. I am gliding effortlessly, the cliffs of Malibu on my left and the turquoise waters of the Pacific on my right. Ahead, at the finish line, flags unfurl in ribbons.

I am a fish, slipping easily into deep water, surrendering to the tide. I am a gull, tilting into the clouds. I am one of three thousand strong women, stepping lightly toward the finish line.

Laurel A. Wasserman

JUST A DAUGHTER

After my divorce, I decided to move home for a while. I didn't have a set time frame of how long I would stay, or a Plan B. I didn't even have a Plan A, really. I just wanted to go home. I don't remember all that I was thinking, but I do remember what I was feeling as I drove over the San Mateo Bridge from Burlingame to San Leandro. I was feeling that I desperately wanted to be a daughter and nothing else: not a wife, or a roommate, or a teacher, or fashion queen or faux pas, nor somebody's burden or heartache, mentor, or best friend. The only thing I wanted to be was a daughter, and I remember being so thankful that I still had the option.

Of course, Mom began to make me feel at home right away. I was her youngest, rebel daughter, who was the only one to get divorced in our entire family tree. (Not the only one who *should* have gotten divorced, just the only one who actually did.) She cautiously opened the door to my room as I was unpacking my *life* and offered me a cup of tea to settle my nerves. Of course, I burst into tears at the sound of her familiar comforting tone, not being able to recall the last time someone offered to take care of me.

"Why did this happen?" I sobbed uncontrollably. "I thought I did everything right." I stopped unpacking and sat on the floor sobbing, "I don't want this to happen." Because we are from such different generations, I didn't expect that she would be able to offer me the advice I was looking for or have answers to my questions. I just wanted to say out loud the words that were pounding in my chest.

She handed me my cup of tea, already prepared with just the right amount of milk and sugar, the way I like it. The pain and empathy in her face spoke a thousand words, but all she actually said was, "Well, you're home, and tomorrow is another day." I sucked up my sobs and exhaled loudly. "Drink your tea," she said. So I did. The next sentence out of her mouth was typical, "Your father has been driving me crazy. Do you know what he did the other day?" I laughed, sniffled loudly, and drank my tea and felt happy to be sitting on the floor in my old room listening to stories about Dad.

She helped me clear off the bed and find places to put my things as she told me stories about my father; all of them ended with him doing something that irritated her. That's what my dad lives for. I remember once he walked out the front door without any pants on, *to make a statement,* because she was rushing him. Another time, he offered to touch up the paint on the side of the house. This made my mom happy since she always has an ongoing "to do" list laying around. The only problem was that when my dad was done, he dumped all the leftover paint and dirty brush water in her flowerbed. "Ay, yie, yie," my mom sighed with aggravation, as she recalled the incident, then she shook her head and laughed. "I kill him." On that note, I crawled into my old bed and pulled the covers up to my chin. My mom turned on the closet light for me, like she used to, and left to do her "before bed" rituals. "Good night," she whispered. "Good night, Mom."

I looked up at the ceiling that I looked up at every night for fifteen years and had a newfound liking for the sparkles on the acoustic ceiling. I lay awake listening to the familiar sounds of the house. My mom's slippers clicking on the kitchen floor, the sound of the TV on downstairs, knowing my dad had fallen asleep in front of it while watching Johnny Carson. The sound of my mom checking the locks on the front door, the sound of my heart beating slowly, as I dozed off to sleep in my old bed.

The next morning I woke up to my dad's face about an inch away from mine. "What the hell!" I exclaimed with a sleepy, scrunched-up face and a slight bit of annoyance. "I check if you asleep," he said, laughing, knowing he was being a pest. "Why? So you could wake me up?" I said, rubbing my eyes and rolling to my side.

The truth is, my dad would be happy to have all us girls back under his roof. He loved to have his family around him, but more so, he loved to make us laugh. He left the room loudly singing a song he wrote about himself. He was happy because his job was done: waking me up an hour and a half before I actually had to get up.

I pulled the covers over my bare shoulder and folded my hands under my chin. I could see that my mom had already come in, while I was asleep, and left fresh white towels on the end of the bed and pulled up the shades to let in the warm sun. I could smell the sweet aroma of pancakes and fresh coffee brewing in the kitchen. "Breakfast is ready for anyone who wants it," my mom called out from the kitchen. My mom was right, I *was* home and today *would* be another day.

Beverly Tribuiani-Montez

TEACHING THE TEACHER

They told me it would be very difficult. They told me it would be extremely frustrating. They told me I could handle it. But, they didn't tell me it would change my life.

I decided to take the temporary position as a dropout-prevention teacher while searching for work in my field. After all, I was a two-day graduate with a master's degree in counseling—how difficult could three months with high-risk high school students be? I was confident that my education would enable me to meet the challenge. Granted, I was somewhat hesitant about teaching one class of algebra, since math had never been my forte, but visions of Dickinson danced in my head as I got ready to teach two classes of my passion: English literature.

True, I had been forewarned that my new students might be a little difficult or even lacking motivation. But *nothing* prepared me for my first week of high school hell. My lessons on paragraph structure were returned with paper wads and crude noises. Those who had smoked pot for breakfast responded to my welcoming smiles with blank stares. My attempts at stern discipline were rebutted with "I hate you's," followed by a few colorful names (none of which sounded remotely like Mrs. Moore). As a result, my five-foot-three, one-hundred-ten-pound stature began dwindling as my morning restroom trips to calm the nausea became ritual.

I felt weak, anxious, and afraid, but I was determined to remain tough. So, I broke up fights between boys twice my size, battled constant disrespect, and refused to let them sleep. I spoke even louder when they didn't listen, sent them out of class with commanding control, and did not flinch when I noticed the felony anklet strapped to a student in the front row. I fought back tears and held my head high . . . as I survived the first five days.

And, by day six, I was mean, ugly, and tired. *I* didn't even like me anymore. As I began a stale lesson on common and proper nouns, attempting to tune out their noise and total lack of concern, I lost what little sanity remained. I threw my teacher's manual to the floor, looked into their frozen smirks, and admitted those agonizing words: I give up. With tears of defeat, I left the classroom. I made a feeble attempt to regain composure, then returned to gather my belongings and call in a replacement.

Certain that a victory celebration was taking place, I was shocked at the total silence when I entered the classroom. I curtly apologized for my outburst and gathered my things.

Silence.

Then, a stirring in my soul urged me to take advantage of the moment, and for once to be completely forthcoming with these hardened, calloused teens. With my eyes cast downward, I admitted that I could not teach them. I shared with them my refusal to become the bitter, angry person that I felt myself becoming. I told them that I cared a lot about them and wondered what would happen to them in life. I told them that they were labeled "troublemakers" that no one wanted to deal with, but that I actually thought I could make a difference. I shared that I wanted to love them and teach them, but since they refused to give me a chance, I would leave and wish someone else better luck.

Then, I heard a quiet sniffle. As I raised my eyes, a gruff senior spoke in a trembling voice, "Mrs. Moore, we've never had a teacher care about us." A girl in the back said, "Please don't go." And to my amazement, others began to chime in with apologies. I was astounded to see tears running down the cheeks of many of these seemingly numb, careless students. Then, the bell rang, and they exited in an orderly fashion. Shocked, I sat alone and considered my two options: I could give up on them and continue in the pattern that they knew so well, or I could believe in them and start fresh.

I came back the next day and true to their words, they had transformed. They were smiling, eager to learn, and demonstrating respect. But I wouldn't be honest if I didn't admit that I was the one who had changed the most. In a few short moments, I learned that all people must be loved before they can be disciplined; trusted before they will trust; and believed in before they will perform. My three years of graduate studies would be worthless if I couldn't apply the principles to real people who deserved a chance, or maybe a second, or third, in life.

My three-month teaching assignment became a two-year career. And during that time, I was both rewarded and challenged. In 2000, my colleagues named me Rookie Teacher of the Year and I was deeply honored. Yet, I know that the true reward revealed itself through the ecstatic student who rushed to my classroom to tell me he finally passed the state-standardized exam. It came through the tears and thumbs-up at graduation ceremonies. And it comes now, in 2002, as I sit in my counseling office and listen to the stories of those who feel abandoned and forgotten. I look back on my brief teaching career and thank God for my personal education from students who gave me a chance, changed my life, and taught me how to offer hope to the hurting.

Cheree Moore

Giving thanks is one course from which we never graduate.
VALERIE ANDERS

CHOOSING SIDES

"P*lay with me!" my voice whined in my head, then* I half shouted at the dark streak in the bushes, "How can we bond if you won't play with me?"

That darting shadow was Kia, my two-year-old black lab. A service dog, she had been trained to help people with disabilities. I had spent three weeks in Pennsylvania working with her at Canine Partners For Life. We had been home a month and were supposed to be bonding.

"Kia—leave it!" I shouted.

I'd planned to play catch, but on my first meager toss, she scooped the tennis ball and bolted to the bushes where two Alaskan malamutes waited in the next yard. Because of the slope of the property, the neighbor's yard dropped below ours. Kia could run along the fence behind the bushes, tormenting the dogs from above. Back and forth she raced, barking out her superiority. I tried to direct her to the ball, which gleamed yellow from among the dried brown leaves, but she paid no attention. She suspended all the rules during playtime.

Living with a service dog turned out to be more of a commitment than I had imagined. Kia went everywhere with me, attached to my power wheelchair with a retracting leash. I had to work her constantly to teach her new skills and to maintain old ones.

Being naturally curious, she stuck her nose into everything and had to be watched until she learned the rules. She needed her exercise. She needed her medicine and frequent bathroom breaks out at the end of the driveway. Although I was grateful for her, I felt like I had a demanding child as I struggled to meld her life into mine.

In order to bond with Kia, no one could interact with her in any way, except me, for six months. This would cement her loyalty and devotion to me no matter what else happened, the trainers had told me. As I watched her race through the branches, I felt none of that. We did everything else together; couldn't we play together?

One month stretched into two. When we worked, Kia was nearly perfect. At playtime, however, she had her own agenda.

"Should I let her do what she wants or should I keep trying?" I asked my trainer during one of our monthly phone calls.

"Try different toys," Joanie suggested. "How did you guys play up here?"

"She spent the entire time playing with an old basketball and ignored all her brand new toys."

"All the dogs love those basketballs," she laughed, adding, "I guess we could ship you one."

I thanked her, but said that my sister's kids probably had some spares. A few days later, I held the partially deflated and useless ball in my hands as we headed outside. As soon as I cleared the door, Kia snatched it, barely missing my fingers with her eager teeth.

Around the yard she flew, past the pecan tree by the garden, behind the swing set. She ran several laps before stopping to shake the ball hard. It flew from her teeth and she pounced on it as it hit the ground. She was crazy for it!

The malamutes barked. Kia paused for a second, torn between two loves. She looked from the new ball to the bushes and back.

Decision made, she ran one more lap with it before ducking beneath the branches.

"So much for that idea," I muttered as she abandoned even this ball for the excitement of barking at her neighbors.

I kept trying, playing tag as she ran her laps, cutting her off so she'd swerve around me. But in the end, she always returned to the bark-fest in the bushes.

On the Saturday after Thanksgiving, almost four months into the "bonding process," we ventured yet again into the backyard for playtime. It was quiet. The neighbors had gone away for Thanksgiving.

As Kia ran her laps, I tried to find a warm spot in the weak Georgia sun. I didn't feel like chasing her, but continued coaxing her to me.

"Kia—come! Bring me the ball."

Kia trotted up to my chair then ran off with a flick of her tail, swinging the ball with the rhythm of her stride.

"Cheater!" I teased. "Kia—come!"

This time she stopped in front of me, watching my face and ready to run.

"Grrrr!" I growled and started toward her. Off she dashed to the end of the yard. She whirled and ran past me.

"Come back here!" I said, then when she did, "Gimme that ball."

To my surprise, she dropped it on my footstools. We froze, looking at each other for a moment, her tail wagging.

With the ball between my feet, I turned sharply, carrying it with me. Chasing along my side, she snatched the ball and sped toward the house.

"Kia—come! Gimme that ball!"

Again she dropped it on my footstools. I whirled my chair as fast as I could on grass and she followed, grabbing the ball and loping across the yard.

"Good girl!" I yelled, chasing after her.

The next sunny day, we raced outside. I heard the dogs next door and prepared for the worst. Kia ran her laps, then surprised me by stepping up on my footstools to deposit the spit-ladened ball on my knees.

"Off!" I said and she jumped down, waiting. I backed away, dropping the ball as my chair bounced over the grass. The ball had barely touched down when Kia caught it and ran, kicking her rump up like a bucking bronco. I had to laugh.

Alternating the ball on the footstools and in my lap, Kia ignored the barking malamutes next door. Dirt turned into a slimy paint as she drooled on the leather. Up and down the yard we raced. Twenty minutes later, we both wanted to go in.

Dog spit and ball slime spotted my gray sweatpants. My tennis shoes sported dried grass and dirt blobs. Brown streaks decorated my sweatshirt's front. Kia panted loudly beside me, her spooned-tipped tongue layered in grit. Stray bits of grass poked out at the corners of her mouth, and red dust gave her nails a freshly manicured look.

"You're a mess!" my dad exclaimed as we came on the porch.

"But we played!" I said.

Kia flopped to the floor, the water bowl between her front paws. She lapped noisily.

"Uh-huh," he said distractedly. "Stay here while I get something to clean you up." He disappeared into the house, grumbling, "You shouldn't let her get you so dirty."

"Whatever," I muttered and looked down at my grinning pup. She stretched against the cool tile, her tongue wiping a circle in the dust as she panted. Catching my eyes on her, she thumped her tail on the floor and sighed.

AMY MUNNELL

VII
THE GUYS IN OUR LIVES

It's not the men in my life that counts,

it's the life in my men.

Mae West

JENNIFER'S FEET

My father sat on the spindly chair in front of my mother's Singer sewing machine, and Betsy, my three-year-old sister, stood beside him. A worried frown fought with a look of utter confusion on her face. I was fifteen and usually concerned with more worldly issues than my little sister's fears, but I could really sympathize with her. After all, Jennifer, a baby doll that had once been mine and was now my sister's favorite companion, was in serious trouble.

Suffering from an overdose of loving, Jennifer's soft muslin body had fallen apart. Mother had sewn patches to keep the stuffing from leaking away, but with the doll's right leg hanging by a few threads of the original cloth, my parents knew something more serious than patching was required.

"Can we fix her?" My sister's eyes swam with unshed tears.

"You love Jennifer, don't you?" Dad asked.

She nodded wordlessly, fingering the dangling leg.

"Well, I love her, too," he said, gently removing the doll from my sister's reluctant hands. "She's been in the family about fourteen years now, gone on many vacations with us, and shared Thanksgivings and Christmases." He inspected the seams, the construction, and the way the head and limbs were attached. "This looks like a man's job."

Betsy's eyes opened wide. "Mommy . . . ? " Betsy looked down the hall toward the dining room where my mother was cutting out fabric for a sundress.

"Honey, I wouldn't know where to start. I need printed instructions." My mother whipped up dresses and shorts and skirts from Simplicity and McCall's patterns with practiced ease, but the notion of disassembling the doll, cutting a new body, packing the stuffing back in, and reattaching the head and limbs was beyond the range of her design and engineering abilities.

"Hey! I said I'd do it, and I will. I'll make her a new body, the likes of which have never before been seen." So my father, far more mechanically minded than my mother, had taken on the task of fashioning a new body for Jennifer.

And my sister looked very worried.

But Dad didn't think much of the material Mom had bought for the project. "This muslin isn't sturdy enough," he said, tossing it aside with disgust. "I'll use an old sheet, good sturdy 100% cotton. It'll never wear out."

Minutes later, Jennifer was in pieces, Betsy was in a quandary, Mom was in a state of barely controlled amusement, and Dad was in Heaven. Jennifer's rubbery head, arms, and legs sat on the table beside the sewing machine. My father laid the shreds of the tattered torso on the white sheet as a pattern, cut two upper arms, two upper legs, a front, and a back, and carried them to the old Singer.

That machine was probably one of the first electric models Singer made after the original treadle machines went out of production. The shiny black paint had elaborate gold scrollwork decorating it across the front and down the right side. Dad got my mother to thread it for him, but when she tried to show him how it operated, he elbowed her aside, saying, "I can see how it works; it's perfectly simple. I lean my knee against that lever thing underneath, and it sews. That's all there is to it, right?"

She choked on a giggle, nodded, and walked back to the dining room. In the fifties in Kansas, men just didn't operate sewing machines. Especially not to make dolls.

"Um, Mommy . . . ? "

"Jennifer will be fine, Betsy. Daddy knows what he's doing."

"You hope," I muttered under my breath, but no one heard me.

Dad always loved a project; so, tickled to bits with himself, he began sewing. It took him a few minutes to figure out how to keep the stitching from speeding out of control and how to lift the presser foot, but he soon had the Singer humming along nicely. He pinned and sewed and snipped, measured and basted and even used Scotch tape a couple of times, chortling to himself like a mad scientist.

"Oh-ho-ho, if my brothers could just see me now." He anchored a rubber leg to a cotton thigh and stitched up to the waist.

Betsy drew close and leaned against his side, looking hopeful as Jennifer began once again to assume a baby-like appearance. She helped poke the old stuffing through a hole he'd left in the middle of the doll's back, but Daddy's fingers proved incapable of blind-stitching that seam.

Mom took over, threaded the needle, and placed about twenty stitches, completely invisible, right along Jennifer's spine. Then she nipped the last thread with her teeth and held Jennifer up for inspection.

Her smile faded. Dad frowned a little, and he and Mom exchanged glances, something unreadable in their faces.

I looked closely at the doll. "Oh gee, Daddy, the feet . . ."

My mother yanked my sweater and I hushed. With a huge smile, my little sister lifted her arms and captured Jennifer in an impassioned hug before dashing off to take her for a walk in the doll stroller.

"But the feet . . ." I said when Betsy was out of hearing.

"She won't notice . . . I hope," said Dad, looking awfully embarrassed.

And, much to his relief, he was right, for it was two years before Betsy noticed that Dad had switched the doll's legs. They angled in at the thighs and out below the knees—and her big toes were on the outside edges. But my sister's tender heart was touched by the strangeness of the doll's legs; from the day she finally saw that something was amiss, she loved Jennifer even more.

True to my father's predictions, Jennifer's body of cotton sheeting will probably last forever. My little sister is more than forty years old now, and Jennifer is still in her life. Looking queenly in an old christening dress, knock-kneed Jennifer sits in state on Betsy's bedroom dresser, and if you should want to play "This Little Pig Goes to Market" on her toes, you'd have to start at the outside of her foot and work your way to the middle.

All the children in our family have played with Jennifer over the passing years, and each child in turn has eventually noticed something odd about those feet. I was in my sister's kitchen one morning when Hannah, my four-year-old niece, wandered in with Jennifer in her arms.

"Aunt Peggy, is something wrong with Jennifer's feet?"

I took Hannah onto my lap, kissed her worried frown away, and said, "Hannah, let me tell you about Jennifer's feet. It's a love story."

Peggy Vincent

Whenever I try to recall that long-ago first day at school
only one memory shines through; my father held my hand.
Marcelene Cox

CULTIVATING CHARACTER

My son and I are off to a great start where our relationship is concerned. We share the time before naps and good night kisses cuddling together and reading his favorite books. We spend time in the kitchen concocting macaroni and cheese and tuna salad. Walks in the woods on our property are filled with tree climbing and rock gathering. And Sean loves to help me in the garden, watering the flowers and picking weeds; always careful to ask me, "Is this one a weed, Mama?" when he isn't quite sure.

But Sean also has a wonderful relationship with his father, and it is this relationship that I smile about, marvel at, and fervently hope will last a lifetime, even if I don't completely understand it.

My husband did his part when Sean was an infant—he took his turn feeding him, diapering him, and taking care of all of his needs. Yet I could tell these things definitely weren't on Jeff's top ten list of ways he wanted to spend quality time with his son.

But as Sean grew older and became more mobile, the bond between the two of them grew stronger. Along with that, it began to take on a new dimension.

We live on a farm. In fact, one of my son's first phrases was

"John Deere." In the spring, my preschooler's greatest joy is to help his father and his uncle get ready for planting. He runs tools back and forth to them as they work on the planter and eagerly opens the lids on the bins so seed can be loaded. During harvest, he will ride in the combine for hours, perfectly happy to be sitting next to Dad or Uncle Jon as they pick corn or soybeans.

At night, Jeff and Sean come trudging into the house, their canvas coveralls covered with dust and their work boots caked with field dirt. They are tired, but there is a glow in their eyes and a smile on their faces. Farming is a legacy that has been passed down in my husband's family for five generations. But while I live on the farm and share in the lifestyle, the joy of fieldwork is a secret shared only between father and son.

Many times when father and son, the two most important men in my life, finish their work on a warm summer day, they'll sit outside, drink root beer, and see who can belch the loudest. My son's peals of laughter drift over the fields they've planted together, and I can't help but smile, even though root beer belching is an art I will never find appealing.

There is nothing that gives me more joy than standing on our front porch watching Jeff and Sean walk across a field together toward the combine, heading out to do what they both love. As they disappear into the early morning haze, my husband reaches down and takes his son's small hand into his own—and I realize that it doesn't matter that I sometimes don't understand what passes between them. What matters is that it does; thereby cultivating another generation to love family and love the land.

Michelle Guthrie Pearson

THE WEDDING HANKIE

Crinkly, aging tissue paper cradles the tiny white bonnet. Delicate batiste trimmed in scalloped lace and satin ribbons to tie under a new baby's chin, it came as a gift to my firstborn son on September 19, 1973, along with a poem clumsily pecked out on an old typewriter. He wore the bonnet home from the hospital. Afterward, the treasured keepsake was neatly folded and carefully packed away.

The new baby outgrew his soft blue booties and took his first awkward steps. The little boy dug in a sandpile, hopped through mud puddles, and pedaled a bicycle. He walked into his first grade classroom all by himself. He ran around bases on a grassy field, constructed cities with Legos, and earned merit badges with scouts. The teenager ran up and down a wooden court in a shiny uniform, bouncing a basketball and scoring points. He learned to drive a big old Ford and escorted pretty girls to parties. One spring evening, he wore a purple cap and gown, made a speech in a crowded gym, and got a diploma. The young man packed up all his favorite things, slipped into a new red Toyota, and drove away to college. Soon, I'd cut the apron strings for good. Soon, he'd stand at the altar, waiting for his bride to walk down the aisle.

All through the years, I had kept watch over the little bonnet—folded neatly, wrapped in tissue paper, and tucked away in the corner of a drawer. From time to time, I'd take it out, unfold it, and read the poem, sniffling and wiping away tears born out of a mother's emotion. All through the years, I had waited for the special moment to present the treasured keepsake to his bride.

A gown of white peau de soie silently waited. All the arrangements were made. It was almost time. Time to follow the bridal tradition of "something old, something new, something borrowed, something blue." To hand over to the bride the old bonnet my son wore on his head as he began his life. I had rehearsed it over and over in my mind. The ritual of snipping strategically placed stitches to create a dainty handkerchief for the bride to carry on her wedding day—his wedding day—as she pledged her love to him, whisking him away to cleave unto him only and him to her instead of me.

Alas, the bonnet remained packed away in the crinkly, yellowing tissue paper in the corner of the drawer—because the wedding didn't happen. The young man picked up the pieces of his life and resumed college. Grandma told him in private, "If you ever want to get married again, just elope! Don't go through all this mess again!"

One day I got a call. "Mama," he said, "I need my birth certificate. The school wants it *now.* Can you send it to me quickly?" His voice had a sense of urgency.

"Why do they need it now? You've been enrolled for years." But I responded and mailed it in a rush. He always had that effect on me.

Then I began mulling it over. And wondering about the fair new lady who had come along. Grandma and I kept the phone lines humming.

"Do you think they eloped?"

"Yes, I think they ran off and got married!"

I called him every evening, teasing, probing for an answer. "Are you married?"

He just laughed at me. Finally, after a fortnight, he called. "Nicole had to get up the courage to tell her parents first. Yes, we are *married*!" he happily confessed.

"You are *marr-i-i-i-ied*?"

"Yes, we're married. That's why I needed my birth certificate.

You fell right into our scheme. We drove to Louisiana and had a private ceremony."

"But, but . . . you didn't have your wedding hankie!" I stumbled over the words.

"My *what*?"

"Your wedding hankie. It was a gift when you were born."

"I didn't know I had one."

"Yes, you have one. Your bride was supposed to carry it down the aisle."

"We didn't have an aisle."

"Well, she could have held it while repeating her vows. It's the bonnet you wore on your head when you came home from the hospital. We were supposed to present it to your bride."

"I didn't know."

"She was supposed to remove some stitches and make it into a handkerchief to carry during the ceremony. It has a poem and everything."

"Our ceremony was pretty without it. We had candles and wrote our own vows."

"And then, some day, your bride is supposed to add back a few stitches and make it into a bonnet again for your baby to wear home from the hospital. It is an *heirloom*!" I shrieked.

"Oh."

Ohhhh? I've waited twenty-five years for this special moment—never to be.

The bonnet remains a bonnet. Its white satin ribbons hang loose, untied. Motherhood has taught me to hang loose, much like the satin ribbons on the bonnet. My children haven't always tied loose strings into neat bows. They don't cross, loop, and pull according to my fancies. Handsome strands of satin are left to their own design.

"I can't *be-lieve* you got married without your wedding hankie," I sputtered under my breath. "Well, we'll just save it for your first child to wear home from the hospital."

My head whirling, I set my sights down the road a bit. By golly, when the first grandchild is born, I'll *personally* deliver the bonnet to the hospital. I'll place it on the newborn's head and loop the loose ribbons into a neat bow—ensuring that one child in this family makes it to the altar with the hankie once worn on his father's head.

KATHY HARDY RHODES

A ship in port is safe, but that's not what ships are built for.
GRACE MURRAY HOPPER

DYLAN'S DERBY

I *am blessed in countless ways, but one of the things* for which I am most grateful is my remarkable husband. Tom had never been a father when I met him, and I worried when we fell in love and got married that his instant family would overwhelm him. My four children had always been the focus of my life and my first priority was their best interests. My fears were dispelled, however, when I saw how hard Tom tried to be a good father. When his biological child was born, our youngest son, Owen, Tom was concerned that the other children would feel threatened or insecure.

Our ten-year-old son, Dylan, is a member of the local Cub Scout troop. One of their projects was building a pinewood derby racer. The racer comes in a kit that the boys and their dads assemble and customize together. The finished cars are then raced in competitions. Tom and Dylan worked very hard putting Dylan's car together. We were caught unaware, though, when we met one of the other parents in the neighborhood grocery store and found out that the cars were going to be raced the following night. Tom rushed home and stayed up for hours painting the car.

He finally came to bed, full of worry that the car was good enough. We lay in bed and talked as we often did before going to sleep. Tom explained to me that he didn't want Dylan to be embarrassed by his efforts. "I just want him to feel good about his car and enjoy himself," he said.

I could tell there was a lot more to his anxiety than simply winning a Boy Scout car race. I put my hand on his arm. "What's up?" I asked.

He was silent for a few moments and then his face grew thoughtful. "You know," he said, "I guess it doesn't matter if Dylan wins or loses the race tomorrow night."

"And?" I said, encouraging him to continue.

"What really matters is that I'm there to cheer him on. When I stayed up late tonight to finish the car, it told him the car and the race were important to me and that made him feel important. I think it showed him that I believe in him."

"I think you're right," I answered.

Tom put his arm around me and held me close. "That's what it's all about, isn't it? Believing in them, letting them know that they can count on you."

I hugged him back. "Right again, Dad."

He turned out the light. "I've got a lot to learn."

I laughed. "Join the club, sweetheart."

I smiled to myself. Faith in himself and hope for the future were beginning to take the place of self-doubt and apprehension.

We arrived just as the test races were about to start. Dylan's car was in the first heat. I held my breath as the race began. My heart sank as his car placed a dismal last. The cars raced again and, once more, Dylan's car was last by a significant margin. I sighed and glanced at Tom and Dylan. Their sorrowful expressions told me how discouraged and defeated they felt.

One of the other boys laughed. "Man, your car is slow," I heard him say, and I saw Tom wince.

I began to pray. "Okay God, I know this is only a kid's car race, and I know Tom realizes there is far more to being a good dad than building a champion pinewood derby racer, but he needs a boost. He needs to know that his best is good enough. Could You please use Dylan's car to encourage Tom and raise his spirits?" I felt foolish and guilty asking for God's attention in what could be perceived as a minor matter, but I wanted the belief that Tom was beginning to have in himself and his confidence as a father to take root, to grow, and to thrive.

Then a very strange thing happened. The next race started and suddenly Dylan's car shot down the track. *It can't possibly be the same car,* I thought, and I looked again. Sure enough, it was Dylan's car speeding down the track. I wasn't the only person standing there with my mouth hanging open. The entire group had fallen silent, watching Dylan's car. When the car arrived in second place, Tom cheered like one of the boys, and the look on his face was one of pure amazement and shock. Dylan was bouncing up and down as though his feet had springs in them.

"Thanks, God," I whispered, but it was as if God responded to my appreciation by saying, "You ain't seen nothin' yet," because the same incredible event occurred three times in a row. Dylan's car came in second place. Then, in the finals, his car placed first in one heat. The other boys crowded around, slapping Dylan on the back, their excited voices offering praise and congratulations. But Dylan's eyes were looking our way, shining bright with love and gratitude for his dad.

SUSAN B. TOWNSEND

ENOUGH LOVE TO GO AROUND

I can still see my Dad leaning over the worn planks of the dock, his hand immersed in the river, hidden by the light dancing on the water's surface.

I must've been sixteen. My parents and I were at the marina. Nearby, fishermen were packing up to leave. Dad struck up a conversation with them, and they offered him a fish. He dipped his hand in the water before taking it. Thanking them, he watched them walk away. The fish lay still as death in his hand. When the men were out of sight, he knelt on the dock.

Leaning over the water, his hand and wrist were lost under the surface. The muscles in his forearm flexed and relaxed patiently, rhythmically. He began to look pensive and sad. But then he smiled. With a splash, the little fish shuddered, revived, and darted into the cool depths. Satisfied, Dad dried his hand off and explained to me the finer points of fish-CPR. The first step was to never touch a fish with your dry hand.

I guess Dad knew before he ever laid a hand on that apparently dead fish that he would try to give the creature its life back rather than take it home for supper. I always knew my dad was tender toward animals. Perhaps it takes the vantage point of time to really see *how* kindhearted he was.

My father has been gone for a decade now. How fitting it was for his love of animals to be shared at his funeral, including a stray cat. As a young girl, I remember riding in the car with my parents when they saw kittens in the road. There were no houses nearby, only forest. Pulling over to investigate, they found a bony little mama kitty carving out a place for her family beneath a huge fir tree. When Dad approached the mama, she ran and hid. There was a bite in the air; autumn's chill would give way to winter soon. These kittens were born awfully late.

Those cats troubled Dad all the way home. Pets were out of the question in their rented home, even if he could catch the felines. But to Dad, the need was clear.

I don't know anyone else who would drive twenty miles one way to feed a stray cat and her kittens. But he did. Once, twice, three times, then I lost count. He managed plenty of excuses to be in the area, shopping or eating out. A trip to the beach, perhaps. When it started to rain, he made a "cat house" from a heavily waxed cardboard box and carefully covered it with waterproof plastic—and plenty of duct tape. I realized he was serious and the cat was staying put, so I took on the task. It was much closer for me and, as it turned out, freed Mom and Dad up to drive in a different direction.

My parents were in Portland one day, taking clothes to a shelter. They saw a young man with a grocery cart holding a few belongings . . . and a tousled dog faithfully walking at his heels. Dad wanted to meet the young man. My parents talked with him at length and set up a rendezvous later in the week. So began a series of trips in the homeless man's direction. They took clothes, coats, blankets, food . . . and lots of dog food, getting a young man and his dog through a difficult time.

Dad helped me repair and shelter wounded birds until they could fly away, coming up with some magic food that kept them going. Dad took treats to hungry-looking horses and always took time to break leafy alder branches off for our nasty, ornery goat. He fed ducks and geese. And he never gave up trying to make friends with our deranged but beautiful barn cat Shotgun, who craved affection but rarely failed to bite the hand that fed him.

Mom and Dad took me to look at a litter of golden retriever

puppies when I was in high school. We came home with Oly. Dad even managed to convince me I had picked him out. I didn't notice until much later, but one of Oly's paws was malformed. Dad mentioned many times over the years how it was a good thing we brought him home as a pet, since his foot would've never held up in field trials or hunting.

Chance? I'm doubtful.

And when the burden of years was too great and Oly's health failed, it was Dad who knelt beside the gray-faced friend as he was put to sleep. On the long drive home, my mom didn't weep alone.

There were many words spoken when Dad was in the hospital in the coronary and intensive care units. Most of them I don't remember. But I do remember telling him good night one cold December evening, taking his hand, and thanking him for giving me such an enduring love for animals. It has been a legacy of compassion and kindness, and I treasure it.

Recently, I've noticed a furtive little stray calico cat peeking through the weeds at the edge of my yard, looking optimistic. I think I'll call her Stella . . . and I'll ask her if she got the address from Dad.

Christy Caballero

MAGIC WORDS

For the third time, Aunt Maggie tried to coax a "thank you" out of my son. She held a cookie just out of reach. "Thank yooouuuuu," she sang. "Say the magic word."

Cameron snatched the cookie, crammed it into his mouth, and gave her nothing but a crumb-filled smile. At fourteen months, he had yet to utter a single intelligible sound, other than the obligatory "mama" and an occasional "no!" I talked to him, read to him, and labeled every object in sight. He seemed interested, but not inclined to participate.

Aunt Maggie, the designated Old One Who Knows Everything in our family, thought she knew the source of his communication blockage.

"The boy needs prunes," she announced, and sent us off to the organic market. I strolled through the aisles doing my usual labeling routine. Did he like the pretty oranges? I wanted to know. He was silent but busy, dropping apples over the side of the cart. And where did he think the dog food was?

He looked up at me, appearing to give this question some consideration.

"I dunno," he said seriously.

Good answer, I thought. No knowledge, no culpability.

"Aren't you a big boy!" the cashier cooed at Cameron.

"I dunno," he grinned back and licked his lips. The words tasted good.

He tried them later on his grandfather, after losing his car keys and breaking his fountain pen.

"Where did you put Papa's keys, Cameron?"

"Mmmmmm . . . I dunno?"

"And what happened to Papa's pen?"

"I dunno!"

Cameron now had an answer for any question and every situation. He didn't know why he wasn't sleepy, how the juice got on the carpet, or where he'd left his choo-choo.

I tried dropping his magic words into my own conversations with amazing results. After eight "I don't knows," my second grader will look for and find his own skates/hamster/Pokemon T-shirt/basketball. After four "I don't knows," the PTA will stop calling me to bake cookies. Six firm "I don't knows" and a shrug, and my teenage daughter will microwave her own pizza.

Aunt Maggie did not approve, but Cameron's magic words were proving far more potent than the traditional please and thank you.

He started waking up in the middle of the night, dizzy with his new power, chanting "I don't know!" During one of these late-nighters, I carried him downstairs to the den and plopped him on a pile of stuffed toys. While he forcefully reminded Barney and Pooh and Elmo that he didn't know, I fell back to sleep on the sofa.

It was the televangelist who jolted me awake. Cameron had discovered the remote control, the Spanish cable station, and the volume button. He had also removed his diaper. (I didn't ask why. I knew what the answer would be.)

My daughter stumbled down the stairs to complain about the noise. She stared at his naked backside in silence. "He's going to wet the floor," she said finally. "I'm not cleaning it up. And since when does he get to watch cable?"

I didn't know the answer to that, either.

After I unplugged and re-diapered him, I carried my sleepy boy back to bed. I suggested to him, between tummy twirls and butterfly kisses, that perhaps it was time to learn some new magic words.

He gave me a drowsy smile and asked, "Why?"

Hey, it has possibilities.

Kay Bolden

RISK, DARE, AND TRY

Vince Lombardi once challenged his players, "It's not whether you get knocked down, it's whether you get up." Several years ago, my then eight-year-old son needed to learn that same truth.

During the end-of-the-year award ceremony, David's shoulders drooped as he watched his friends receive ribbons and awards that he had worked so hard for. He stared for a few moments at the small participation certificate in his hand.

"I got A's on all my work." He choked back tears. "Why did I try so hard?"

That night I found the certificate crumpled on the floor in his room.

Afterward, David refused to do his homework or care about what he learned. Fortunately, school ended the following week and I breathed a sigh of relief. But how could I help my son cope with disappointment? How could I encourage him to keep doing his best?

The answer came a few days later in the mail. It was an exhibition booklet for the upcoming county fair. As I leafed through the pages I came across a children's cooking division. Would David want to try? When I asked him, he answered, "I want to win something."

I drew him close and nodded. "I do, too." I smiled. "But winners must try and try again until they succeed." We looked at all the categories and decided to make biscuits. The rest of the summer we baked biscuits once a week.

Finally, the day came for David to bake his entry for the fair. The rules stated that he had to handle the baking alone, so I left him in the kitchen. Despite the heat and squeals of his friends outside, he measured flour, poured liquids, and stirred. He rolled out the dough, cut the biscuits, and placed them in the oven. When they were done, we took the best four to the fairgrounds.

On the way home he asked, "Do you think I can win?"

I told him his biscuits looked better than mine and tasted delicious.

"Your hard work has already made you a winner," I said. "But, as for a ribbon, we will wait and see."

The following day we headed for the Home Arts Building at the fairgrounds. We searched through rows of cakes, pies, canned fruit, and jellies until we found the children's baking division. David was the first to spot his entry and, there . . . on the plate next to half-eaten biscuits . . . a blue ribbon! He was the best second-grade biscuit baker in the county! I took his picture as he held his ribbon and the plate of biscuits. Confidence radiated from his smiling face.

That ribbon dangled at the head of his bed for a long time. It encouraged him when he didn't make the soccer team, or failed a spelling test, or when his first attempts at a martial art were awkward and weak. That blue ribbon taught us both that there is always a place in the winner's circle. You just have to keep trying.

NANCY MAFFEO

VIII
LIFE'S BIGGEST CHALLENGES

Nobody can take away your future.

Nobody can take something that you don't have yet.

Dorothy B. Hughes

SHAMAN'S FLIGHT

"And what do you say
of Fear?" I asked.
And the river answered:
"Look out upon my ripples . . ."

A bird then circled in
downstream and dove
into a flight path
all its own.

Inches off the river's
white-water it flew
as if on a mission,
unparalleled.

Still, a common bird
I thought it to be
until it rocketed
past me—
a flash of emerald
green,
a shaman's flight.

Its mallard wings
whispering,
showing me all things—
even courage of my own—
that I would miss
if I gave Fear
my heart, my soul.

SHEILA STEPHENS

Character cannot be developed in ease and quiet.
Only through experiences of trial and suffering can
the soul be strengthened, vision cleared, ambition
inspired and success achieved.
HELEN KELLER

TWO PINK LINES

Two pink lines! I couldn't believe it! I couldn't wait to tell my husband. When I did share the exciting news with him that afternoon, he replied, "Yeah . . . so? You've been sick for weeks. We already figured you were pregnant."

He was right about one thing. I had been sick—and I was still ecstatic. His less-than-enthusiastic response didn't deflate me, yet somewhere in the stillness of me, I did wonder if it was a sign of things to come.

I knew he had a temper. He kicked things. He said things he didn't mean. But I thought all that would pass. I didn't think I would have to celebrate alone for the next several months. But I did, and for the next twelve weeks experienced morning sickness twenty-four hours a day, seven days a week.

Along the way, I felt some changes. Even in the midst of nausea and my husband's detached attitude, I felt an extraordinary love come into play. And something strong in me declared itself. *I would be a mother. I would answer that call for love.*

In preparation for our larger family, we found a larger house. A good thing, I thought at first. Then my husband's sister moved in, along with her fifteen-year-old, and I realized I was the only one with a consistent, full-time job. Now, when I came home from work each day, it was with a heavy heart and slow steps. My hand paused before I opened the front door, for I knew some turmoil would invariably need to be diffused before I could make dinner, do the housework, and then finally collapse into bed.

As if caught in a whirlwind all their own, there were reasons they didn't get along. All three of them were habitual liars, alcoholics, and drug addicts. But even though my husband and sister-in-law were drunk more often than not, I didn't know where I'd go. So I tried to address the issues. Each time I tried, it made the situation worse. *Couldn't we work this out?* I wondered, desperate for a solution.

At least when I was at work, things felt better, and I think my baby did too. But when I was home, I really became concerned—for she wouldn't move at all. It was then, when my worry got so intense, that I started praying—and she'd wiggle just enough to let me know she was okay. Suddenly I was praying every day for the first time in years.

At seven months, complications seemed to reflect my complicated life. "You have gestational diabetes," my doctor explained. "The cause: genetics, diet, and/or stress." In my case, all three applied. How was I to manage stress and have a peaceful pregnancy as the violence that had always been present in my marriage escalated, like a windstorm gaining momentum? All three of the people I was living with were throwing things, hitting, and screaming as if it were natural. One night the turbulence came too close and my sister-in-law and nephew erupted, knocking me down—first into a coffee table and then, again, into a wall.

By this time, the police were on a first-name basis with me. "Please, get out of this situation," they urged me. Still, I fooled myself into thinking that if my husband and I got away from his family, things would get better.

At eight months pregnant, we moved to our own place. As I neatly folded my baby's soft, sweet clothes, I knew this was the last chance I was giving my marriage. I wouldn't let my daughter grow up with abuse as the example. It was going to change—or else.

One week after our move, my doctor scheduled an induction for the following Monday. Almost as soon as we arrived at the hospital, my husband tried to leave. "I want to go home and take care of the dogs," he said. It felt as though an elephant had just charged into my room and now sat upon my chest. Certainly, I knew I meant less than his liquor, but for my baby and myself to be less than the dogs? As I struggled for breath and composure, he headed for the door. But as I cast the elephant off me, the words finally popped out of my mouth. "If you leave now, don't bother coming back." He stayed.

After twelve and a half hours of labor, our beautiful daughter made her entrance into the world. Almost immediately, my husband went home. During my hospital stay, he came to see me once—for ten minutes. I knew he must be drinking, but I didn't know where he was getting the money to do it. Much later I learned that he'd been using my credit card without my consent.

After our daughter's birth, I noticed I continued praying. I started going back to church, and when I told local church leaders what was going on, they offered support. "Tell us what you need, and we'll come pack you up and move you to a safe place." My family learned of the abuse in my so-called marriage and also tried to persuade me to leave. We scheduled the moving truck to come while he was at work. That day, he quit his job. I canceled the move and decided to wait one more week.

Since I was unable to return to work full time, the money had stopped coming in. Our landlord called and said, "We'll be up your way over the weekend. I need your rent, or you need to move." I told them I'd figure something out, but I knew in my heart that we wouldn't be able to come up with the money.

When my daughter was two and a half months old, I realized

that, no matter what, today was the day. I don't know exactly what urged me to pick up the phone—maybe because of all those times of prayer and silence as I listened to that small still voice. I called the police to warn them I was leaving my husband and I didn't know what he would do.

Later that afternoon my husband came home, higher than I had ever seen him. Coming too close to me, he bragged about racing my car, the one we'd just repaired. "I just beat the crap out of a Porsche!" he yelled as he swaggered his way down the hall.

"That's enough!" I said, right on his heels. "I'm tired of this! I don't want to deal with this anymore." Even in his delirium, I had his attention. "Get your stuff, and get out. I never want to see you again!" Now his pace picked up. Running into the bedroom, with me right behind, he picked up something. I figured it was his stash. But it was a gun. I didn't know the gun was in the house, but I knew it was loaded and ready to go. *God help us now,* I thought, knowing I didn't have anything else to lose. We were dead if I delayed. Clutching my infant daughter to my breast, I ran for the phone. Fingers quaking, I dialed 911. And with strength I'd never used before, I told the operator that our lives were in peril.

Gun in hand, my husband stared at me in disbelief. "I'll kill anyone who tries to catch me," he snarled. Then he flew from the house. As I held on to the phone, the world whirled around me; my world had changed forever. Still struggling to focus, I answered the operator, telling her that he was wearing black jeans and a blue-and-black plaid flannel shirt. After what seemed like long stretches of time, the operator told me they'd caught him. Within three blocks—with no shots fired. The next morning, members of my church kindly came and packed us up. And my family drove us home, where they immediately had a new alarm system installed.

He did go to jail. And I did press charges. The things I did surprised me, but then again they didn't. I went to the police station. I identified the gun. I even went to court to testify against him, and when he realized I was serious, he pled guilty. He stayed in jail for ten months. Long enough for the new me to get a lot of therapy, file for divorce, and move out of state.

I'm a lot healthier and happier now. I don't think of him often. But when I do, I know his abuse of me was not my fault. I stand a little taller, and square my shoulders a little more, and I'm able to let it go. My daughter is also healthy and happy, thriving in her new surroundings. She asks for a daddy sometimes. I tell her we'll find her one, someday. But I'm not in a hurry anymore. With a newfound peace, I carry a new kind of hope. And in that still place I've found, I realize this is nowhere near the end. That someday, I'll even see two pink lines again.

Annette V.

UNLEASHED

The new dog park opened with a ribbon-cutting ceremony that lasted far too long for the four-legged set. They strained at their leashes as if they sensed they were about to run free. Fanciful imagining perhaps, but every dog there seemed to stand a little taller, with eyes a bit brighter, including my own small doxi cross, who had never been off a leash outside his own backyard. How could I have known that as I unleashed my dog, I was also setting myself free?

Sometimes the most profound moments come from the simplest acts.

This moment actually began months before when I was diagnosed with a pituitary tumor. The pituitary gland is located at the base of the brain and I was struck with Fear the minute I heard the words "brain" and "tumor" together in the same sentence.

Fear became my pet, my constant companion. He sat with me as I ate breakfast with my family. He took baths with me as I attempted to relax him away. He followed me on the long, daily walks I took with my dog. Even the doctor's reassurances that pituitary gland tumors are usually benign and fairly easily removed (comparatively) didn't chase away my pet.

My eleven-year-old daughter snuggled up to me one night in bed, and under the cover of darkness she asked me about my new pet.

"Mama," she said quietly, "are you scared?"

I struggled with the truth: Should I tell her or not? She lay with her head tucked under my chin. I could smell her hair. Fear lay next to her like a calico cat pressing down on my chest like a weight.

"Yes," I whispered as Fear settled itself more comfortably against me. I held my daughter as she cried about a world in which her grown-ups were suddenly afraid.

Fear went with me into surgery and stayed during the long nights in the ICU. He kept me awake, fearful of sleeping lest the nurses make a mistake with my various drains and tubes. I thought I would lose him after the surgery, but the pain I endured seemed to make him stronger. What if the tumor was still there? What if I had to do this again? What if I had to have radiation? Fear is an expert at what-ifs.

My family helped me with my recovery. My children and husband surrounded me as I got on with the business of living. It would be months before I would know the status of the tumor and I struggled to put Fear behind me as I tried to enjoy the life that had become so precious and sweet.

But Fear leaves a bitter taste in your mouth and makes it hard to savor the sweetness.

As I stood waiting for the ribbon to be cut, I realized I had kept Fear with me for almost six months. I was tired of my pet. My own dog pulled at his leash in excitement. He kept looking up at me with deep brown eyes that begged to be unleashed. Fear sat next to him, fat and complacent. He knew he was well loved and kept close to me at all cost.

The ribbon was cut and people began moving toward the park gate. My dog pulled me along, his tail wagging excitedly. How eager he was to be free. The sun glowed down on us and my heart lightened to see the laughing people and joyous dogs. I was tired of taking Fear with me everywhere I went.

People were bending and unleashing their animals. They bounded away, tongues lolling from their mouths in doggy ecstasy. I wanted to be free, too. I bent down and unsnapped the latch on my dog's leash. He was free. He smelled flowers and barked at the other dogs. Mostly he ran, happy to be unleashed, happy to be free.

"You can go too," I told Fear. He was surprised and didn't want to budge, but I just smiled at him. "Go on, scoot. I don't want you anymore."

My dog ran back to me and jumped delightedly about my knees. He wanted me to play with him. I set off at a brisk pace and left Fear behind me. I didn't know what the future would hold, but I did know that I wasn't going to let my fear be in control of it.

Teri Brown

A PLACE WE CALL HOME

Outside our freshly painted door, the gentle wind rushes through the bare winter branches of our towering pecan tree. The chimes tinkle a welcoming tune, and I flip on the Christmas lights, their twinkling warmth reflecting what I feel. My husband, the cozy armchair of a man I married two decades ago, will soon come home. My heart grows eager at the thought, and I marvel at the things we've endured, the changes that have taken place in this home, in this family, in this marriage we began so long ago.

On the early spring day we had moved into this old homestead, a steady drizzle had soaked us all. My husband and extended family members carried our meager belongings from trucks and cars into the old ranch house that we'd looked idealistically forward to as home.

My two-year-old son chattered as he "helped" us move in. Carrying a few light toys up the walk, he was easily distracted by an earthworm rising from the rich, dampened soil I couldn't wait to start a garden in. Or by a mocking bird that guarded a nearby nest, chirping a warning call from the big acacia tree coated in yellow blooms. Sheltered from the rain beneath the tree, I stood holding my newborn in tiring arms, his angelic face holding the promise of our bright future here.

My toddler came close, tugging with chubby fingers at my jeans. I tucked his fleece hood back down over his damp blond curls, watching as he pointed to another bird. I'd get a bird feeder soon, hang it where we could watch them flutter about while we peeled sweet, homegrown oranges in the summer. I imagined us letting the tangy juice dribble clear to our elbows in the hot summer sun. It would be a happy life, full of the simplicities of nature, of family togetherness, and the comfort of a place to call home.

For the first several years, we worked like tireless ants to improve our home and make a happy productive nest for the family. Then came another baby, a poor economy, and the worries of bills, of putting food on the table and clothes on our children's backs. Worries that my husband shouldered. I stayed home, happy and sheltered in my little world as caregiver, companion, and wife. I sewed and cooked and grew a garden and instilled morals in my growing children.

Increasingly, work interests took my husband away from our old home. He didn't have time to mow the grass, keep our fruit trees pruned and healthy, or fix the sprinkler system. He spent his time in the pursuit of money, getting ahead, providing his family with the material possessions he thought we wanted. The meager belongings we'd moved in with had multiplied into a pirate's booty of furnishings, toys, and entertainment devices. Christmas came every day, yet never seemed enough. The real needs—togetherness and companionship—which are the real heart of a home, went unsatisfied.

With the children's growth came their increased independence. Interests and activities took them away from the safe simplicity of our little house, down the asphalt driveway with its ever-widening potholes, and out into the world. The grass grew waist high sometimes before we found time to mow. Spring showers evaporated into long, hot summer days, then into fall and winter . . . again and again.

The children reached their teen years. I found interests outside the home—work, friends, and a business of my own. We were successful, yet our old house no longer felt like home. The orange trees were neglected. The bird feeder hung empty. Swaying gently in the afternoon wind, it seemed to mock the occasional bird that fluttered to a stop on the feeder perch and peered in at the emptiness. Across the dinner table on the odd night we gathered there as a family, that same emptiness was present in my husband's eyes and gaping like a dark hole in my heart.

I blamed him at first. I lashed out at him for not caring about our family, our relationship, and our home. But he had cared. He'd cared so much that he'd spent all of his time doing what his conservative upbringing a decade earlier than mine had taught him to do—provide materially for his family. And along the way, I'd grown busy. The business I'd always dreamed about had somehow taken precedence over my simpler dreams, and over the homey intentions that had blanketed us with hope and happiness on that wet spring day so long ago.

Instead of gathering my husband back to the nest where, thank goodness, I'd managed to keep my children close, I'd let him go. I'd found other interests for myself as the children had grown.

Was it possible now to backtrack? To find our way back to the path that led home? We tried, only this time the path was rocky. No spring moss softened our falls as we stumbled, fighting our way back from the slippery cliff of a marriage teetering on divorce. But as the path narrowed, our children and our memories of a happy beginning made us lean closer together. We began to do things together again, and one day late in October, a family outing made us realize just how much we'd missed.

Arriving at a local farm where I'd taken our children throughout the years, my husband commented, "The trees are huge. Last time I was here there was no shade at all." He was referring to the lush canopy of leaves that blocked all sunlight from the picnic area. As he looked out at the vast field of pumpkins, I realized he had never been along for this annual outing.

Confused, I later dug out some old photos that memorialized our last visit to the farm as a complete family. A much younger man grinned up from the glossy image. Our now thirteen-year-old daughter wore diapers and stood, full height, just to her daddy's knee. There were other family events and holiday photos, too. Each taken at around that same time, they marked the end of our togetherness. Somehow, an entire decade had passed while each of us veered slowly off on paths of our own. Now, with our fingers entwined, we gripped each other tightly. With the crisis now evident, we weren't about to let our future go. We'd already lost too much of the past.

Today, in the little house that has become bigger, with a new roof and bird feeders filled every other day, I finish some paperwork for my business and call it a day. As a couple we've learned to schedule our priorities and fulfill our personal dreams together. I go to the window that overlooks our neatly swept deck. The fifty-foot pecan tree my son towered over at age two when we first moved in stands sentry over our property. Its mighty, enduring limbs hold the memories of tire swings, of children's laughter, and even a time of neglect.

The Christmas lights shed a warm glow that reflects my feelings. Caressed by the early evening wind, our homemade chimes tinkle a welcoming tune. Then the wind ripples away to find my husband and gently urge him home, where we still have Christmas every day—only now, the gift isn't material at all.

Sheri McGregor

SOMETHING IN COMMON

In my work as a breast pump salesperson, I visited area hospitals to consult with new moms about breast-feeding. At one of these hospitals I would regularly see a statuesque woman stride down the hallway. She was quite beautiful with a flair for distinctive fashion. The other noticeable factor in her appearance was her lack of approachability. Her demeanor evoked an image of an outstretched arm with hand splayed to prevent anyone from entering her personal space. Day in, day out, she strode down the hall, head held high with her eyes fixated on some unknown object in the faraway distance.

I often wondered about this mysterious lady who remained coolly aloof. I asked a few of the nurses on the floor about her. She was a clinical manager, quite efficient in her job and well respected, but intimidating and demanding. She consistently maintained an air of detachment, except with a few select people. I decided it was in my best professional interest to not attempt to break in to her inner circle. During the next few years, we never acknowledged each other. That is, until need overtook protocol.

My husband of twenty-three years decided to change his life by leaving mine. Overnight, my days became a nightmare of worry, anguish, and despair. Work became almost unbearable. My job demanded a happy face. Seeing these loving families reveling in the miracle of birth with husband and wife united in complete harmony was enough to put even the moderately lovelorn onlookers over the brink. In my condition of total emotional annihilation, I experienced an uncontrollable disdain for the display of familial bliss. I was jealous to the core.

One day as I trudged through the hallway leaning on the wall for support, going from one patient's room to the next, I saw a woman performing the exact same ritual on the opposite wall. It was the clinical manager with whom I had shared this walk space for five years, but had never made eye contact with, much less conversation. Suddenly aware of the image of the two of us on opposite sides of the hall, groping our way along, lifting one weighted leg after another, pushing our unwilling spirits to get us through another work day, I started laughing. Somebody just pull the plug, please, and put these two pathetic souls out of their misery. I turned my head so she wouldn't see my face, I was so afraid she would think I was laughing at her.

I did not know why she was so miserable, but the fact of her misery was blatant and it made me realize what I must look like to everyone whose path I crossed. A few days later, one of the floor nurses informed me that the clinical manager's husband had left her. So, that was it. We shared pain. I made a decision. Her office was right next to the nurse's station. I did not hesitate or knock. I stuck my head in her door, startling her. She looked at me with such anxious eyes as I blurted out, "We have something in common." I uncontrollably burst into tears. She replied in kind. It took less than ten seconds to open up entirely to each other.

This began a supportive friendship that was one of several I entered based upon a foundation of shared divorce anguish. These friendships were life preservers in a sea of tears. Together we forged the strength to fight loneliness and the fear of our unknown futures. Our solidarity allowed us to find humor in our predicaments. We devised plans and goals for one another and we became one another's cheerleaders.

Six years later we are all firmly planted in new, happy lives. We don't speak every day or even every week, but we are one in our history. Like veterans of war, when we gather together, we tell our stories and we look upon one another with a knowing recognition of pride for having gone through the same battle and returned safe and sound.

PATTY SWYDEN SULLIVAN

Both within the family and without,
our sisters hold up our mirrors; our images of
who we are and of who we can dare to become.
ELIZABETH FISHEL

ONE OUT OF FOUR

W*e've had a unique relationship, my sister Judy* and I. We're "mid-kids," she and I. We dwell in that netherworld of being neither the much-anticipated first child nor the cherished last, as befits the baby of the family. We simply were. Separated by five years, I was the proverbial thorn in Judy's side, tagging along and making mischief whenever I could.

Over the years, ours has been a prickly relationship at times. Tossed together in the middle, we battled as often as we laughed. I threw a lamp at her once, in the heat of an argument. She could have told, but she didn't.

Judy hauling me along—none too gracefully—to a Sunday matinee with her friends, ordering me to "shut up." I do, but not before telling her that I'm telling Mom and Dad.

And so it went, all through our growing years, into adulthood. Vying for attention, competing without realizing it. Standing together against outside forces, at odds with each other over matters mundane and trivial. So it often is with sisters. Words hurled in anger during childhood and youth still hold some small power to wound years later. And yet, when I needed her most, there she was.

One year older, another year closer to looking like Mom.

So read the inside message on a popular birthday card about five years ago. That year on my birthday, I received two of them from two of my siblings.

We number four, my sisters and I. To one degree or another, all four of us resemble our parents. Some more than others. Make that *one* most of all. Make it me.

Upon receipt of those cards, rather than evoking smiles or giggles, which I know the senders intended, a shudder ran through me. *Looking like Mom indeed.* What they didn't know then, and wouldn't for almost another year, is that I not only had inherited Mom's physical traits, but I was also the recipient of the gene or propensity toward alcohol abuse.

Hide. Deny. Act as if. However, as 1997 drew to a close, even I knew that I could no longer squelch the ugly yet honest voices that spoke to me from the darkest recesses of my soul. "You're a drunk!" they hissed. "You need help," they insisted. "You're just like your mother!" they taunted. And of course, I knew they were right. I had known for a long time that my "social drinking" had long since passed social. At what point had it spiraled out of control? The event or events that transpired to lead me on that lonely and dangerous path matter not one whit. The inescapable fact was I'd lost control of my drinking, and in so doing had lost myself, without ever realizing that the real me had gone missing. Until it was too late. Nevertheless, although my children knew and my spouse knew, no one else in the family knew. Never my sisters. But that all changed in December 1997. They found out in the worst possible way.

"Aunt Judy," my son said haltingly, "Mom's in the hospital ICU."

I was told all this much later, of course. I was incommunicado at the time.

I'd attempted to wean myself from booze. A foolish idea, given the strength of my addiction. My body refused to adjust—or was simply unable to. In essence, every system in my body was in shutdown mode. To add to the problem, there was the small matter of my pneumonia. I was fair game for every virus; my immune system was nonexistent. The prognosis was grim—the medical community gave me a less than 10 percent chance of survival.

And so it fell to Judy to take up the burden of notifying our two other sisters so far away: Vicki, the youngest, living in St. Cloud, Minnesota; Carmen, the eldest, in Washington Court House, Ohio. The burden grew. Day after day, week after week, she kept up a grueling schedule that I, in my wildest imagination, would hardly have deemed possible.

More importantly, however, was the message that Judy brought to me, day after day, week in and week out. In bone-chilling cold and ice-encrusted snow, she trekked each day to my side. "Get well. Come back. Fight," while she continued to work full time and care for her own family.

I don't remember any of that, of course. For days I was lost in a hideous nightmare of demons and monsters, laughing and chasing me, to God knows where. "I have to go home!" was my plaintive cry. No one heard. No one listened. No matter how hard I tried, I couldn't find the exit that would permit me to return home.

Carmen and Vicki also played a huge role in my physical, mental, and spiritual healing, sending love and prayers telepathically. In addition, I had the unwavering love and support of my husband and son.

One day, however, through the fog I heard a voice. "There's Judy!" I said out loud. It was *her* voice that I recall hearing first, *her* smile peeking around the corner of my hospital room. After that, there were *her* cheers, leading me forward into the land of the lucid and alive.

Imagine. Judy. A taunter in my childhood—the sometime

nemesis of my youth who bolstered my flagging courage when gremlins whispered doubt in my ear. Her love remained constant, her compassion unwavering. How blind could one person be? For most of my life, I'd seen only the thorns, not the rose. As my life hung in the balance, she reminded me that I had the strength within to pull through—at a critical time when push had definitely come to shove.

PATRICIA R. REULE

A FRUITFUL OBSESSION

We had just boarded the plane that, in a few hours, would land all of us in Honolulu. I was set apart from the other passengers because I would have been as thrilled if my destination had been Kankakee. Mine was a journey that had taken years. Hawaii was a bonus.

I leaned back against the headrest, closed my eyes, and my mind made a quantum leap back to when I was seven. A neighbor had deemed it her business to tell me I was not an only child. She insisted I had a brother somewhere. Of course she was lying! How could a neighbor know something so important if I didn't know it?

Never have my feet carried me faster than on that trip home. Running to my mother, I blurted out the revelations, knowing she would say the neighbor had confused us with some other family. The look on her face told me I had hoped in vain. The story was true. Mama reached out to clasp both my arms and looked directly into my eyes. "Yes, it's true," she said, "but you are too young to understand it all now."

I pulled free of her grasp and ran out the door, racing to the playground two blocks away. All of my anxiety took the form of strength as I pumped a swing much higher than I had ever dared. When the dark of night matched my mood, I went home, the only place I knew to go.

Mama did not scold me. She sat me down and made her first attempt to explain. The only words that registered were, "He was given up for adoption as a baby." Mama cried as she told me, and

I cried listening. She added, "You should try to forget it. There is nothing to be done now. I have no idea where he is, nor can I find out."

Fear clutched my heart. When would she give me away? I had spent a lot of time with an aunt and uncle when my alcoholic stepfather made life difficult. Would Mama want to make our separation permanent? Or worse, perhaps she would prefer not to know where I was, like my brother.

My brother was four years older than I, but my child's mind did not assimilate that fact. My dreams were filled with my discovery of a baby brother. Sometimes he was in the woods in a basket hidden near the water, much like Moses. Once he was found inside a huge oyster shell. The dreams continued for a couple of years. Fear subsided and was replaced by an obsession to one day find my brother.

Mama confided the whole story when I was fifteen. When Mama was fifteen, she married my father who was sixteen. Her mother had died when she was eleven, and her father was an indifferent parent. However, her parents-in-law were outraged by the marriage, and they lost no time in having it annulled. When it was discovered that Mama was pregnant, her father shipped her off to an institution for girls in the same predicament.

I had long known that Mama was always blue on New Year's when other people celebrated. I learned my brother was a first-of-the-New-Year baby. The child was taken away from Mama immediately after birth, and she was told he would be cared for with other infants until she was trained in mothering. She later learned her baby had been adopted, and there was no recourse.

She and our father remarried when they became of legal age.

The story was acceptable when I was fifteen, and I only ached for Mama's pain. I promised that one day I would find her son—and my brother. She responded reluctantly, and the father who might have furnished me with needed encouragement died when I was sixteen.

During World War II, Mama placed a star in a window. She said she was sure my brother was serving his country.

I matured, and holes appeared in the fabric of the story I had believed at fifteen. There was the bit about Mama never having signed a release form. I told myself she had been young and probably didn't know what she had signed. They couldn't have taken her baby and placed it for adoption without her written permission—could they? My doubts continually nagged me.

When I actively began my search, I encountered many blind alleys. Even my mother refused to tell me where the infant had been taken prior to the adoption. Every obstacle made me more determined in my quest.

Eventually, I approached Judge Burns in our city and persuaded him to open the court records. The adoption form was on file. It had my mother's name on it, but it was not her signature. Mama had only a third grade education, and her signature had been barely legible. The name on the form was an obvious forgery. The important thing was that I finally found the name of the institution from which the adoption had been made.

When I told Mama of the signature on the release form, she was sure it had been signed by her caseworker. There was a tinge of bitterness, but mostly Mama had an attitude of resignation. When she learned I had discovered the place from which the adoption was made, she suddenly realized I intended to make the search more than a dream.

I needed her signature for authority to request an opening of the records. It did not come easily. Mama was so sure her son would hate her. I was asking her to make herself vulnerable. I didn't press. I knew what I was asking. Let her have time to assimilate the fact I had come closer to the solution of the secret than she ever expected.

Finally, she told me to bring the forms, that she was ready to sign. "You've been deprived of your brother for these many years," she said, "and I owe it to you to help all I can." When she signed the forms and I looked at her name, it was like a weight being lifted. I was so grateful to her.

Memories of all the times, over the years, when I had been asked if I was an only child came flooding back to me. There was no doubt in my mind, as I hurtled toward the capital city, that by the next day I would know where to find my brother. The wait for my interview seemed endless.

Once ushered in, I was shocked by the cold attitude of the worker. The woman held up the file folder containing all the answers I had sought for such a long time. She made no move to open it. Total numbness enveloped me when she told me those documents were permanently sealed.

I explained that we were both adults now. "How could we hurt anyone?" I asked.

She admitted that both adoptive parents were dead. However, she dismissed me, saying she would take the matter to the board for a decision. This appeared to be a concession. Once a decision was made, I would be contacted. I requested they phone me. It was hard to think of anything but that call. I vacillated from optimism to the depths of despair. Four days passed before the woman telephoned. She was sorry, but the board had decided to keep the records sealed. She would not listen to my pleas.

Totally dejected, I placed the receiver back in its cradle, and sobs tore at hope. It all seemed so futile. It was the first time I doubted I would reach my goal.

A friend suggested that I take the story to a man he knew in the capital. "He knows practically everyone there," my friend said. "I'm betting he will be able to help."

When I met this man, I felt foolish unfolding my story. It wouldn't have surprised me if he had asked what I expected him to do about it.

"The board probably fears you want to open an old can of worms." He smiled. "I know one of the board members rather well. I'll take him out to dinner and explain your case. It should lend weight that you know your mother did not sign a release document."

Hope buoyed me again.

Three days later the verdict was in. I could write a letter to my brother and send it to the board. It would be forwarded to him. He could answer, or not, as he chose.

Here was the day I had waited a lifetime for, and I couldn't think of a word to say. Many drafts were discarded before I was satisfied with one to mail.

I tried not to watch the mailbox too soon, realizing the letter was to be channeled. I decided not to tell Mama unless an answer came. One of us eaten by anxiety was enough.

Actually, not much time elapsed before an answer came, with a Honolulu postmark. Once in my hands, the letter suddenly seemed frightening. It was finally here, and all of my expected joy had turned to fear. Not at all rational because he surely would not have written to say he wanted no contact. Would he? I quickly opened the first of many letters to come from my very own brother. It began, "Dear Sis . . ."

It had to be read several times because it is hard to read through tears. Learning his name, Bruce, made him real, as did his wife and five children. He told me he had always wanted a sister, and his wife could vouch for the fact because he had told her often. The letter was lengthy, warm, and open. He wrote that he would also write our mother and assure her he did not blame her for anything. The letter ended with love and a request that I answer very soon. When I had it thoroughly digested, the only words that came to mind were, "Thank you, God. My cup runneth over."

The flight to Honolulu went fast. Everyone was anxious to get off and see the beautiful sights. I wanted to get off and show whoever would watch that I'm not an only child.

We entered the airport to be confronted by a sea of faces. One loomed out in a split second. There was no mistaking my brother because he looked so much like our mother. I quickly wove my way through the crowd. Before I knew what was happening, leis were being placed around my neck. I was being hugged and kissed. As I inhaled the fragrance of flowers, my brother said, "Welcome to Hawaii!"

I held him close and answered, "Welcome to my life!"

EDNA MINER LARSON

THE KEYHOLE

U*nlike before, the upstairs bathroom door closes* tight and Mom says she doesn't want me to wash her back. I stand beside the door listening to rushing water fill the old four-legged bathtub, wondering how awful Mom could look—certain it's not bad enough to refuse my back-washing. Since the mastectomy, Mom has quit getting dressed on top of the living room register, the only warm place in the house. Now she dresses in her bedroom behind a closed door. And when a bra commercial comes on TV, she runs into the kitchen bathroom crying. I know her breast is gone, but I don't know what that means. At seven it's hard to understand the importance of breasts.

Quietly I bend toward the keyhole, relieved to find a towel doesn't cover it. The water has quit running but Mom hasn't gotten into the tub. I don't know what's taking her so long. All the sounds have stopped. If I hadn't seen her go into the bathroom, I wouldn't know there was anyone in there.

When I peek through the keyhole, I find Mom standing near the door, looking at herself in front of the mirror. I can see her fleshy back, sagging rump, and muscular legs, not her breast. The floor creaks as I move to the left a bit, trying to get a better view. Then I hear Mom crying. She lifts her arms over her head and squeezes her fists together, wrapping her head in a tight embrace. The more she squeezes, the louder she cries, yet it's a stifled cry, one that she smothers by sucking the side of her arm. This is something she doesn't want me to see. Something even she doesn't want to see.

Slowly she lifts her legs into the bathtub and sinks into the water, still crying. I remain crouched by the keyhole, staring at her missing breast, finally understanding the loss of so much flesh. Mom's skin is red and raw, crusted with wounds that will become thick scars. She looks bruised and off balance, but not untouchable. I can see she'll never have another breast to replace this one. All that will remain is a scar and memories.

Mom's been cut off from her womanhood and now wants to be alone with her body, which means cutting herself off from me. But I want to scrub her back again. All I want to do is wash her neck and back. Her developed woman's body is so unlike mine. It isn't until she's naked that I realize how different we are in age. She's a woman and I'm a girl. With clothes on, we seem more the same.

When she was in the hospital, I could only wave at her through the window since I was too young to be admitted as a visitor. And now she's home and I can only peek at her through the keyhole, unable to comfort her. I watch her cry and begin to cry softly, stifling tears by sucking my arm. I must be with Mom. That missing breast isn't enough reason to separate us. After my tears are wiped away, I open the door and Mom screams, "I'm in here!" She holds a washcloth over her missing breast. There's not enough cloth to cover the wounds.

"It's all right, Ma." Nothing else is said. The washcloth remains clenched over the wounds and I pick up the bar of soap and wash her back. "Does that feel good, Ma?"

"Yeah."

"You can take that washcloth away. I still think you're beautiful."

Tears roll down her cheeks again. "You're too young to see this."

"I saw it through the keyhole, Ma. It ain't that bad."

"Are you sure?"

"Yeah."

Mom reaches over her shoulder and squeezes my hand. Without saying anything, her touch reminds both of us we need to be strong.

DIANE PAYNE

IX
FINDING PEACE ALONG THE WAY

Dreams are . . . illustrations from the book your soul is writing about you.

MARSHA NORMAN

A BLUEBIRD'S LESSON

If there was a survey floating around the universe, one that dealt only with issues pertinent to who we are as humans, who we *really* are, I think it would have one major question. Not "What is your favorite color?" or "If you were stranded on a desert island, what one thing must you have with you?" or even "Who is your perfect mate?" I think the question would be "What do you believe in?"

Now, for many years my answer would have been "nothing." Raised in a family with one agnostic, one atheist, a Christian, some Buddhists, and one "I'm not sure but I know the world is goin' to hell in a handbasket," a crisis of identity seems unsurprising, to say the least. While the way my parents met may appear to be fate (they were the only two to show up at the gate; everyone else heard the flight was delayed), our family discussions go back and forth from meant-to-be to luck-of-the-draw, to karmic-energy whirlpools. My head actually *became* the whirlpool after a while, sucking variegated notions into the maelstrom of my mind and spitting out . . . nothing. After all, how could one belief system find its way up through all these poles-apart ideals?

So I went along in my "non-belief" way and did just fine. I got a college degree, even. I became a teacher. I leaned toward my father's belief system—he's the atheist—because I couldn't see any evidence to the contrary. And, I felt way too intelligent to believe in the other stuff. Self-righteousness became my conviction, acute moralism my faith. I spent much time arguing for tolerance and against extremism, without realizing the extreme intolerance of my own position. It was a glorious place to be, atop a mountain created from the littered remnants of others' shattered conceptions.

It was a pretty long way down, too.

My dethroning came in April 1994. After a lifetime blessed by the gods of . . . oh, that's right . . . we're still in the non-belief phase. After an extraordinarily lucky life, untouched by death or dysfunction, enriched by support and success, I was diagnosed with multiple sclerosis. I was just twenty-four.

The diagnosis stunned me, panicked me, and, most of all, pulled me headfirst back into the vortex. I left the neurologist's office with my father, and as we exited the big double doors of the building, I saw him cry for the first time. I could see the question in his head, this man who believed it was all random and luck of the draw: *How could this be happening to her? She is definitely not that unlucky.* Seeing his face was almost harder than the diagnosis itself.

My mother couldn't believe I was meant for disease and sickness, and all the Christians and Buddhists saw it as part of a larger, if hard to understand plan, and my grandma, well—if this wasn't proof eternal that the world really was going to hell in a handbasket.

I was just plain mad. Whether multiple sclerosis was part of a larger plan or was pure bad luck, I felt it monumentally unfair that it should happen to me. Some early symptoms (like double vision and dizziness so bad I couldn't lift my head) did nothing to improve my outlook. My mother even came to California from Colorado to help me grade essays, since I couldn't read them. I wasn't grateful, only scared. Wasn't coping much, but crying often. My past seemed to be too easy, and I started blaming my wonderful life for not preparing me to handle something like this.

I ended up moving home to Colorado, needing some of the support and success that had marked my first twenty-four years. I settled into my old bedroom, pored over albums that sang of an earlier time, watched the posters of forever-young men pose from my wall, and wished it all back again. I took walks around the block whenever I felt able and remembered who had lived in which house in my neighborhood, which roads I had conquered on my bike, which trees I had climbed. I prayed . . . no, I wished . . . no, I hoped to make some sense of it all.

And then the strangest thing happened. One morning I awoke from my tiny twin bed, pulled the curtains, and saw a bluebird sitting in the tree outside my window. Well, probably a blue jay, since I'm pretty sure that bluebirds aren't indigenous to this area. Whatever, it was a beautiful cornflower blue, with animated eyes and a navy crown on its head. It fixed me with a look from one side of its face and settled into the tree. Every time I glanced out of that window, there was my new friend. But the wild part, the part that turned me inside out, lifted me from the undertow and dropped me whole on the beach, was what happened when I left that room.

I walked outside for my daily stroll around the block, and that bluebird followed me. No, he didn't fly from tree to tree; he literally jumped down on the ground and hopped along with me. Slow, fast, watching him, or whistling nonchalantly as I looked the other way, there he was. And when I drove away, he'd perch on successive trees and see me off. It was the most fantastic thing, this bird!

Sometimes I cussed him out, "Whaddya want with me, ya crazy bird? Don't you know I'm sick?" Sometimes he walked alongside me and watched me cry—his penetrating stare darting from one side of his head. Always his look said, "I'm here. I'm still here." And he was. Until I figured it out and didn't need him anymore, there he was. This disease wasn't fatal, and you know what they say about that which doesn't kill you. Besides, that whole self-righteous thing gets old after a while. A chronic illness can do amazing things for one's compassion and ability to empathize with all kinds of differing lifestyles and viewpoints. Sometimes, it even makes one think that her viewpoint might not be the all-time best one.

What was he? Guardian angel, messenger from God, positive energy from the Universe? A bird in need of therapy?

I'm not sure, but I am sure of something—that bird gave me something to believe in. I now have no doubt that we are a small part of something larger—be it force, presence, or energy. That bluebird showed me this and now that I understand it, I'm seeing it in every aspect of my life. If you gave me that survey question today, I'd be able to answer it with pride and confidence. It's me—I believe in me. And you, and you, and the endless possibilities of the whole darn parade as it passes before my chronically ill body but free-flying spirit, and dances before my compassionate and wide-believing eyes.

Kelley Bowles Albaugh

EXACTLY LIKE ME

I'm *not sure when I became obsessed with heredity or* why it even mattered, but I believe my obsession culminated within hours of the birth of my first child. Amidst the joy and astonishment of his arrival, I clearly recall thinking, *Finally I have a blood relation.*

As an adopted child, I was minus a genetic link. A small thing, perhaps, to the masses of kids who are told that they have Grandma Ida's red hair, Uncle Joey's blue eyes, cousin Hilda's chubby cheeks, or Grandpa Herman's big feet. A physical link to what has come before. Your mother's freckles, your father's bushy brows, the spitting image of your big sister. Even buckteeth and lanky limbs come with a connection that can't be denied.

"Who do I look like?" I often asked my mother, knowing full well that I was adopted; yet, still not comprehending the depths of that lost connection.

"Your Grandma Alice," she would lie. Except the truth was, no one could tell me where my big emerald eyes came from, why I excelled at English and stank in math, or whose hideous stubborn streak I had inherited.

Who did I look like, act like, speak like, and think like? No one, it seemed. And why did it matter so?

After a lifetime of missing my hereditary links and marveling at those of others, I finally understand my obsession. I presumed that the link to our past, to our people, and to our hereditary characteristics meant that we belong. Most of us belong to the people who share our name, our heritage, our hazel or almond-shaped eyes, our auburn hair, our left cowlick, our hay fever, our propensity toward mystery novels. We are forever linked to those who share common physical, social, and moral distinctions—we belong with them.

And so if I had no link—no connections or characteristics passed from those who've gone before me, or even alongside me—did I belong?

For a long time, I thought not. I held fast to my husband, the youngest of six, happy in the thought of a "real relative," if only by marriage. The clan he was born into embraced me, and I marveled at the physical resemblance of him and his siblings. The common characteristics they shared with their parents and the many traits that banded them awed me. I yearned to belong in a way that it appeared everyone else took so complacently for granted.

Then my first child was born. A wisp of blond hair, the color of mine, crossed his otherwise bald head, and I realized for the first time that I was connected. I had grown my own branch of the family tree. Finally I knew someone who might resemble me, act like me, love the things I love, or hate the things I hate. Eventually I had two someones. I watched and waited while I made connections.

One has my hair, the other my eyes. Both resemble me. They have my teeth—and years of orthodontics to prove it. She stinks at math and has my hands; he tells a story in exactly the way I do—excruciating detail.

And so it dawns that my free-falling existence, untied genetically to any who had come before me, never meant that I didn't belong, but instead that I was waiting for ones to belong to. It seems my genetic link was suspended, not in the past, but in the future.

Today I search for—and often find—the connections that bind my children and me. Whenever I spot one I share it with them. Funny, now they do it, too. "I don't ever get sick," I overheard my son tell my daughter recently while she sniffed and sneezed through the misery of a cold. "I take after Mom," he bragged.

I smiled at the similarity and hugged my red-nosed daughter in sympathy. Finally, it feels like I belong.

JENNIFER NELSON

Life is pure adventure, and the sooner we realize that,
the quicker we will be able to treat life as art.
MAYA ANGELOU

TAKING A CHANCE

*One of the walls in my living room had been taunt*ing me for fifteen years. Behind the wall, a bed, a bureau, two turtle tanks, and a bookcase crowded into a small room. The room had once been a porch. Whoever owned this house during the hundred years of its existence had decided to build a narrow passageway to the spare room in which one had to be of a certain height and weight to complete the journey unscathed. For the fifteen years I've lived here, I made the trip through the hallway, often bruising an elbow or a knee, and always thinking someday I would create another entrance into the room.

But each year, there seemed to be another reason to leave the wall untouched. Other issues were more important. Siding for the house. New windows. Plumbing repairs. Now and then, especially in summertime, I would suggest to my husband that we let in the ocean air from the windows on the other side of the wall. But he would reply, "I'm afraid we might open up a bag of trouble with this old house if we begin to open up any of these old walls. The whole house will probably fall down." And I could not disagree with him. The house had its own history and one move in the wrong direction might create havoc.

So I forgot about the wall. For a while. Gradually, we accepted the narrow hallway as a constant in our lives. Whenever we used it to reach the spare room we'd complain, but the doorway was not mentioned again. And after a while, we forgot about the irritating wall and the ocean air trapped on the other side.

After my husband passed away, the house suddenly seemed too small, too full of memories, too crowded with grief. One year, I moved around the furniture. The next, I changed my way of life. I read all the books about closure and moving on and felt quite good about the progress I had made. And yet I yearned to do more, risk more, change more. As a widow, I had lost my old life and was searching for a new one. But after eight years of widowhood and a determination to be independent, I was beginning to lose faith in myself and in the world around me. Friends suggested a vacation but I did not know where I wanted to go.

And then one day, I again noticed the wall. It seemed to stand there, taunting me. "You wouldn't dare," I heard it chuckle. "The whole house will fall down on your head. I'm an old house and I do not enjoy anyone tampering with my structure." Day after day, I felt it daring me, until I could not bear to look at it again. It grew to represent my fears and my lifelong inability to take chances. One day I awoke, looked at the toolbox, and had the urge to grab a hammer and knock the wall down myself.

Instead, I confided my frustration to Julie and Joseph, two young people who had recently moved in as neighbors. I shared my dream of a doorway into the spare room where everything good seemed to be trapped. I thought, to begin, I might call an engineer to study the structure of the house. But that would take time. And today, I felt time had run out. Perhaps there was desperation in my voice. Perhaps they understood through the pain in my eyes that I needed to do something immediately. I wanted my old life back and I knew it would not return. Perhaps they felt me losing faith in my ability to live alone, to be a single woman, to make it all come together.

Two hours later, my new neighbors arrived on my porch with saws and hammers and equipment I had never seen before.

"We're here to make your doorway," they said.

I knew they had done much to upgrade their own property, but I did not know about their ability to deal with an old house. My husband's words echoed in the room. I hesitated. What if the house did fall down? I shared my fears and they just smiled and responded with their youthful enthusiasm, their confidence, and their caring. And so the work began. We laughed together when we found the original siding from the house on the other side where the porch had once been. We worried together when there were decisions to make about the beams and electrical wiring. But Julie and Joseph never gave up.

Often I would interrupt their work and say, "This is too much. I had no idea what it would take. What have I gotten you in to?"

Slowly, the faith that it could be done slipped away with the passing hours. The project was taking a day of their lives, a day when they could have been on the beach or sitting on their own porch, relaxing. It was taking their energy and I could see the fatigue shadowing their faces.

"Don't get discouraged," one or the other would reply. "We'll do it. We're having a great time."

The wall was now challenging them and they were determined to win.

It took seven hours, but at the end of it, a large doorway faced the living room and through it swept the cool ocean air and the bright sunlight. And, as if by magic, the living room increased in size. Neighbors came to celebrate the doorway and to inspect it. Others helped rearrange the furniture in the living room now that there was more space. It was as if I had just moved into the house. Only this time I was alone, and I had shaped the room to fit my needs.

Somewhere, between staring at the doorway, the disbelief that it was done, and the wonder that the house truly did not fall down, I regained my belief that all things are possible. That human beings have a quality of goodness and beauty just waiting to be shared, and that it is never too late to take a chance.

I wanted to pay my neighbors for their work. Reimburse them in some way. But they refused. Someday I will find a way. It will be their turn to need help and I will be there.

It is a special doorway I now have in my house. It has love and faith built into it. And it reminds me every day that my house and I are stronger than I thought.

Neither of us falls apart easily.

HARRIET MAY SAVITZ

MOM'S KIDDIE POOL

At the playground, my mother watches my daughter gleefully running from the swing to the slide to the crawling tube and back again. "I'm so glad Stephanie likes to play outside," she says. "You never did."

She's right about that. When I was Stephanie's age, I did my time at the playground as though it were some kind of punishment. "Can we go now?" I asked every two minutes, until my mother finally got sick of the question and took me home.

I have never been an outdoor person. While the other kids in my neighborhood were climbing trees, catching fireflies, and playing forty-seven-inning kickball games, I preferred to be inside with the air conditioner and a book.

As a teenager, I never had a tan like the other girls my age. I hated lying in the sun. Between the bug bites, the sweat, and the embarrassment of being a 32AA in a bathing suit, I was miserable every time I tried it.

Even as an adult, I would listen to friends talk about their camping trips and summer barbecues, and think, *Better them than me.* And then on a beautiful summer day when my daughter was six months old, a friend suggested taking our babies for a walk in their strollers.

"Great idea," I replied. "Let's go to the mall!"

My daughter, on the other hand, has never been an indoor person. As a baby, she loved long walks around the neighborhood. When she got older, she and her daddy would go to the playground and not return for hours. She begged me to take her to the zoo, or to her uncle's pool, or just out to the backyard to ride her tricycle, kick her soccer ball, or run through the sprinkler. As I did all these things with Stephanie, I found myself asking her the same question I used to ask my mother: "Can we go now?" No matter how much fun I had with my daughter, I couldn't stand being outside for long.

Then, on one of our many trips to the toy store, three-year-old Stephanie spotted an inflatable kiddie pool. It was love at first sight. "Oh, Mommy, can I have it? Can I have it? Please?"

"I don't think it'll fit in the car, sweetie," I said with my fingers crossed.

"No, Mommy, the one that's set up stays here in the store," she explained. "We get one in a box."

I thought it over. A little pool might not be so bad . . . if we could keep it in the house. As I was fantasizing about setting it up on the kitchen linoleum, Stephanie said, "I'm being very good. So can I have a pool . . . pleeeeease?"

That weekend, Stephanie and I got into our bathing suits while my husband inflated the pool and filled it with water (in the backyard, of course). We took a few bath toys out with us, along with a watering can, some measuring cups, and a funnel.

I lifted Stephanie into the pool and her joy was instantaneous. "Come on in, Mommy!" she yelled, splashing me with water.

"I'm coming in and I'm going to get you!" I yelled back as I climbed in with her and started splashing. For the next two hours—until our skin wrinkled and shriveled—we floated boats and kicked and poured water on each other, and had a great time. Stephanie and I loved the kiddie pool! We both whined when we had to get out.

Stephanie and I spent part of each day in our little pool. We accumulated a huge collection of pool toys. We splashed and played "Marco Polo" in six inches of water, and we giggled for hours. I taught her how to put her face in the water and blow bubbles. She taught me how to enjoy being outdoors.

But I didn't realize how much Stephanie had taught me until she spent a day with my mother, and I couldn't find anything to do. Sure, my house needed cleaning, but I couldn't see wasting a day to myself on that. Then I looked out the window and felt a huge smile come to my face. I ran outside and put the hose into the pool. Then I headed upstairs to put on my bathing suit and grab the book I had just checked out of the library.

A few minutes later, I was reclining in the pool with my book in one hand and a big glass of iced tea in the other. It felt like Heaven, or at least an expensive spa. And I didn't even care if anyone saw me in a kiddie pool without a kiddie.

I'm still a 32AA who hates wearing a bathing suit. And I'm still not an outdoor person. But every time I see the deflated kiddie pool waiting in the garage for summer, I smile and think to myself, *It won't be long now.*

Carol Sjostrom Miller

If you judge people, you don't have time to love them.
MOTHER TERESA

EGYPT CALLING

I *was afraid to go to Egypt alone. Afraid of the many* long flights that would take me nearly halfway across the globe. Afraid that the Muslims would hate me because I was a Christian, an *infidel,* a "faithless one." Afraid of terrorists, lurking around corners, just waiting for my arrival. Afraid of yellow fever, diarrhea, rape, torture, and land mines. Afraid of the people in a country strange and different. My mother was worried that I'd be abducted into a harem, but I let that one go. Still, I was afraid. And yet, I went. With ten places I felt I *had* to see, two weeks of time, and not enough money to spend, I would call on Egypt. In her turn, with her demands and her offerings, Egypt would call on me.

By the time I reached Cairo, thirty-six hours and ten time zones from Oregon, I had been propositioned, scammed, delayed, exhausted, hung over, and scared spit-less by a maniacal cab driver. All I wanted was to check in to my safe, quiet, little room at the Nile Hilton, take a long, hot, steamy shower, and indulge in twelve solid hours of dreamless sleep. I would wake up the next day, gather my wits and senses back together, and figure out a plan for exploring Egypt. But . . . the Hilton lost my reservation.

Autumn is high season in Egypt and tourists go then to avoid the blazing heat of Egyptian summers. Every hotel, restaurant, airplane, and monument was packed with people. I hadn't planned on *that* either. Most people would have had a plan before they left the United States. But no, I was alone on the Make-It-Up-As-You-Go plan in the strangest land I'd ever seen, amongst people more mysterious than I had ever known.

I finally found a vacancy in the Grand Hotel in downtown Cairo. It came recommended to me by James, a traveling textile consultant from South Africa, who was drinking beer in the bar at the Hilton. (Where I was having peanuts and red wine for dinner.) I could have kissed James for his help. His help and the fact that he looked like a blond version of Dennis Quaid. But I didn't. I was in enough trouble already.

The Grand Hotel was busy, noisy, rustic, old, and off-the-charts charming. I didn't see one other tourist in the entire place. There was, however, an armed guard outside the entrance, smoking a cigarette while he leaned on an automatic rifle.

The staff at the hotel didn't speak much English and I knew zero Arabic, except *ma'as salama,* which means *go in safety.* (I had memorized that particular phrase and had it engraved in a tiger's-eye, set in gold, and strung on a chain around my neck.) Though I would later have absurd conversations trying to get toilet paper and orange juice, the man behind the desk and I communicated well enough for me to secure a room for three nights. After I surrendered my passport, that is. With luggage in tow, the lift slowly lurched me to the second floor.

My room had a mirrored armoire for my clothes, Persian carpets on hardwood floors, a bathroom the size of my living room at home, and a double bed with a sunken divot in the middle the size of a coffee table. French doors led to a balcony, which overlooked an open market. Vendors and shoppers crowded a narrow street, buying and selling bananas, eggs, live chickens, pots and pans, produce, and just about anything you could, or could not, imagine.

From this noisy, cozy, odd little sanctuary of space, I would set out upon Cairo. Down a flight of white marble stairs (the edges worn soft and round through the decades), past the Cinderella Cafe, waving to the man at the front desk, offering greetings to the armed guard outside, I went out into the hot dry streets of Cairo.

I learned in those first few days in Cairo how to exchange money, cross a street, speak the basic pleasantries in Arabic, e-mail home, and close my eyes at the end of the day in gratitude. It was the simplest things at home that became adventures of spirit in Cairo.

The traffic, for one, is unimaginable. Like an orchestra without a conductor, the cars, carts, goats, bikes, and pedestrians move in a chaotic symphony of beeping horns and darting bodies. The sidewalks are for selling; the streets are for walking. Constant communication, combined with a heightened state of alertness, keeps everyone alive and moving, from the hearty and young to the little old ladies dressed in black from head to toe.

Above the sounds of horns, which beep and blare from dawn until midnight, comes the call of the muezzin. This is the signal, five times a day, that calls the Muslims to prayer. There was a time when the muezzin climbed the stairs to the minaret, the tall spire on every mosque, to wail his prayer over the city. But in modern Cairo the sacred call is amplified over loudspeakers throughout the city. I came to love that sound, the long low chant, calling, calling.

Over the next two weeks, for better or worse, great adventures unfolded all around me: Leaving Cairo, I took an agonizing bus ride a hot long way to paradise, on the southeast coast of Sinai. I was the only woman on the jam-packed bus, on a ride that lasted all night. As a violent movie blared in Arabic overhead, I sat next to a man I was certain was a terrorist, with my backpack on my lap for protection.

Safe, finally, in Dahab, I would listen to the sound of quiet. I would sit isolated on a beach chair, ignored by the tourists, while I cried into my sweater because it didn't look as though I'd ever reach Mt. Sinai. I would hear myself invite a shy young waiter to join with me in conversation over dinner, because I was—again—the only customer in the open-air restaurant on the beach, and had had such a tumultuous day. Eventually, I would climb the mountain of Moses to watch the sun rise, hear the pilgrims chant, and search the face of God.

Back in Cairo, I drank hot, sweet tea with a merchant in the enormous Khan el-Khalili bazaar in Old Cairo, where buying and selling is as delicate and intricate as the spun-glass perfume bottles.

One evening, through happenstance or great luck, I found myself alone at the Great Pyramids of Giza at sunset. The monument had closed, and I was there with only a tour guide who called me *habibi* (sweetie) and a few tourist police. I took the greatest roll of film ever taken in all time at one of the most sacred places on earth, as the sky turned from gold to orange to red and the sphinx lorded over a solitary and ancient landscape. Later that night, I accidentally broke my camera and ruined the whole roll.

In Luxor, I blew kisses to the children who didn't get to go to school because they were selling cigarettes and bookmarks to help feed their families. I touched ancient stones and walked sacred paths, lingering in amazement long past the time I should have left.

I thought I was forever changed.

I came back to myself, though, when I returned to America. It was as if I had passed unwittingly through some cultural decompression chamber over the Atlantic Ocean. America welcomed me home, clean and easy. I was re-embraced by the familiar and the ordinary: money I didn't have to calculate, shopping malls, good-mannered traffic, the English language, "The Simpsons." Still though, the drop of dye cannot entirely disappear once it's dispersed through the water. A trace lingers, and calls to me in sudden, distracted moments, loud and certain. It is saying, if I will listen: *You. You there. Pay attention. You are more than this. Remember. Remember . . .*

And I remember. And what I see first are faces. Before I recall the land, the cities, the ancient monuments, the great river, I see the faces of Egypt. I was wrong in my judgments and fears of the Muslims. I fell in love with the people of Egypt, whose warmth, humor, and kindness made the world smaller and offered me all the promises of travel—and the great adventure on the other side of fear.

KYLA MERWIN

RAISING DAUGHTERS DIFFERENTLY

On the front of my journal is a photograph of a pair of black, strappy, high-heeled sandals. Beside the sandals rest a pair of black, Mary Jane–style baby shoes. The first pair belongs to my blonde, green-eyed daughter, Kristin, eighteen, and the second belongs to my brunette, brown-eyed daughter, Makenna, two. Very different daughters. And even though they are both mine, I suppose one day they'll compare notes and say they had very different mothers as children.

I raised Kristin while working full time (and more) outside my home as a legal secretary. When I was on maternity leave with Makenna, I dreamed about being a working mom with flexibility and control over my schedule. While cleaning the house, I came upon my daughters' shoes lying side by side. It seemed like yesterday when those little shoes were Kristin's. *If there is ever a time to do things differently,* I thought, *it's now.*

I snapped the picture and began making plans to be a work-at-home mom.

I wish I could say it was clear sailing from that point on, but I've made more starts and stops than the metro bus. I changed my mind three times about what business to choose the first year, finally settling on writing. I've endured the skepticism of family and friends who weren't sure if it was postpartum depression or midlife crisis that started my big ideas. My plans were well into the second year before my husband agreed that reducing time spent at my secretarial job to three days per week to build a home business had merit.

Now, in my third year, I finally see progress. I've written several published articles and, as a commercial freelance writer, I'm beginning to see my first clients. On Thursdays and Fridays, Makenna and I run the home writing biz. On those days, I'm not a secretary, I'm the president, and she . . . well, she is the trainee.

During one important training session in the boardroom (known to the rest of my family as the dining room), I discussed with Makenna over chocolate cookies and milk the importance of using her new potty-chair. She looked a little perplexed, probably because she uses the potty-chair quite frequently. She uses it to reach high shelves when I hide the footstool. "The potty-chair is for potty. Tell Mommy when you have to go," I instructed.

Later that day we went to a meeting at the bank. As I sat in the banker's private office discussing business, Makenna abruptly darted out the door. Before I could catch up to her, she ran to the center of the lobby surrounded by four tellers and several other bank employees. Spinning around, she cupped her hands around her sweet little rosebud mouth and shouted at the very top of her lungs, "Hey, I hafta poop now!"

Being the only customer in the bank at that moment, I had to claim her. I strolled out to the center of the lobby where all eyes were focused and said, "You'll have to excuse my business partner. Her stomach is a little upset over the recent activity of the stock market."

She and I are still working on the "timing is everything" principle.

Louisa May Alcott said it best, "Far away, there in the sunshine, are my highest aspirations. I may not reach them, but I can look up and see their beauty, believe in them, and try to follow where they lead." I don't know when I'll be a full-time work-at-home mom. Yet, I am making progress, and I continue the journey with the same drive I felt on day one of this decision.

When I'm up late at night working on a marketing strategy, completing a client project, or writing, I often reflect on my photo of two pairs of shoes that represents, to me, two distinct ways of raising my daughters. The picture may be unremarkable to anyone else, but it is my motivation to follow this dream wherever it leads.

Barbara Carr Phillips

CHRISTMAS CRUNCH

'T*was the week before Christmas and I was doing* the "Christmas Crunch."

I had waited too long, Christmas was only a week away, and I was just starting my shopping. Gifts for nieces and nephews, sisters, brothers, parents, sisters-in-law, brothers-in-law—in-laws of all types. Many of them were difficult to shop for because I didn't know them all that well, being newly married.

The air was as bitter as my mood. I had been in enough malls and department stores to witness the crying of begging children and the yelling of moms with short tempers to last me the rest of my life. As I walked through each department store, I was bumped, pushed, elbowed, run into by strollers.

People seemed to be shopping just to get it over with. I watched a lady pull a man's orange sweater with green stripes off a rack. "He can bring it back and get something else," she said to her shopping companion in a crabby voice. *Ya, that's the spirit,* I thought sarcastically.

I left a mall department store hoping to find a less crowded one. I entered into the big hall, all decked out for the holidays. This time, I found myself in a crowd of laughing, screaming, and wiggling children. They stood in a long line, moms gripping their tiny hands and trying to keep order.

Looking ahead, I saw what they waited for. Saint Nick with his silky long white beard. He wore a beautiful red velvet suit; his black boots stuck out from beneath his pants. He sat in a huge rocking chair with cheery people dressed as elves and oversized candy canes and Christmas trees all around him. Poor guy, a baby screamed in his lap, but Santa kept smiling and a photo was shot of the two of them. *What a treasure,* I thought. *Title this one, Baby's First Terrifying Meeting with "The Clause."*

I scouted for a fast exit around this pack of kids and couldn't help noticing a small girl sitting on the floor. She had tears streaming down her chubby cheeks. The look on her little face broke my hardened heart.

Assuming she was lost, I approached her and got down on my knees.

"Honey, are you lost? Where is your momma?"

"I can't talk to strangers."

"My name's Linda, there, now I'm not a stranger."

She looked up at me with huge brown eyes, tears still spilling out, her long black eyelashes soaked from crying.

"Honey, are you lost?" I asked again. "Should I help you find your mom?"

I looked around for a security guard, then saw a woman seated against the wall rocking a tiny baby in her arms. She shrugged her shoulders, looking at me, and put one hand in the air . . . like "go figure." The crying child on the floor looked just like her.

"Is that your mom over there on the bench, the lady with the baby?" I asked.

"Yes. She's holding my brother, he's hungry, I guess. I want to see Santa, but . . . but . . ." More tears spilled from her eyes.

"But what? Why can't you see Santa?"

"He can't come to my house."

"He can't? Why can't he come to your house?"

She took a few sobbing breaths and said, "Santa can't come because we don't have a fireplace, and he would just be stuck on the woof."

When I was a child, I just figured he landed in our front yard and walked through the front door, like any normal elf.

I couldn't stand the sad look on her little face any longer. I had tears in my own eyes by this time.

I reached into my coat pocket for some change. I pulled it out and looked it over. A dull quarter, an old nickel, two dingy pennies, and, alas . . . one shiny penny.

I dumped all but the shiny coin back into my pocket.

I held out my hand and the girl looked at the coin.

"Dat is money . . . Santa won't come if you pay him."

"No, sweetheart, this is a magic penny. When I was a little girl I didn't have a fireplace at my house either. If Santa would have come down my chimney, he would have landed in the furnace and burned his buns!"

She giggled and listened intently.

I continued, making up the story as I went. "Every Christmas Eve, I would leave this magic penny next to the milk and cookies I left for Santa. When he arrived, the magic in the penny would turn into a fireplace complete with a big chimney so Santa wouldn't get stuck!"

She giggled a little more. "Or burn his buns!" she said.

We both giggled. I looked over at her mom. She smiled and nodded. I guessed she was so stressed out she didn't care what I was saying as long as Little Miss Long Lashes was now smiling.

I took the girl's hand and placed the penny in it. I told her if she ever lost it . . . she would surely find it again. Sometimes these magic pennies end up in Daddy's pocket!

"Now, hang on to that penny and go tell Santa what you would like for Christmas, and I promise that on Christmas Eve, that little penny will turn in to a huge fireplace and Santa will visit you . . . and your baby brother!"

We both stood up; she hugged me around the waist and headed in the direction of the Santa line. Suddenly she swung around and said, "What 'bout you, how will he get into your house without the magic penny?"

"Oh, I have a fireplace now, a big one, so Santa won't get stuck!"

She smiled. "Or burn his buns!" She giggled and found a place in line.

I found myself humming along with the mall Christmas music

as I walked away, excited now to buy gifts for my family. I decided to purchase some holiday decorations, too, to make my house look more like Christmas.

Maybe that really was a magic penny after all.

Linda Aspenson Bergstrom

X
LAUGH LINES

I think I've found inner peace. My therapist told me the way to achieve inner peace was to finish things I had started. Today I finished two bags of potato chips, a dozen chocolate chip cookies, four Reese's cups, a lemon pie, a fifth of Jack Daniel's and a box of chocolate candy. I feel better already.

AUTHOR UNKNOWN

DOUGHNUTS FOR HEROES

I *am a newspaper editor in Wisconsin and have had a* long and storied career writing about crime and accidents. As a result, I have gotten to know more than a few law enforcement officers, whom I respect as brave people who put their lives on the line for us, every day.

It takes a certain personality to be a good and dedicated cop. One must be honorable and courageous, but have a wry sense of humor that lets one live with what one does.

It's a full range of expression that I've always appreciated. Some of my most serious conversations, and funniest moments, have come in the company of these boys in blue. There is no group quite like them.

We have a lot in common as reporters and police officers. We must do our jobs in the face of tragedy. If there is a bad accident, it's likely that the first people on the scene are cops and rescue personnel, and then the journalists. We all know what we're supposed to do and try not to get in one another's way. There is often a satisfying, shared respect.

Throughout the years, I have made it a habit to show my appreciation by stopping in occasionally with doughnuts or bagels. Each and every time, these goodies have been received with appreciation readily expressed before the treats disappear into the coffee room to be enjoyed by the current shift. Taking them snacks doesn't cost much, but it sure helps create goodwill.

My newspaper is undergoing a redesign, and I recently invited my group of columnists to come in for new photographs. We bought a huge box of doughnuts to celebrate the gathering, but most of my writers declined the offer. As a result, we had twenty-four leftover doughnuts, minus the glazed croissant, which I consumed.

Rather than let them go to waste, I carried the pastries across the street to the police department. The chief was holding a meeting with his officers, but the secretary told me to go on in.

I waltzed into the meeting with the large box of doughnuts, leaned across a couple of sheathed shotguns, and plunked them on the table. The chief paused with his lecture, goggled, and asked, "What are these?"

I smiled. "These are doughnuts, you are cops, and if you can't figure out what to do with them, I give up."

Everyone laughed, including myself, and I went back to my office with another tale for my storied career. After almost twenty years in the business, I've come to realize that most of my stories don't end up in the newspaper. But they are wonderful and heartwarming, all the same.

A little kindness goes a long way, and doughnuts for heroes is a good place to begin.

Jennifer Gordon Gray

THE NO TREAT RETREAT

Savoring the thought of a relaxing massage to soothe my sore neck muscles, I scheduled a thirty-minute neck and back massage. I imagined my healthy back restored, my spirit renewed, and my body rejuvenated.

On the appointed day, I rushed to finish my errands and soon found myself racing through yellow lights to get to the day spa. The clock seemed to speed up as the scheduled time approached. I became more tense, knowing my precious thirty-minute time allotment was disappearing. What was the purpose of getting stressed out to get to a massage so I could relax?

When I arrived, time slowed down. The receptionist handed me a crystal goblet of cranberry juice with ice and led me to a small meditation room. I listened to water trickle over pebbles in a fountain. The bright red, bittersweet drink ran cold down my parched throat, helping me to recover from the race to the spa. I was handed a key to a locker where I found a terry wrap and robe waiting for me. I ignored the paper slippers that looked like decorations for a sushi platter.

A large white candle flickered in front of a mirror and filled the massage room with the scent of vanilla. Suspended on the walls were displays of brightly colored eye shadows and lipsticks. The massage table beckoned me from the center of the small room, with a pastel-colored sheet draped over it. I stretched out on the bed, pulling up the cover sheet to stay warm.

The tall, blonde masseuse entered and introduced herself. "I do a deep massage," she said. "I've been doing this for twenty years." I breathed in deeply, ready to melt into the World of Relaxation.

"Sometimes I don't realize how strong I am." She lathered her hands noisily with lotion. "My fingers are stronger than most." I closed my eyes and listened to the soft background music, the sound of waves crashing.

Then the onslaught began.

She pounded my upper back like a butcher tenderizing meat. "I'm also a reflexologist," she said, "and a part-time nurse." She punched my lower back like it was bread dough. "I care for an eighteen-month-old baby three days a week," she said, pummeling muscles in my back that I didn't know I had. "The baby's a quadriplegic," she continued, "on a ventilator, from a car accident." Not only did my muscles hurt from the kneading, but hearing this depressed me.

"What do you do for a living?" she asked.

Must the masseuse talk during the massage? Talking about work and trying to relax is an oxymoron.

Of course, anyone else would have just said, "Shsssh, and ease up on the massage there." Or perhaps, "Your voice is so melodious that I'm afraid I'll fall asleep and never wake up—if you keep talking in your smooth manner. And by the way, your hands are so strong from all your experience as a reflexologist-masseuse that I will never be able to get up from this table when you're done. So if it would be no trouble, please, lighten up just a tad." But none of these words entered my mind while I was being flattened like a filet of chicken. And even if they had, I was too much like frosting stuck to a cake to lift my head and open my mouth to speak.

My head was wedged into a donut pillow, hanging off the massage table. It felt quite stuffy as the masseuse continued her diatribe, something about how important nurses are and how they should be more valued in society.

"Are you having trouble breathing? The sheet draped over the headrest gets in the way," she said.

Was she trying to kill me?

"I put the sheet there to keep your face from getting stuck to the support." She paused to move the sheet and then resumed drilling into my back. She had deceived me like a blonde villain from a James Bond movie.

Thank God this massage was only thirty minutes, or twenty-two, if she deducted time for lateness. I was praying she would. I heard snapping and felt popping as she played my tendons like guitar strings. *Was she a chiropractor, too?* She whispered something about how much stress there was in my back. Yes, this was stressful. I tried to speak, but I was paralyzed.

There was a knock at the door.

"Thanks," Miss Helga called out, without resting her hands.

Time's up. I had survived.

Then she began a karate chop up and down my back that reverberated in my bones. Her hands felt like ginsu steak knives.

"You might be sore tomorrow," she chirped.

Might be? I was sore now.

Maybe when I get home, I thought, *I'll listen to music and recover in a hot bath.*

ELIZABETH KANN

She who laughs, lasts.
BARBARA JOHNSON

PRAYING FOR DEEP WATER

A *recent sunny day found me at the mall trying on* swimsuits. I hadn't purchased new swimwear since Ronald Reagan was our president—his first term of office. I had postponed this as long as possible, but a move to our new house in Arizona, the year-round warmth, and a backyard pool shook me out of my Twinkie-induced stupor. It was time to dive in.

The sight of my swimsuit-clad body, reflected in a three-way dressing room mirror, was an unsettling experience. I looked like I had been fed a steady diet of mashed potatoes and cheesecake. My knee-highs, which pushed my knees into bulbous shapes, added to the trauma. I told myself I didn't actually look like the Pillsbury Doughboy's big sister, but who was I kidding?

Heaving bosoms may be spicy in romance novels, but I'm here to report that there can be too much of a good thing. Today's swimsuits are designed with women in mind who are shaped like boys. Jiggling body parts, both fore and aft, are quite a distraction. A skirted version hides a multitude of sins, but women who have reached the point in their lives when they should be enjoying themselves shouldn't have to don tutus to swim.

I'd never lost the baby fat after giving birth, but when my baby registered with Selective Service, I had no one to blame but myself.

Customers in the surrounding dressing rooms were having their own personal epiphanies. Some overheard comments included, "Get me out of here. I'm hyperventilating." And, "My problem is that I keep getting Jenny Craig and Sara Lee mixed up." And, "I beg upon my dimpled knees. Don't give us thongs—we want sarongs."

Then there was this memorable exchange.

"I bought two suits at the end of last season," said the first woman.

"Just like that? Didn't you try them on?" asked the second.

"No, because they'd've looked horrendous on me," replied the first. "I figure if the suit's too big I can always put on weight. And if it's too small, I'll file it away with all the other clothes that don't fit."

I turned back to the three-way mirror and sighed in stereo. My husband envisioned me in a bikini, but I was stuffed with linguini. I resembled Queen Victoria on one of her bloated days. In desperation I scooped up the least objectionable model from the bevy of swimsuits tossed about in my dressing room. This came at a higher price than the beautiful formal I'd worn to my senior prom, which included many more yards of fabric.

On moonless nights, my husband knows where to find me. I can be found hiding in the pool submerged to my neck.

Lana Robertson Hayes

ONE DAY AT A TIME

I sat in the dirt of the vegetable garden Gene planted before we were married. Maybe if I put my hands in the earth, I could find the secret of belonging on a farm. Then I began plucking red root weed from the rows of vegetables, remembering the directions Gene gave me after breakfast.

"It needs a little weeding," he had told me as we walked to the garden spot. "You can get that done before lunch. Then, if you want, you can come with me over to Dad's while I check the water on the fields."

"What do weeds look like?" I asked.

"Haven't you ever been around a garden before?"

"Not really. Mom grew some string beans during the war. I wasn't allowed to touch them."

"Well, just look for the rows. See? The corn is here, these are the carrots, beets, beans, and onions." His hands indicated there were edibles lurking in the mass of plants that all looked the same to me. I reached down and pulled something feathery and weedy looking.

"No! That's a carrot. The vegetables are in the row. If you just pull the weeds between the rows, that will help."

"I really don't see any rows," I said, becoming as testy as he was, and it was true. While we were on our honeymoon, Gene's garden had grown into a matted rectangle of various colored greens. Only an expert could have known where the rows were.

"Oh, for Heaven's sake! Just pull the red root. I'll do the rest when I get back."

"What does red root look like?" I shouted as he jumped into our old black Studebaker.

"It's got red roots. Just look for the red stems!"

He didn't have to yell, I had thought at the time, and then I found myself in the middle of all that leafy plant life. Running my fingers through each growing thing, I searched for the obvious red root, pulling them up one by one. Maybe the day would come when I could kneel in the sun with my eyes closed, and my hands would know instinctively which was food and which was weed. But for the present, Gene might as well have invited me to go to Mars and raise rocks because I found out later that beets have red roots, too.

Gene had also warned me to always keep an eye on Goofy, our milk cow.

"If she gets out, chase her back in," he said, as if that were an easy thing to do.

Goofy weighed seventeen hundred pounds and was the deranged Holstein with twisted horns that had frightened me the first time I saw her. She had a mean streak that was legend with the Thiel boys, who had had to milk her before Gene's dad gave her to us for a wedding present. I wanted to grind her up for hamburger, but she was a good milker and we sold her milk and cream for grocery money.

Goofy was an escape artist. I had watched Gene herd her back into the pasture several times. I even helped him once by standing in the road waving my arms to keep her in the yard; but when she charged me, I let her go past.

"What did you do that for?" Gene had said. "You've got to turn her around."

"She was going to hook me with her horns." I was surprised Gene didn't show any concern about that fact.

"No she wouldn't have. Just stand your ground. She's a coward."

But she had frightened me beyond reason, whipping the air

with her drooling nose. She was the very picture of conflict with one curled horn pointed down, like a gun, and the other horn jutting straight out like a finger, accusing no one in particular. I always prayed she would only run away when Gene was home. If two of us had a hard time turning her around, I wondered how I was supposed to stop her by myself.

When I finished with the garden, I walked over to check the corral gate. Gene had repaired it that morning after milking, after patting Goofy on the flanks and saying, "Good girl," as if she might believe him and behave.

Now she stood with her back to me, her deformed neck allowing her to half face me at the same time. She was watching me with her floating eye. The gate looked secure, and I continued my round of chores, feeding and watering the chickens. Goofy waited until I was backing out of the chicken coop, arms loaded with eggs, before she pushed down the gate. She took a detour to climb on Mrs. Wackerly's potato cellar, leaving two inch deep hoof prints in the dirt roof.

By the time I could put the eggs down and lock the chicken coop, Goofy was trotting down the road, her huge pink udder swinging wildly between her hind legs.

I sprinted down the fence line on the pasture side, put my hand on the fence post and, without thinking about consequences, leaped over the top string of barbed wire with several inches to spare and landed in front of her. Until that point, she was not aware of me. Because of her deformity, Goofy could not see where she was going, only where she had been.

I was alone with a crazy cow seventeen times my weight. Turning, she took a side step and lunged at me, hooking her bent horns in all directions. Keeping my distance, I tried to frighten her by imitating Gene's language and gestures.

"Git, you old cheese factory!"

Goofy belched sour hay breath, an eye-stinging vapor that could power a tractor, and stamped her feet, causing herself to stumble off the road. Grabbing a stick, I scraped it across the road, making a rasping, ominous sound, while I screeched and howled at her. Goofy and I stood face to face, which meant she had started to turn around. She knew I was not Gene, but I decided I could not be bossed around by a cow and survive my new life.

Turning toward home, her tail swatted at flies attracted to the dried manure on her hind legs. It seemed a pitiful view of my personal triumph. With hooves dragging against the pavement, she shuffled forward. I wondered what her world was really like. Perhaps a bit like mine: split in two, seeing her days with one focus pointing ahead, the other observing hindsight. Maybe she was born under Pisces, like me, trying to go in opposite directions but stuck in the middle, frozen in time.

"Haagh!" I yelled, waving my stick to keep her going. That strange throaty language coming from the gut was easy to speak. No real words, simply a communication of power. If Goofy had showed her teeth and bellowed from the depth of her triple stomach or had turned on me with the same conviction of survival as mine, she would have conquered. But she didn't know I was frightened and she backed down first.

My first conquest in life was a cow, and I had triumphed over fear. However, Goofy would not be taken for granted. She still needed to be guided through two gates. To my relief, she was not interested in traveling where she had never been before and made the turn into our farmyard by herself. Not to be mistaken as an easy mark, she insisted upon following her own difficult trail back, climbing Mrs. Wackerly's potato cellar one more time, punching more deep prints next to the ones she had made earlier. I ran from side to side behind Goofy, acting like a far more deranged animal than she, making her believe the corral was the safest place to be as I wired the gate behind her.

At lunch Gene said, "I see Goofy got out again. Have any trouble?"

"No." I did not have the energy to explain my terror and knew he wouldn't understand it if I did.

"I knew you wouldn't. Should have kept her off the cellar, though."

"I tried."

"Should have headed her around the front. Wait till Mrs. Wackerly sees that. After lunch I'll teach you how to drive."

"How about tomorrow. I really don't want to learn anything new today."

"Tomorrow I need you to follow me with the pickup when I move the tractor over to Bloomberg's place."

"But I don't know how to drive. I don't have a license."

"Don't need one. We'll go the back roads."

EILEEN THIEL

DORIS

"R*emember the time you carried your life-sized doll* to kindergarten?"

Gina e-mails me questions like that about once a week as we reminisce about childhood. We've known each other since we were five, but now that she lives in California and I live in North Carolina, we have little in common but the past. But to answer her question, I say, "Of course I remember. That's what started my career with mannequins!"

A minute later, my PC beeps with another e-mail. "Details please!"

I start at the beginning.

We adopted Doris after a long modeling career at Kmart. The store was doing away with mannequins, and my husband, Webb, found her out in the Dumpster. Knowing my weakness for quirky collectibles, he asked the store manager if he could have her. And that evening, he drove up with a plaster woman sprawled on the backseat.

She had no hands and no legs, but she did have a nice blonde wig and eyelashes to die for, and I wasn't sure what to do with the dummy except stand her in the spare bedroom, which gave me a start every time I walked by. By the next day, she had been put in the closet.

The name Doris came about when Webb's spunky coworker, Shirley, borrowed her one evening for a ride around town. Shirley was going through a divorce and thought it would be great fun to dress "Doris" up in a man's hat and shirt and take her for a spin because her soon-to-be ex-husband was the nosy, overbearing type and deserved some torment after what she knew he had been up to. The plan worked. Shirley and Doris were spotted near a convenience store and Hubby took off after them in hot pursuit. It wasn't until she pulled up alongside him at a stoplight that Shirley reached over to have Doris wave her handless wrist at him. I suppose Hubby's eyes nearly popped out of his head. That was the last Shirley saw of him until they met in court and he claimed she was a nut case with a dummy boyfriend.

I went on to tell Gina that Doris has had many lives since. Early on we threw a party and set her up so she'd be just visible behind the shower curtain. You couldn't help but think there was a naked woman in there because you could see her in the mirror immediately when you turned on the light. It wasn't long until one of the guests had to use the bathroom and you should have seen the look on his face when he backed out of the bathroom. We laughed for years.

Another time I dressed Doris up in maternity clothes to attend a baby shower I was hosting. It so happened this circle of friends had already met Doris, so the shock value wasn't nearly what it could have been, but to the uninitiated, we were lunatics.

And then there was the time Doris went for a dip.

"Anna and Larry, our next-door neighbors, had a swimming pool. We were good friends and we'd played jokes on each other for quite a while," I tell Gina.

Every Friday evening like clockwork, the couple would go out to eat and then go for a midnight swim. One evening Webb and I dressed Doris in some of my old panties and a bathing cap, and we sneaked her over behind the hedge and carefully slipped her into the pool, floating facedown. We waited. It was well past dark before they finally came home. Webb and I had kept our windows open and when we heard a commotion next door, we figured Doris had been discovered.

Around 10 P.M. our doorbell rang and there she stood propped against the porch post in sagging, waterlogged panties. Her bathing cap was wrapped in a stranglehold around her neck.

Larry stood next to her, his eyes narrowed. "You need to keep better track of this wench," he said. Then, he proceeded to tell us how he had spotted what he thought was a dead body in his pool and almost had a stroke. "Anna!" he had shouted, nearly tripping down the back steps, racing to the pool edge.

Anna only laughed.

That December, Larry approached us about borrowing Doris for a special assignment. His church had a life-sized nativity display out front and someone had stolen Mary. A police report was made and the congregation was naturally upset. It wouldn't do to depict Joseph as a single parent and it was too late to order a replacement figure. Someone suggested that one of the Wise Men be transformed into the Blessed Virgin, but two Wise Men would look odd. Larry joked that he knew Doris had less than a spotless reputation, but she would be the perfect life-sized replacement for Mary.

Webb and I agreed that church might be the ideal place for Doris to make amends. It was heartwarming to drive past the First Baptist Church on Christmas Eve and see Doris there in an oversized blue robe and shawl, her arms lifted in adoration over Baby Jesus.

When we moved to our new house, Doris came along, I told Gina. We just packed her up along with all our other stuff. Along with the rest of our household items stacked in the carport, the movers picked her up, wigless, and loaded her onto the van when Webb overheard one of the burly men say, "I guess it takes all kinds."

Doris was relegated to the attic for much of her residence in our new house until I took a job with the college. One day I was talking to one of the sociology professors and learned that the International Students Association needed a mannequin for a display at the library. Impulsively, I volunteered Doris to help them out. I drove her over to the library and next thing I knew, Doris was in the front display case wearing an Indian sari and surrounded by brass bowls, elaborate baskets, and books on Sanskrit and Hinduism. As a model, she is a natural.

The display remained a good while, and when it came time to change it out, the students asked if it would be all right to keep using "your mannequin" for future displays. I saw no harm in it. In fact, Webb and I dropped by the library every month or so just to see what Doris was wearing. One time she was in a German dirndl, with overgrown sleeves hiding the fact that she had no hands. The next time, she was wearing a Japanese kimono. Inside of six months, she had circled the globe in foreign attire. But by Christmas, I grew concerned to see that the students had given up their display project. I asked around for Doris, but no one, not even the professor, seemed to know where she had gone.

On a college campus, I knew there was no telling where she might be. Losing her was something like missing a prized possession, even a favorite pet goldfish. She didn't say much, but she did add some color and fun to our lives. And after all these years, how could I let her slip away? Like a neglectful parent, I had let go of her tether just a little too far, and she had wandered off with the wrong crowd.

Even Webb felt bad. When his boss was getting ready to turn sixty, he lamented the fact that we didn't have Doris to dress up and leave in his office chair.

After three semesters passed, we had pretty much given up hope when Webb was reading a newspaper article about the college's TV broadcast studio. Accompanying the story was a photograph.

"It's Doris!" he said.

The figure was wearing sunglasses, but I would know that vacant face anywhere. Sure enough, there she was, dressed in a rain parka; her stubbed wrists cleverly disguised with prosthetic gloves, her knees stood up on a table to conceal her missing legs.

The next day, I was over there in the studio, demanding my mannequin back. Regretfully, they let her go.

"Of course no one claimed to know who had kidnapped her from the library and no one would own up to where she had been for eighteen months. And Doris sure isn't telling," I told my old friend. I suppose I should have seen it coming, turning her loose on a college campus. The newfound freedom was bound to come to no good.

"So where is she now?" Gina asks.

"Locked away in the attic," I reply. "She might have got an education, but we learned our lesson: College is no place for dummies."

Tammy Wilson

OF GOLF TEES AND EVERGREEN TREES

W*hen thinking golf, I sound like a Dorothy* wanna-be skipping through the Land of Oz chanting, "Lions and tigers and bears, oh my." My chant speaks of tigers and bears and trees. Of course the tiger is Tiger Woods, who works hard to make golf look effortless as he annihilates his competition. The bear is none other than the Golden Bear, Jack Nicklaus, the Tiger Woods of my generation. And the trees, evergreen trees, remind me of my last golf lesson.

Golf has been my husband's passion since he bellied up to his first tee a few decades ago. Over the years he has cajoled and dragged me to the golf course, nurturing the hope that I would excel at his favorite sport.

Sadly, I have no hand-eye coordination or depth perception. When estimating how much energy it takes to move a ball the distance from my putter to the hole in the middle of the green, my cognitive skills approach zero. Golf is a game of pure luck for me, and most of it is bad.

On those rare times I accompanied him, he knocked strokes off his game while encouraging me. "You're doing better. You're getting the hang of it. Absolutely!" When my husband uses that word, "absolutely," I know he's not being truthful. But, I followed him across the course, racking up scores that the Lakers would have admired. If only we'd been playing basketball.

But, on these outings I learned a few things—mostly about people—and I gathered memories. To my surprise, community golf courses are nothing like the sedate, reverent Master's tournaments I've watched on television. Public golf courses overflow with colorful characters, and I'm not describing their knickers.

With each visit I saw big, burly men crawling through bushes looking for little white balls. Others threw golf clubs farther than they hit their drive, and then waded into the water after that same club. "Fore" and other four-letter words floated on the air. And golfers in carts, intently watching someone's swing, drove off the path and up to their wheel wells in a sand trap. I understood the term "hazard" much better after just one visit to the local course.

In a last attempt to convert me, my husband arranged a foursome: the two of us and a couple from his workplace. It was a rare chance to socialize; he knew I'd say yes.

By the time we reached the fifth tee, the husband, let's call him Arnie, decided he knew what was wrong with my game. Like a preening peacock, he confidently said, "Just watch me." Reverently he placed the ball on the tee. He stepped back, admired the placement, then demonstrated his interlocking grip on the club. Arnie took a couple practice swings to show me the proper stance and followthrough. All of this zoomed over my head, but I smiled and nodded.

He motioned me off the tee with a flip of his hand, then turned to the ball. He addressed it with authority. "Show it you are in control," he said.

Arnie shifted his weight from one foot to the other and back again, flexed his knees, took a deep breath, drew the club back and, like Casey at the bat, whacked the ball a mighty blow.

The ball apparently had conflicting thoughts of who was in control. It chose a trajectory that sent it directly up a stately old evergreen tree that shaded the tee and right back down again. The pong of golf ball against wooden limbs resounded in a staccato rhythm, running up the scale and back down again as it rose and fell, landing three feet from our golf expert.

I sat nearby on a bench beside his wife. We both planted our hands firmly over our mouths to stifle the laughter that bubbled inside. Our eyes watered, but we worked hard to maintain proper decorum.

Arnie was a hearty soul and resolutely picked up his ball, put it back on the tee, and mumbled something about, things like that happen. He squared his shoulders and addressed the ball a second time. If nothing else, this golfer was persistent, and consistent. He whacked the ball even harder, watching for it to soar over the fairway. Instead it found the same tree. It played a similar song, this time pinging even faster as it bounced up the trunk and back down again knocking off needles that floated in its wake as this ball landed smack where his previous ball had stopped.

Our control gone, his wife and I laughed, hooted, and cried until we couldn't catch our breath. My husband, the stoic and dedicated golfer that he is, stood silent and intently examined the contents of his golf bag. But his shoulders developed a strange shaking. The golfer, face red, club clenched tightly, picked up the ball and gave it a mighty heave sending it out onto the fairway before heading toward the golf path and his next stroke. Arnie perfectly defined the term "teed off."

That was my last golf lesson, and the last time we saw that couple.

Recently, as my husband polished his favorite scarred and battered seven iron, I asked about Arnie and his wife. He said they had bought a new boat, and Arnie now casts for fish rather than par.

"You know," I said, "every time I see a big old evergreen tree, I think of him."

My husband eyed me with that long-suffering look. "Golf is a serious game."

I grinned. "Absolutely!"

DAWN GOLDSMITH

Nobody can be exactly like me.
Sometimes even I have trouble doing it.
Tallulah Bankhead

MECHANICAL PARIAH

My toaster hates me. So do my coffee maker, dishwasher, vacuum, and all the other mechanical "servants" that I own—but the toaster can be really vindictive.

I never would have known how much so, except that the alarm didn't go off this morning . . . because I had set it. It's something I normally don't do—the alarm clock hates me, too, you see—but my husband, Jonathan, had fallen asleep while reading in bed last night, and I hadn't the heart to awaken him for such a menial task.

This morning, late for work, we were dashing around the house getting ready. "I'll make instant coffee," Jonathan said. "You put some bread in the toaster."

He couldn't have been thinking clearly. Nor could I, since I did as he asked. The bread was inserted and the lever depressed. Nothing. Minutes went by—still nothing. I jiggled the lever, checked the plug, and shook the toaster. It was a waste of time.

"Forget it," I said, "we can grab something to eat at the office," and sat down to sip at the coffee. By the second sip, the kitchen was filled with thick, acrid smoke spewing forth from the burning toast.

With a yelp, Jonathan rushed from the table and wrested the

plug from the wall, muttering under his breath, "I should have known better." And he should have.

I watched, helpless, as he upended the toaster over the sink, dropping carbon-like slabs into it that might well have been used to pave a walkway through our garden.

Now, it's not my fault. I have no idea why everything electric chooses me to vent its animosity on. I've never done anything to one of them that I know of, and I'd be happy to apologize to it if I did. When anyone else in my home uses an appliance, it works perfectly.

Everyone I've told about my "condition" tells me that it's all my imagination. I'd like to believe them, but I can't. Even Jonathan tried to convince me of it, once, and tried to prove it by conducting some experiments.

First, he'd use some appliance, the air conditioner in one case, letting it run as smoothly and efficiently as the salesperson had said it would. When we were both satisfied that it was in perfect working order, he turned it off, stood back, and watched as I took my turn.

Hesitantly, I touched nothing but the SLOW START button, as he had done, pressing it slowly but firmly. Nothing happened. The air was as quiet and still as it had been before I'd pushed the button. But then, just as I was turning to Jonathan, the mechanical monster threw itself into HIGH EXHAUST, creating a maelstrom in the living room that nearly tore the buttons from my blouse as it tried to draw me through its vents.

Coincidence? That's what Jonathan believed until all the other appliances tested with the same result: electric mixer, iron, microwave oven (we'd decided by then that the real oven was much too risky), food processor, hair dryer, and—I get chills when I think of it—the lawn mower.

Happily, Jonathan does not believe in divorce.

To those who ask about the scars on my ankles, I usually say that I received them during a rough tennis match. Much easier than trying to explain that it's the result of my one-time shaving encounter with an electric razor. The permanent puckering in the outer corners of my lips is a reminder of my single exposure to a sunlamp.

But, aside from the restrictions my handicap forces on me, I don't really mind it too much—as long as someone is on hand to operate my adversaries for me. Problems arise when, for one reason or other, I find myself at home alone, when my solitude comes unexpectedly, when contingency plans have not been enacted in the form of automatic timers for the lights, thermostat settings, etc.

It gets lonely sitting in a silent, chill, darkening house, surrounded by gleaming objects lying in wait, daring me to lay a finger on them. The TV set, for example. It just sits there like a mine ready to detonate, poised for my slightest movement, ready, literally, to burst into life.

It wasn't always like this. When I was growing up, everything worked as well for me as it did for everyone else. It's hard to remember exactly when the change came about, but the first time I remember noticing something strange was after I'd moved into my first apartment—alone. It was a mindless thing for someone with my condition to do, I now realize, but who knew?

The only gear my car would tolerate was reverse. The carriage return on my old electric portable typewriter sent the roller flying off to the left, rather than to the right, and my building's elevator refused to take me anywhere but to the basement if I'd pressed UP, or the roof if I'd pressed DOWN. That is, if it chose to stop for me at all!

After long deliberation, I decided that something was truly amiss and, knowing little about electricity, decided to consult with the experts, electricians, to see if they could answer any of my questions. Most of the ones I talked with eyed me quite strangely, not that I blamed them. Two of them, however, grinned knowingly.

"I wouldn't be telling anyone else about this," one said. "They'll think you're touched in the head. But, sure, there are people I know of who have the same problem as yours. There's something about them that makes electricity do peculiar things. Like some people can't get along with cats and dogs. There's really not a thing you can do about it except keep your distance."

I'll just have to live my life as a pioneer, a do-it-yourselfer, creating my own energy sources, using my initiative, developing dexterity.

I just wish I didn't have to write all this in longhand. I have no choice after what the computer did to me.

Alleyne McGill

THE KING OF HEARTS

One recent Valentine's Day, my son came home from school, opened his sweaty little hand, and revealed a small pink sugar heart inscribed with the words, "I Love You." He tossed me a smile.

"Whew! I was afraid I'd lose it, Mom, so I've held it real tight ever since after lunch. I want you to have it," he said, prying it from his damp little palm and dropping it onto mine. My eyes misted a little.

"My friend gave it to me, Mom. She's a girl," he added, as though that made a difference. I looked at the slightly worse-for-wear candy heart. There was something brown around the edges.

"Aren't you going to eat it, Mom?" he quizzed, blue eyes anxiously searching my face.

"Eat it? Yeah, sure. Just a minute," I said, the candy now sticking to my palm like a wad of tape. I wondered what the brown stuff could be. Dirt or maybe a marker, something benign I hoped.

"I was afraid I wouldn't get it home, Mom. I nearly lost it in the restroom, but lucky for you I found it. It rolled under the sinks." He smiled with triumph.

"I think I'll just put it over here for a few minutes, okay?" I asked brightly, peeling the heart from my hand and placing it on the kitchen counter. I made a mental note to spray the spot where I put it with some sort of anti-bacterial cleanser once I'd gotten rid of the candy. But first I had to get rid of the kid and he was sticking to me like a short shadow.

"Why don't you go play?" I said, giving him a little pat.

"Because I want to be with you, Mom," he said.

He wants to be with me, I thought. *This sweet little boy who will someday grow into a sullen teenager wants to be with me. This child I cradled and rocked to sleep, his fuzzy little head in the crook of my arm, this child of the sweet, soft baby cheeks, with the sunny smile and the unique perspective on life. He'll be moving on soon, to other things—big-boy things. He'll leave you behind in his rush to grow up. You should savor this moment and that dirty, germ-ridden, dented little pink sugar heart. Go ahead, Carole, eat the heart. The kid kept it all day, carried it around especially for you. Eat the heart or break his.*

My mind made up, I turned and slowly walked toward the counter where the heart, which was probably crawling with more bacteria than a toilet seat, rested, a small, dirty pink smear on the counter. But I was saved by the bell—my husband walked into the kitchen.

"How was your day, honey?" he asked as he absently reached down, snatched up the heart, and popped it into his mouth. He smiled at me as he crunched it in his teeth.

"Well, it's had its ups and downs, but ever since you walked in the door, it's been terrific," I said with sincerity. He sauntered off into the den leaving me alone with my son.

"I'm sorry I didn't get to eat your heart, honey," I said. "But it was the thought that counted."

"That's okay, Mom," he said. "It didn't taste very good to me and Ryan when we licked it, so I thought I'd just give it to you."

And they say there's no such thing as a guardian angel.

CAROLE MOORE

MORE CHOCOLATE STORIES?

Do you have a short story you want published that fits the spirit of *Chocolate for a Woman's Soul Volume II?* I am planning future editions using a similar format that will feature true stories of love, divine moments, family highlights, overcoming obstacles, following our intuition, and humorous events that allow us to laugh at ourselves. I am seeking heartwarming stories of two to four pages in length that feed your soul.

I invite you to join me in these future projects by sending your special story for consideration. If your story is selected, you will be paid $100, listed as a contributing author, and have a biographical paragraph included. For more information or to send a story, please contact:

Kay Allenbaugh
P. O. Box 2165
Lake Oswego, Oregon 97035
kay@allenbaugh.com

www.chocolateforwomen.com

CONTRIBUTORS

Kelley Bowles Albaugh is a thirty-two-year-old English and drama teacher who's been living and working in western Colorado since 1994. She is currently pursuing a master's in Fine Arts—Creative Writing. She's written one novel in the Emma Lovett mystery series and is currently at work on her second. When she's not teaching or having fun with family, friends, cats, and dogs, she's speaking at charity fundraisers for the Multiple Sclerosis Society. kelkay1202@yahoo.com

Sande Boritz Berger began writing as a young teenager because her letters amused her parents and "they finally heard me." For several years she got sidetracked in the corporate world writing and producing promotional video programs, until finally returning to her passion. A poet, essayist, and fiction writer, her work appears in *Every Woman Has a Story* (Warner Books) and in *A Cup of Comfort* (Adams Media). Her essays are also included in *Ophelia's Mom* (Crown) about the trials of raising adolescent daughters. She has completed a novel about a young woman's boredom in 1970s suburbia and its consequences. She lives on Long Island and Manhattan with her "first reader," husband Steven, and has two extremely independent hardworking daughters. MurphyFace@aol.com

Linda Aspenson Bergstrom is from northern Wisconsin where she lives a busy life with her two active children, Hannah and

Beau, and her husband, Jeff. She is a freelance writer and artist, who also enjoys her dogs and spending time at the family cabin in the North Woods. She is working on her first novel. She has been published in the Chocolate series several times. lindapaints@hotmail.com

LYNNE BIANGO is passionate about empowering women by sharing her personal experiences through writing. She has published one other article and has served as an editorial assistant for film book author Tony Villecco on the release of his book *Silent Stars Speak*. She works full time for the NYS Department of Disability Determinations and is a part-time certified aerobics instructor. She is a theatre student at Broome Community College in Binghamton, New York, taking acting courses and performing in plays. Her two favorite places to travel are New York City (it's magical) and Florida (loves beaches and palm trees). When not on the go, she loves to snuggle in front of her television set with her two cats, Happy and Stubby. She is currently writing a book describing in detail her relationship with Larry. (607) 785–4419. IamSparklynn@aol.com

KAY BOLDEN was inspired to become a writer as a child after reading a poetry collection by Gwendolyn Brooks. While she still dabbles in poetry, personal essays are her first love. She and her children live in Joliet, Illinois, where they share their backyard with a family of raccoons, a deaf squirrel, a stray frog, a pair of lost hummingbirds, and a pumpkin patch. kbolden@ameritech.net

KATHY BRICCETTI has published her personal essays, opinion pieces, and feature stories in newspapers and magazines and on public radio. Her memoir, *Blood Strangers*, chronicles the saga of four generations touched by adoption as well as her multiple journeys to find lost family members and reestablish broken ties.

She lives with her partner and their two sons in the San Francisco Bay area. kbriccetti@attbi.com

TERI BROWN is a freelance writer and homeschool author who lives, gardens, and homeschools her two children in Portland, Oregon.

CHRISTY CABALLERO is a freelance writer and photographer who lives in a quiet forested area in the Pacific Northwest. She writes for magazines, newspapers, rescue groups, and herself, and she is most in her element on a woodland trail, beside the river, or at the ocean. She writes about matters of the heart and her love for animals—large, small, pets, and wildlife. Her special bond with animals began with the massive German shepherd who decided he belonged to her the day after he was born in Anchorage, Alaska. She says The Great American Novel is, of course, in the works. greeneyz@cport.com

ANDE CARDWELL is driven to explore her life on paper. She says don't mention this to her husband; he prefers to pretend their personal life is a secret. In addition to first-person essays, she writes poetry, children's stories that are really for adults, and short fiction. andecardwell@hotmail.com

SUSAN DEMERSSEMAN, PhD, is a psychologist in the San Francisco Bay area. She works in schools and conducts workshops on a wide range of subjects. Topics include stress reduction, parenting adolescents, character education, and multicultural issues. She begins most parenting workshops with the statement: " 'Parenting expert' is an oxymoron!" She grew up in South Dakota and brings a Midwestern sense of proportion and humor to her work with children and families. She lives with her husband and two teenage children, who are a frequent source of inspiration for her writing. She consults on media projects related to children and has appeared on TV and radio programs and in educational films. She has written for local and national publications. Demerssemans@yahoo.com

KAREN C. DRISCOLL lives in coastal Connecticut with her husband and four young children. While pregnant with twins she completed a master's degree in elementary and special education. Four years and four kids later she has embraced life as a stay-at-home mother. Looking for something creative to do while her children napped, recording her life with kids became a way of keeping in touch with friends and family. With naps now a distant memory, she continues to write and has been published in both books and magazines. kmhbrdriscoll@hotmail.com

JENNIFER R. FINLEY is a Southern scribe who makes her living as a technical writer from her home in Atlanta, Georgia. She has a BA in Journalism and has authored numerous spiritual fiction and nonfiction works, including her first book, a spiritual memoir entitled *God Makes No Strays.* Her stories often revolve around her passion for animals and her love of travel. She is currently working on a set of books specifically designed to prepare handicapped children for hippotherapy. Jfinley66@aol.com

PATRICIA C. FISCHER received her bachelor and master's degrees in Social Work from Aurora University in Chicago, Illinois. Her articles and short stories have appeared in United Airlines' inflight magazine, *The Forum,* and *The Storyteller,* where she won first place for her story titled "Gunplay." Her recent retirement from United Airlines has afforded her more time to devote to her love of writing. She lives in Charlotte, North Carolina, with her husband, Fred, and stepson Ted. She has four children and two grandchildren.

DIANE FLEMING has a diploma in advertising arts, a BA in Sociology and English, and a certification in Clinical Hypnotherapy. She has been published in *Woman's Day* and has had children's stories and current events stories published locally. She has her own hypnotherapy and counseling business and writes in her spare time. Her three adult children and three grandchildren all live in Edmonton, Alberta, Canada. She lives with her husband, Mike, and Cayman, their big white cat.

JOANNE M. FRIEDMAN was born and raised in New Jersey. She has a BA in Psychology from Clark University in Worcester, Massachusetts, and a MEd in Special Education from University of Hartford. She has been a teacher and a writer for thirty years and is currently teaching high school English. She lives with her daughter and her partner in Sussex County, New Jersey, on the horse farm she owns and operates. She writes a humor column on the subject of horses, which appears in several local newspapers in Massachusetts. jmfriedman@nac.net

LYSSA FRIEDMAN is a freelance writer living in Mill Valley, California. As a teenager, she learned that cars, books, music played loud, and the sound of the ocean contribute meaning to life. It wasn't until she grew up, though, that she learned the value of showing up on time and studying algebra.

JENNIFER GALVIN received her bachelor of science in Art from Oregon State University in 1992. She writes and illustrates from her home in Northern California. In addition to writing and drawing, she enjoys reading, walking, camping, and being with her family. www.jennifergalvin.com. JenniferLGalvin@aol.com

JEAN JEFFREY GIETZEN is a freelance writer whose work has appeared in *McCall's, Reader's Digest, Catholic Digest,* the Chicken Soup books, and many small press magazines. She is the author of the best-selling Christian gift book *If You're Missing Baby Jesus,* available from Multnomah Publishers. The grandmother of six, she is a former Midwesterner who now writes from her retirement nest in Tucson, Arizona. In addition to her writing, she is a writing coach and offers readings and workshops in creative writing. (520) 296–1550 (October through May), or (414) 352–2009 (June through September). octodon31469@cs.com

Elizabeth P. Glixman writes humorous essays, poetry, and short stories. Her recent work can be seen in the upcoming issues of *Snow Monkey, In Posse, 3 A.M. Magazine, A Cup of Comfort for Woman,* and *Spinnings Magazine.* Elizabeth has a master's degree in Education. She used to work with children in arts and educational programs, but found that writing was her true heart's desire. glixman@mindspring.com

Dawn Goldsmith is a multi-published writer of nonfiction, short stories, and essays, and she also reviews books for *Publishers Weekly* and *Crescent Blues* eMagazine. www.crescentblues.com

Jennifer Gordon Gray has worked as a writer, editor, and photographer in the newspaper industry since 1983, and as a correspondent for several publications serving members and friends of Soka Gakkai International. She loves hiking, snowshoeing, and hugging her cat, Bear. http://TartanPony.Homestead.com. TartanPony@yahoo.com

Melissa Gray is a freelance writer living in Springfield, Missouri. With more than three hundred bylines to her credit in regional, national, and international publications, her column on raising a child with learning differences, "Greater Expectations," recently won the LDA of Missouri Journalist of the Year Award. Admittedly, her life is a comedy of errors so she recently began writing about some of her mishaps and humor and is honored to be a contributor to the Chocolate series. She leads a busy life shuttling her two children around and sharing the parent duty with her loving husband and her desk with a neurotic cat. mdjgray@mchsi.com

Dawne J. Harris is the founder of SPEAKSTRENGTH Motivational Seminars for women and enjoys sharing the Good News. She is a faith community representative and committee member of the Annual African American Health Conference. Appointed by the Church of God in Christ, Inc., she is Jurisdictional President of the Young Women's Christian Council in Michigan. She hosts conferences for Christian singles and is the president of the singles ministry at Rewarding Faith Church where her father is pastor. She is working on her first book, *Every Woman Needs a Well.* (313) 933–3000, (313) 933–3300 fax. djharris8@msn.com

Lana Robertson Hayes has an MA in Education and has authored many humorous essays and articles, as well as the "Sonoran Sampler" column in *Arizona Garden Magazine.* In a world divided by those who see the glass half empty or half full, she alone is left wondering why she received the glass with the lipstick on the rim, and who left it there. Britishtea@aol.com

Tracey Henry is a newly published author. Her various works include moving personal essays, children's stories, and short stories. Currently, she is working on her first novel. This particular story is dedicated to the memory of her mother, Ellen, her sister, Wendy, and her new niece or nephew. Tracey currently resides in the Tampa Bay area with her husband, Sean, and two young sons, Steven and Matthew. TraceyHenry70@aol.com

Sheila S. Hudson is a freelance writer/speaker and a wife, mother, and grandmother. Her company is called Bright Ideas, and her credits include *Chocolate for a Woman's Dreams, An Expressive Heart, Chocolate for a Teen's Heart, Chocolate for a Teen's Soul, Chocolate for a Woman's Blessing, Chocolate for a Woman's Heart, God's Vitamin "C" for the Spirit of Men, Taking Education Higher,*

Casas por Cristo: Stories from the Border, and *Life's Little Rule Book.* (706) 546–5085. (706) 546–7419 fax. sheila@naccm.org

Pamela Jenkins lives near Henryetta, Oklahoma, with Stanley, her husband of twenty-one years, and their four children. She is the office manager for her husband's veterinary practice and receives inspiration for her writing from her family and through witnessing daily the bond between people and pets. She is a contributing author in *Chocolate for a Woman's Dreams, Written in Stone,* and *Chicken Soup for the Grandparent's Soul,* as well as being widely published on the Internet. She is a member of the Church of Christ. ramblinrabbit@juno.com

Elizabeth Kann lives near Youngstown, Ohio, with her husband and son. She is a physician who has earned degrees from Vassar College, Columbia University, and Albany Medical College. She is a self-appointed chocolate connoisseur. pekann@pol.net

Shirley Kawa-Jump and her husband, Jeff, live in Indiana with their children, Mandy and Derek. She spends her days writing and running after the kids, trying to contain messes and maintain her sanity. A fan of happy endings, she is the author of two nonfiction books and also writes for Silhouette Romance. www.writingcorner.com. shirley@shirleykawa-jump.com

Kathleen Coudle King is married and the mother of four young children. She has a BFA in Playwriting from NYU, and an MA in English from UND. She's written more than a dozen plays and several screenplays, which she hopes to see made into movies. Her first novel, *Wannabe* (2002), revolves around the rites of passage of a group of friends in a Cuban-American town in New Jersey—first bras, first kisses, and the guts and glory of friendships are all explored in humor and detail. When not writing or chasing after her lil' darlin's, she teaches writing and women studies at the University of North Dakota in Grand Forks. Please visit her at her website where you are encouraged to share your own stories: http://www.angelfire.com/nd/wannabe.

EDNA MINER LARSON (Edina) is a published writer of poems and short stories. She has worked as a salesperson, stenographer, bookkeeper, and supervisor of a hospital admissions office. At the time of her early retirement, she was the administrative director of a large physicians' exchange. Her college education was wedged in along the way. Since becoming a widow at the age of fifty-two, she has been a hospice volunteer, taught a literacy program through a local college, and enjoyed creating and teaching the art of Eggery. She thinks writing is something you do akin to decorating a Christmas tree: You take a plain piece of paper and bring it beauty by the adornment of your words. And publication is putting the star at the top of the tree.

MARY DIXON LEBEAU is a freelance writer and employment counselor. Her work has appeared in such publications as *ePregnancy Magazine, The Christian Science Monitor,* and *Baby Years.* She also writes a weekly column for *Gloucester County Times.* Mary and her husband, Scott, share a home—and a drawerful of socks—in West Deptford, New Jersey. mlebeau@snip.net

RUTH LEE is a feature writer for her hometown newspaper the *Drexel Star.* From 1987 to 1996, her column, "A Little Bit of Life," was anticipated and enjoyed by her readers. She is a seven-time first-place-award–winning member of the Missouri Writers' Guild and a member of the Ozarks Writers' League. Her poetry, inspirational fiction, and personal essays have appeared in a wide array of publications, including *Stories for a Kindred Heart* and *Chocolate for a Woman's Spirit.* ruthlee2@casstel.net

Nancy Maffeo is a former schoolteacher who lives with her husband of twenty-six years in San Diego, California. She has written a column on parenting for a webzine and has contributed articles to books, regional papers, and Christian magazines.

Marilyn McFarlane is a freelance writer and the author of numerous travel books, including *Best Places to Stay in the Pacific Northwest* (5 editions), *Best Places to Stay in California* (3 editions), *Quick Escapes in the Pacific Northwest,* and *Northwest Discoveries.* Her most recent book is *Sacred Myths: Stories of World Religions,* a vividly illustrated, award-winning book of beloved stories from seven spiritual traditions. She coleads a women's spirituality group and has made pilgrimages to sacred sites around the world. She lives in Portland, Oregon, with her husband, John, and visits her eleven grandchildren as often as possible. mmcf@easystreet.com

Alleyne McGill is originally from New York. She is a parent and a former airline executive. Her published articles, essays, short stories, travel pieces, creative nonfiction, poetry, and a play have been, or will soon be, seen in *The New York Times, The Writer Magazine, Newsday* magazine and newspaper, *Unity Magazine, Modern Drummer, Intro, NY Air,* and *Mexico City News.* She has numerous online credits as well. She was a semifinalist in a Phyllis A. Whitney "Writing To Win" contest. She moved to Mexico fifteen years ago where she writes and takes part in English language theater. aljons@prodigy.net.mx

Sheri McGregor is an internationally published writer whose women's, parenting, self-help, and psychology articles appear in publications including *The Washington Post, Sunset, Australia's InfoWeek, USA Weekend,* and *Reader's Digest.* Her novels have been translated internationally. A mother of five, she uses the lessons she's learned to inspire other mothers who have dreams to pursue. She is currently finishing her psychology degree. She speaks to women's groups on overcoming physical and mental obstacles. Her website includes her writing and profiles successful mothers who share their joys and sorrows and practical advice. (760) 746–2949. www.motherswhodream.com. smcg@sbcglobal.net

KYLA MERWIN lives and writes in Bend, Oregon. kyla@empnet.com

CHRIS MIKALSON lives with her husband in Alberta, Canada, and has two daughters and three grandchildren: two girls and a boy. She works full time as a bookkeeper for a car dealership. On weekends and evenings, when not spending time with the grandkids, she pursues her love of writing. She has had articles published in *Grandparents Today* and *Woman's World,* and writes for the "Soapbox" of her local newspaper. Her biggest project, a romance novel, is waiting for its second draft. i-mik@telusplanet.net

CAROL SJOSTROM MILLER is a freelance writer and stay-at-home mom. Her articles, essays, and humor pieces have appeared in *FamilyFun* magazine, *The Christian Science Monitor, Chocolate for a Woman's Courage,* and many other publications. When she isn't in front of her computer, she loves scrapbooking, and her goal is to get all the baby pictures into photo albums before her kids leave for college. She lives in New Jersey with her husband, Jack, daughters Stephanie and Lauren, and beagle, Tapper. miller_carol@usa.net

MARLA HARDEE MILLING is the director of communications at Mars Hill College in Mars Hill, North Carolina. Her articles and essays have been published in *The Christian Science Monitor, ePregnancy Magazine, Pregnancy Magazine, Healthgate, Smart Computing's PC Today, Armchair Millionaire, Smoky Mountain Living, Blue Ridge*

Country, Debt Counselors of America, the Myria Media network of websites, Babycenter.com, and others. She lives in North Carolina with her husband and two children. marla@reporters.net

Eileen Modracek was first published in her local newspaper at the age of ten with a poem about her cat. She has since been published in *Guideposts Magazine.* Prior to her retirement, her career was spent working with special needs children. Her two sons are now grown. Recently widowed, she shares her home with her dog, Katie. After hearing Divine inspiration, she has returned to writing and looks forward to the journey ahead. modracek@olypen.com

Gayle Montanez is the author of "Kara and the Swing" online, and the story will soon be a listener essay on NPR's "Living On Earth." gmmontanez@cs.com

Carole Moore is a writer and newspaper columnist based in North Carolina. A former police officer, she has also worked in television news and as a radio talk show host. Married and the mother of two, she is the author of "The Perils of Eileen" serialized fiction, which is carried on her website: www.thehumorwriter.com. carolemoore@ec.rr.com

Cheree Moore is a Christian counselor who developed a passion for writing at the age of nine. She is a former high school teacher who enjoys working with teens, reading, and scrapbooking. For the past six years, Cheree has enjoyed competing in scholarship pageants and now directs a local Junior Miss program. She holds a master's degree in Marriage and Family Therapy and resides with her husband in Florida. chereemoore@hotmail.com

Amy Munnell has been a freelance writer/editor since 1987. Her work has been featured in such magazines as *ByLine, CAREERS*

& the disABLED, Georgia Journal, and *Athens Magazine.* She is on the board of directors for the Southeastern Writers Association. She lives in Athens, Georgia. (706) 354–0361. nega_writer@yahoo.com

JENNIFER NELSON is a freelance writer based in north Florida. She writes about a variety of topics, including health, nutrition, fitness, writing, and family. Her work regularly appears in *Woman's Day, Parenting, Fitness, Shape, Health, Energy, Writer's Digest,* and others. Her essays have appeared in *The Christian Science Monitor* and *The Washington Post.* She also teaches an online writing course, "Selling to the Sisterhood—Breaking into the Women's Magazine Market." She speaks at writing conferences around the country and is currently working on her first nonfiction book. She's also the mother of two teens. nelsonje@bellsouth.net

LY NGUYEN was raised in San Francisco and currently lives in Oakland, California. She is the founding codirector of Oasis, a young women's art and leadership center in San Francisco. Her work has been published in the *San Francisco Chronicle, Defining Herself Online Publication,* and *Seawood Soup Asian American Journal.* Her writing ranges from short stories to personal memoirs of the Vietnamese-American experience. She has been recognized by the American Association of University Women and was given the Daniel Koshland award from the San Francisco Foundation for her work in the San Francisco community. She is also a photographer.

SUSAN PARKER has had essays in the *San Francisco Chronicle, The Washington Post,* the *Chicago Tribune, The Mercury News, The Denver Post, The Sun Magazine, Hope Magazine,* and salon.com. Her commentaries have been recorded on NPR's "Morning Edition" and KQED's "Perspective." She is the author of the memoir *Tumbling After: Pedaling Like Crazy After Life Goes Downhill,* released by Crown in April 2002. Her memoir is now available in bookstores and can be ordered from www.2ndEDITION.net and www.amazon.com. sqparker@pacbell.net

DIANE PAYNE teaches creative writing at the University of Arkansas–Monticello. *Burning Tulips,* her memoir about growing up in Holland, Michigan, was published by Red Hen Press in 2002.

MICHELLE GUTHRIE PEARSON is a freelance writer and home-based business owner. She lives with her husband and son on a fifth-generation family farm in northern Illinois. Her work has appeared in previous Chocolate books, as well as *The Christian Science Monitor, Becoming Family, God Allows U-Turns, Nudges from God,* and *Chicago Parent.* stoneyknoll@lrnet1.com

BARBARA CARR PHILLIPS is a writer who lives in Whiteland, Indiana, with her husband, Randy. They have five children, Kristin, Tony, Amber, Austin, and Makenna. She writes many nonfiction articles for newspapers, websites, and magazines, and she is also a freelance commercial writer. She is currently working on her first nonfiction book about adopting children from foster care. She enjoys family life, humor, journaling, and hearing from readers. (317) 535–1574. Barbaracarrphillips@msn.com

FELICE R. PRAGER is a freelance writer from Scottsdale, Arizona. Her work has appeared in international, national, and local publications, as well as many eZines. http://www.writefunny.com. FelPager@aol.com

PATRICIA R. REULE is a native of Grand Forks, North Dakota, who retired from a twenty-five-year high school teaching career in 1997. Writing is a creative outlet, but it is important to her as a source of spirit sustenance as well. She has one book, *Metamorphosis,* published in 2001 by PageFree Publishing, which chronicles her first year after treatment for alcohol addiction and includes advice for the newly sober, their families, and friends. In fall 2002, she began studying to become a chemical addiction counselor, which will result in licensure in 2004. She and her husband, Ron, have two adult children and three grandchildren. senora54@hotmail.com

KATHY HARDY RHODES is a published author of nonfiction. Born and raised in the Mississippi Delta, she writes narrative personal essays that reflect the Deep South—warm observations about family, place, and Southern culture, laced with nostalgia and/or humor. A former educator, she currently lives in Franklin, Tennessee, where she is a business administrator in a company established by her husband. Rhodes also enjoys web authoring and photography. She has two grown sons. Her passion is preserving family history; she has researched, authored, and compiled biographical material on her ancestors. She has also completed a collection of essays and is working on her first novel. (615) 591–7516. www.kathyhardyrhodes.com

JULIA ROSIEN lives in Ontario with her husband and four children. Her essays and articles appear in magazines and newspapers across North America. juliarosien@rogers.com

LISA SANDERS is a writer specializing in family and education articles; however, her true peace comes from reading and writing inspirational essays. She lives in northern Virginia with her husband, Rich—who she says is her best friend, boyfriend, and one true love—and their children, Torri and Teague. Lisa is currently working on an inspirational anthology for teachers, tentatively titled *Chalkdust on the Sleeve of My Soul.* www.Chalkdust-Online.com. Lisamarie@Joy-Writer.com

HARRIET MAY SAVITZ was born in Newark, New Jersey, and grew up during the Depression. She is the award-winning author of twenty-one books and two essay collections, *Growing Up at 62* and *Messages from Somewhere: Inspiring Stories of Life After 60* (Little Treasure Publications, Inc.). To learn more, visit www.harrietmaysavitz.com.

LAURA STANFORD has been writing poems and short stories since childhood. She works as a mortgage loan officer and massage therapist in San Antonio, Texas, where she also volunteers with pet adoption efforts. She is most grateful to Lynn—friend, teacher, and healer—who led her through a reconstruction of deep beliefs to an increase of faith. Her desire now is to facilitate spiritual healing for others. 2103517132@archwireless.net

SHEILA STEPHENS is an international award-winning poet, writing teacher, columnist, and speaker who enjoys helping people build their lives "from the inside, out." To her, self-esteem is a spiritual journey of accepting the seed of love that divine spirit places in each heart. She has just completed *Walking With the Flowers: 50 Weeks of Quiet Meditations for a Woman's Busy World*. Her professional services include creativity coaching, personalized correspondence writing classes (available worldwide), and Walking With the Flowers seminars.

PATTY SWYDEN SULLIVAN is a freelance writer living in Overland Park, Kansas. "Sisterhood" is an excerpt from a larger work entitled *So This Is How It Feels to Be Put Asunder.* Special acknowledgment goes to her husband, Robert Sullivan, and to her daughter, Victoria White, who continually provide sage insight and skilled editing to her writing. pss@kc.rr.com

EILEEN THIEL is a freelance writer and helps her husband run an organic farm on the edge of the wilderness in northeastern Oregon. She holds a food processing technology degree and has written a technical food column for *Agri Times Northwest*. Her essays have been published in several books, including the *Fishtrap Anthologies,* stories from the experiences and concerns of writers in the West; *Woven on the Wind,* a collection of essays about the friendship of women living in the West; and *All About Wallowa County: People, Places and Images.* Her work has also appeared in literary magazines, *Country,* and several trade magazines. She was awarded a Fishtrap Fellowship in 1999. She is first and foremost a wife, mother of four, grandmother of thirteen, and great-grandmother of one. eileenthiel@eoni.com

Susan B. Townsend is a writer and stay-at-home mother to five children ranging in age from three to sixteen. Transplanted four years ago from the west coast of Canada, she and her husband, Tom, live on a three-hundred-acre farm in southeastern Virginia with their children and a multitude of pets. She is at work on her first novel. (804) 834–2245. monitor@visi.net

Beverly Tribuiani-Montez is thirty-five years old, married, and has a daughter named Jessica and a chocolate lab puppy named Maddy. Although she has been many things by profession, from a wedding consultant to an account executive to a high school teacher, she says she is by nature a writer. She writes to process her life. She has done freelance work for *The Contra Costa Times* and the *San Francisco Chronicle,* and she has written and directed plays for her local church. Her story, "Just a Daughter," is an excerpt from one of her current projects, a book titled *Did I Mention My Family's Italian?* Her other project is a book of poetry, not yet titled. Bevie1967@aol.com

Annette V. wishes to remain anonymous. She also wishes to recognize the DRW for their love and support.

Peggy Vincent is a retired midwife who has welcomed more than 2,500 babies into the world. She lives in Oakland, California, with Roger, her husband of thirty-six years, and Skylar, their teenage son. Two adult children, Colin and Jill, live nearby. Her first book, *Baby Catcher: Chronicles of a Modern Midwife,* was released by Scribner in spring 2002. In addition to working on a sequel, she also writes fiction and short essays. www.babycatcher.net. PV@peggyvincent.com

Laurel A. Wasserman has taught English for twenty-six years and has published poetry, essays, and travel articles. She lives in California with her husband, Lauren. She looks for the lessons in everyday experiences. Laurelwasserman@aol.com

Anne Culbreath Watkins resides in Alabama. Her work has appeared in publications such as *American Caged-Bird Magazine, Angels on Earth, Bird Talk, Writer's Digest Forum,* and many others. A regular contributor to the Guideposts hardcover book series Listening to the Animals, she also has more stories scheduled to appear in the Guideposts book *Their Mysterious Ways.* She is the author of *A New Owner's Guide to Conures.* http://www.geocities.com/anne_c_watkins

Janie M. West lives in the Deep South, USA, with her husband and teenage daughter. Together they enjoy reading, writing, hiking, two dogs, and an ever-changing number of cats. Three married children provide wonderful in-laws, grandchildren, and richer family gatherings—all the result of that first wedding thirty years ago.

Tammy Wilson is a past contributor to the Chocolate series. She still has a mannequin in her attic. Her work has appeared in the *North Carolina Literary Review, Branches,* and the online *Charlotte Austin Review,* among other publications. A graduate of the University of Missouri School of Journalism, she resides in North Carolina.

Linda C. Wisniewski is a retired librarian who lives with her family in Bucks County, Pennsylvania. She has two sons, ages twenty-five and twelve, a shih tzu named Lucky, and a gray cat named Missy. She can be found reading mystery novels when she is not writing, volunteering at Planned Parenthood, or watching her retired scientist husband cook fabulous gourmet meals. She is very proud that her memoir on domestic violence was included in an anthology celebrating the twenty-fifth anniversary of a local women's shelter. She is an active member of the International Women's Writing Guild and the Story Circle Network.

Jennifer Bialow Zeidler graduated Phi Beta Kappa with a degree in Communications from Tulane University in New Orleans. Her entertainment journalism career has included freelance reporting for *People* magazine's Los Angeles bureau and producing for the syndicated television shows "Inside Edition" and "American Journal." After relocating to Chicago, she was an Emmy-winning producer for Fox News on WFLD-TV and produced segments for "Fox Thing in the Morning." She now works part time from home as the executive producer of "Travel Channel Radio," a nationally syndicated radio show based on the Discovery-owned television network, and she works full time raising her two boys, ages three and seven months.

ACKNOWLEDGMENTS

I am extremely grateful to the Chocolate sisters who shared their soulful, poignant, and heartwarming stories of love, Heaven-sent moments, hardship and triumph, and humor. Their true tales bless women of all ages.

Many, many thanks for all the attention and devotion given to the Chocolate series from Fireside/Simon & Schuster senior editor Caroline Sutton and her assistant, Christina Duffy, and to all those Simon & Schuster chocolate lovers who are promoting and marketing the series from behind the scenes.

Enormous thanks to my agent, Peter Miller of PMA Literary and Film Management, Inc., and his chocolate-loving staff. Thanks to Peter, the Chocolate series is published in eighteen languages throughout the world.

As always, my love goes to my husband, Eric, and our growing family (four sons and two daughters-in-law and the addition of two beautiful grandbabies). Just as the stories in *Chocolate for a Woman's Soul Volume II* lift my spirit, so does the love of family and friends.

ABOUT THE AUTHOR

Kay Allenbaugh is the author of *Chocolate for a Woman's Soul, Chocolate for a Woman's Heart, Chocolate for a Lover's Heart, Chocolate for a Mother's Heart, Chocolate for a Woman's Spirit, Chocolate for a Teen's Soul, Chocolate for a Woman's Blessings, Chocolate for a Teen's Heart, Chocolate for a Woman's Dreams, Chocolate for a Teen's Spirit,* and *Chocolate for a Woman's Courage.* She resides in Lake Oswego, Oregon, with her husband, Eric Allenbaugh, author of *Deliberate Success: Realize Your Vision with Purpose, Passion, and Performance* and *Wake-Up Calls: You Don't Have to Sleepwalk Through Your Life, Love, or Career!*

Look for the other volumes of delicious Chocolate stories.

Chocolate for a Woman's Soul
0-684-83217-8 · $12.00

Chocolate for a Woman's Heart
0-684-84896-1 · $12.00

Chocolate for a Lover's Heart
0-684-86298-0 · $11.00

Chocolate for a Mother's Heart
0-684-86299-9 · $11.00

Chocolate for a Woman's Spirit
0-684-84897-X · $12.00

Chocolate for a Woman's Blessings
0-7432-0308-9 · $12.00

Chocolate for a Woman's Dreams
0-7432-1777-2 · $12.00

Chocolate for a Woman's Courage
0-7432-3699-8 · $12.00

Chocolate for a Teen's Soul
0-684-87081-9 · $12.00

Chocolate for a Teen's Heart
0-7432-1380-7 · $12.00

Chocolate for a Teen's Spirit
0-7432-2289-X · $12.00

Chocolate for a Teen's Dreams
0-7432-3703-X · $12.00

FIRESIDE
A Division of Simon & Schuster
A VIACOM COMPANY